CW00672057

SECRET OPERATIONS OVER OCCUPIED EUROPE

This book is dedicated with affection to:

Arthur Clement Bartter Service number 110875 Service: RAF

*Nicholas Anderson Service number 1542641
PoW number 267429 Service: RAF*

*Brian Henry Atkins Service number 170267
PoW number 267430 Service: RAF*

*Clarence William Fry Service number J 22493
Service: RCAF*

*Ernesto Howell Service number 144194
Service: RAF*

*Walter Ralph Riggs Service number 1600344
PoW number 267473 Service: RAF*

*Stanley Gordon Smith Service number 1890877
PoW number 267479 Service: RAF*

*In the memory of John Evans (1945–2022), who throughout the
preparation of this book gave invaluable support and advice.*

SECRET OPERATIONS OVER OCCUPIED EUROPE

RAF CREW'S STORY OF CLANDESTINE MISSIONS, BEING SHOT DOWN, ESCAPE AND CAPTURE

JAN CHRISTENSEN & NIGEL S. ATKINS

AIR WORLD

AIR WORLD

SECRET OPERATIONS OVER OCCUPIED EUROPE
RAF Crew's Story of Clandestine Missions, Being Shot Down,
Escape and Capture

First published in Great Britain in 2024 by
Air World
An imprint of
Pen & Sword Books Ltd
Yorkshire – Philadelphia

Main Text © Jan Christensen
With contributions from Maxine Harcourt-Kelly, Nigel S. Atkins and Abi Exelby

Foreword and Afterword © Nigel S. Atkins

ISBN 978 1 39907 979 2

The right of Jan Christensen & Nigel S. Atkins to be identified as Authors of this work has been asserted by them in accordance with the Copyright, Designs and Patents Act 1988.

A CIP catalogue record for this book is available from the British Library.

All rights reserved. No part of this book may be reproduced or transmitted in any form or by any means, electronic or mechanical including photocopying, recording or by any information storage and retrieval system, without permission from the Publisher in writing.

Typeset by SJmagic DESIGN SERVICES, India.

Printed and bound in the UK by CPI Group (UK) Ltd.

Pen & Sword Books Limited incorporates the imprints of After the Battle, Atlas, Archaeology, Aviation, Discovery, Family History, Fiction, History, Maritime, Military, Military Classics, Politics, Select, Transport, True Crime, Air World, Frontline Publishing, Leo Cooper, Remember When, Seaforth Publishing, The Praetorian Press, Wharncliffe Local History, Wharncliffe Transport, Wharncliffe True Crime and White Owl.

For a complete list of Pen & Sword titles please contact

PEN & SWORD BOOKS LIMITED
George House, Units 12 & 13, Beevor Street, Off Pontefract Road,
Barnsley, South Yorkshire, S71 1HN, England
E-mail: enquiries@pen-and-sword.co.uk
Website: www.pen-and-sword.co.uk

or
PEN AND SWORD BOOKS
1950 Lawrence Rd, Havertown, PA 19083, USA
E-mail: uspen-and-sword@casematepublishers.com
Website: www.penandswordbooks.com

MIX
Paper | Supporting
responsible forestry
FSC
www.fsc.org FSC® C013604

Contents

List of Figures

LIST OF FIGURES

LIST OF FIGURES

List of Abbreviations

AMF	SOE French Section, Algiers, codename Massingham
BBC	British Broadcasting Corporation
BCRA	*Bureau Central de Renseignements et d'Action* – Free French Organisation under De Gaulle
BOAC	British Overseas Airways Corporation
CC	Civilian Commission
CIGS	Chief of the Imperial General Staff
DFC	Distinguished Flying Cross
DF Section	SOE section responsible for French escape routes
DSO	Distinguished Service Order
Dulag Luft	*Durchgangslager der Luftwaffe* [Air Force Transit Camp]
DZ	Drop Zone
ETA	Estimated Time of Arrival
EU/P section	SOE section dealing with Polish community in France
F2	Polish Network in France
F Section	Run by Buckmaster, responsible for SOE operations in France
FANY	First Aid Nursing Yeomanry
GHQ	General Headquarters
GP	General Practitioner (Doctor)
HCU	Heavy Conversion Unit, a training station to upgrade crew to the heavy bombers such as the Halifax.
HQ	Headquarters
IWM	Imperial War Museum
JIC	Joint Intelligence Committee
KCMG	Knight Commander of the Order of St Michael and St George
LMF	Lacking Moral Fibre
LMS	London, Midlands and Scottish Railway Company
MBE	Member of the Most Excellent Order of the British Empire

LIST OF ABBREVIATIONS

MC	Military Cross
MI5	British Directorate of Military Intelligence Section 5
	MI6 British Directorate of Military Intelligence Section 6
MI9	British Directorate of Military Intelligence Section 9
	MIR Military Intelligence, Research
MUR	*Mouvements Unis de la Résistance* [United Resistance Movements]
NCO	Non-Commissioned Officer
OKW	*Oberkommando der Wehrmacht* [High Command of the Wehrmacht]
ORB	Operational Record Book
OTU	Operational Training Unit
PAT Line	Organised escape route
PDSA	People's Dispensary for Sick Animals
PM	Prime Minister
PoW	Prisoner of War
PTSD	Post Traumatic Stress Disorder
RAAF	Royal Australian Air Force
RAF	Royal Air Force
RAFES	Royal Air Force Escape Society
RCAF	Royal Canadian Air Force
RF Section	liaised with BCRA for their operations in France
SAS	Special Air Service
SD	Special Duties
SHAEF	Supreme Headquarters Allied Expeditionary Force
SIS	Secret Intelligence Service
SOE	Special Operations Executive
SS	*Schutzstaffel*
STO	*Service du Travail Obligatoire* 'Compulsory Work Service' or STO law of September 1942 requiring all men aged 18 to 50 and all women aged 25 to 35 to be registered so that they could be transported for work
STS	Special Training School
TNA	The National Archives, Kew
TVARA	Tempsford Veterans and Relatives Association
USAA	United Services Automobile Association
USAAF	United States Army Air Forces
WAAF	Women's Auxiliary Air Force
W.Op/Air	Wireless Operator /Air Gunner

Foreword

The Bartter crew

The Bartter crew story is a tribute to all the Special Duties crews who flew from RAF Tempsford and the many who sacrificed their lives. The aim has been to look at the human angle of the crew, detailing their different missions. This has been possible thanks to meticulous research carried out by Jan Christensen. The endurance and psychological demands on these crews were immense. Long lonely flights over enemy territory, with little or no knowledge of their cargo or the aim of the operation. The Resistance in occupied countries relied on the moonlit flights of 138 Squadron and 161 Squadron. Much has been written about the agents and how they probably shortened the war. The secret services might recruit and train, but if they could not get their agents, or as they were known 'Joes', to the operating zones their efforts were futile.

My father, Brian Atkins, was only 20 years old when he volunteered for the Royal Air Force in 1941. His father, Charles Atkins, had had a distinguished army career, rising to the rank of Lieutenant Colonel. I am certain that my father wanted to make another military commitment to that of his father, so he chose the RAF. After air training in Georgia, USA, and Ontario, Canada, he was chosen for the Special Duties 138 Squadron (Bomber Command). He was appointed second pilot and bomb aimer based at RAF Tempsford near Bedford. The captain and pilot was Peter Bartter.

My parents had met when they were both stationed at RAF Beverley in Yorkshire during the summer of 1943. After the war they bought a plot of land and built a house in Rickmansworth, then out in the Hertfordshire countryside. At that time there were no street numbers, just the names of the houses; ours was called 'Roskilde'. My mother told me that Roskilde was the town in Denmark where my father's plane had crashed in 1943. At home the war was never discussed. Bomber Command was a sensitive subject due to the massive destruction of German cities by the RAF. My father had participated in the intensive bombing raids over Hamburg and

Berlin. The traumatic events he endured may well have impacted his ability to discuss his experiences.

During my adolescence, I remember my father attending 138 Squadron's veterans' reunions in Tempsford. I married in 1972 and moved to France. My father would often represent the RAF at French Resistance association events, notably *Amicale Action*. With him I met several of the important Resistance leaders: on one memorable occasion in the town hall of Paris in the presence of the then mayor Jacques Chirac. I was fortunate that my father also introduced me to several legendary pilots from Tempsford: Hugh Verity, Lewis Hodges and Ron Hockey.

My father never knew the details of his SOE missions as they were classified under the Official Secrets Act. Once, when I travelled to Algeria and Yugoslavia on business, he mentioned that he had been there during the war. He simply added that his crew had brought back from Algiers, via Gibraltar, Winston Churchill's son Randolph, who had been parachuted into Yugoslavia to meet Tito. It had been my intention to speak to my father about his wartime experiences when he was due to visit me in Paris over Easter 2000. Regrettably, I never had the chance as he died suddenly the morning before leaving.

I found in my father's belongings a two-hour recording of an interview by the Imperial War Museum. My father explains his RAF recruitment and his SOE and prisoner of war experiences. In this interview, he speaks of his time in the PoW Stalag camp near Dresden. This is in general terms and he does not describe the hardships suffered. When in the area in 2008, I visited the site where my father and four other members of the crew were held between January 1944 and May 1945. Today it is a memorial in the form of a park and woodland. With documents researched I was able to identify the location of the RAF compound. It is in a very peaceful setting and it is difficult to imagine that at one time it held over 20,000 prisoners, essentially British, French and Polish. I strongly recommend reading *Survival at Stalag IV B* by Tony Vercoe.

To mark the seventieth anniversary of the crash I, along with my son, decided to visit the site near Roskilde in Denmark in December 2013. Upon my arrival I was surprised to find a welcoming party of nearly twenty people. Among them was Jan Christensen, a local historian and writer who was researching another RAF crash, and who had been advised of my visit by the local archivist, who I had contacted. Jan immediately showed an interest in the Bartter crew story and we agreed to carry out further research, in both Denmark and England. This entailed Jan visiting the SOE and Bomber Command files on numerous occasions in the National Archives at Kew.

Coincidences have been a regular recurrence in our investigations. One day Jan and I were in the National Archives when we received information from Bob Body, who is the organiser of the Tempsford Veterans and Relatives Association (TVARA), that an original painting of the crew's plane, Halifax BB378, was for sale in an auction. I managed to acquire it!

By coincidence, John, the son of the crew's engineer Nick Anderson, bought a summer home near Roskilde in Denmark. Jan was able to meet him during one of his stays and showed him and his family the crash site. Local newspapers and genealogy sites have also been used to locate descendants of the crew, which has proven challenging at times. We are delighted that most of those contacted were interested and happy to engage with the story. I would like to thank the Gerry Holdsworth Special Forces Charitable Trust for their support with this project.[1] Last but not least, a special thanks to our very patient editor Adrian Stenton and to Maxine Harcourt-Kelly, who while completing her Master's Degree at the University of Chichester found time for invaluable support and encouragement.

By now Jan and I felt that the moment had come for a book to be written about the Bartter crew. *Et le voilà!*

Nigel Atkins Paris
March 2022

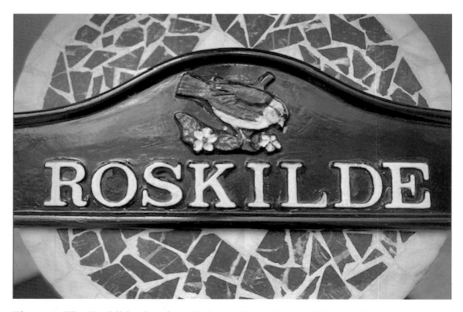

Figure 1. The Roskilde sign from Brian Atkins's home. (Nigel Atkins)

Chapter 1

Seven young men

This is the story of seven young men who, apart from Bartter, the pilot, had an average age of just 21 when they volunteered for the Royal Air Force between 1940 and 1943, and who went on to form the Bartter crew. The Second World War threw together many young people who might otherwise never have crossed paths, and this was certainly true of the Bartter crew with three nationalities represented: an Argentinian, a Canadian, and five Britons. Beyond nationality their livelihoods were also diverse, yet they came together and worked as a tight-knit professional group.

Figure 2. The Bartter crew: (front row, left to right) Fry, Bartter, Anderson; (back row) Riggs, Atkins, Howell, Smith. (Nigel Atkins)

The armed forces in wartime offered a unique opportunity for social integration and for young men and women to interact as never before. The Bartter crew, with the exception of Bartter himself, were in the early stages of their working lives. Their experiences would have a profound impact on them but, as was the case with many of the war generation, they rarely spoke of this momentous time in their lives.

The RAF had been formed towards the end of the First World War in 1918 and was still a very young service compared with the Army (established 1707) and the Royal Navy (established 1546), so there were very few who could follow their father's path into the service. Nonetheless, the RAF had a glamour that the other services did not, and the idea of soaring over the battlefield shooting down enemy aircraft must have seemed appealing to young men when set against the thought of long marches and muddy battlefields, as memories of the First World War would still have been fresh. The recruitment posters of the time encouraged this idea of a glamorous and brave service, but the selection procedure was rigorous, both physically and intellectually. It would have taken more than glamour to attract young men to travel from Argentina and from Canada, and from many other countries, and motivation would have come from a sense of wanting to contribute to the fight against the Nazi regime, and in some cases of wanting to protect their ancestral country. Recruitment took many forms, from posters to cinema promotions to vans with loudspeakers; standards for entry were high but the demand for air and ground crews was equally high.

Between September 1939 and December 1941, almost 790,000 recruits were enrolled in the RAF, with 358,257 joining between September 1939 and December 1940, and 431,526 joining in 1941.[2] The RAF was seen as very much a middle- and lower-middle-class service, and Winston Churchill lamented that in the Battle of Britain the elite schools, including Eton and Harrow, had provided only a few hundred of the 3,000 pilots. Churchill felt that the elite classes had left saving Britain to the middle classes, and that by saving the country, the middle classes had won the right to rule. As we shall see, our Bartter crew fitted the middle-class label. Part of the reason for the number of middle-class entrants into the RAF was simply demand. As George Orwell pointed out: 'Because of, among other things, the need to raise a huge air force a serious breach has been made in the class system', and the other services attempted to maintain an elitism which saw Churchill intervening in some cases.[3]

The new officers in the RAF encountered a level of class snobbery from some who regarded them as mechanics in uniform, but there was also a level of rank distinction within the RAF: for example, in regular squadrons, officers would often be given the same aircraft for every flight, whereas non-commissioned pilots would be allocated whatever aircraft were available. Our Bartter crew had all joined the RAF as volunteers, and we have traced, as much as possible, their pre-war lives through to their coming together as a single crew. In some cases very little information is available, but we know that, during 1943, the crew were involved in several conflict zones, including France, Germany, Yugoslavia, and Denmark.

Arthur (Peter) Bartter

Arthur Bartter was born in 1912 in Kent, and he attended the Harvey Grammar School in Folkestone. He was the oldest member of the crew, and as pilot the most senior – yet he was still only 31 in 1943, the year we focus on in this book. According to his adopted daughter, Julia Castelli Gair, he had initially been refused entry to the RAF as he was deemed to be too old. He was also the only married member of the crew, having married in 1940. He was known as Peter because of his love of the Peter Pan story, which was read to him by his older sister Edith during his childhood years, and the name Peter stuck. It seems to have given him a love for the idea of flying, and his career certainly centred around air travel. Nicknames are a common form of endearment and were also very popular in

Figure 3. Peter Bartter as a young man in his Imperial Airways uniform. (Margaret Fradin)

the forces; as we shall see, all the crew had either a nickname or a name shortened to a more familiar style.

Bartter had worked for Imperial Airways in Egypt, Sudan and Palestine from 1931 to 1936 before transferring to Rome for three-and-a-half years. During these years international travel was glamorous and restricted to the wealthy. Imperial Airways was based in Croydon and flew to Europe and the British Empire, offering great luxury for the time to those who could afford it. Bartter would have enjoyed great respect and probably a very good living. It was not all glamour however; accidents happened with a frequency that would be horrifying today. Bartter's roles included Assistant Station Superintendent and Station Superintendent; he would have been responsible for the operation of the Station, and his fluency in both French and Italian would have been essential in performing this role efficiently. Passenger capacity on these early flights was only around twenty, with about 50,000 people annually travelling world-wide with Imperial in the 1930s. Crews, both in the air and on the ground, were all male and were expected to promote Britain and to represent both the company and the country. Bartter's role would have been a prestigious one, dealing with diplomats travelling around the Empire and those few who could afford air travel. He returned to Imperial Airways in Bristol before joining the RAF in October 1940. He was 28 years old at this point and, despite his initial refusal, his persistence had paid off.

Bartter first trained as a wireless operator at RAF Blackpool, also known as RAF Squires Gate, as well as training camps at Weeton and Kirkham, before transferring to pilot training in RAF Staverton. He was then a flying instructor at RAF Perth, also known as Scone Airport, before moving to RAF Abingdon in 1942 for operational training. He rose through the ranks from Leading Aircraftman (LAC) to Acting Sergeant, and was then commissioned as a Pilot Officer by September 1941. Having qualified as a pilot, he was promoted to Flying Officer a year later.

Within this training he would have been assessed on a Link Trainer. The Link Trainer was designed to train pilots to fly on instruments, rather than by sight. Situated in a darkened room with only the instruments to guide the aircrew, it was a vital tool in pilot training. While rudimentary, it moved in a few directions, and could easily confuse the pilot. Pilots quickly learned to understand their instruments and gain the ability to fly blind. It was, in essence, an early form of flight simulator.

Having moved to RAF Abingdon for operational training, he met Atkins, Fry, Howell, and Riggs. RAF Abingdon would prove to be a useful training ground as it provided challenging terrain which would have been valuable practice for the Bartter crew's overseas missions. In August, Bartter, along with Atkins, Fry, Howell, and Riggs, moved to RAF Riccall in Yorkshire, where Anderson and Smith completed the crew. RAF Riccall was a Heavy Conversion Unit (HCU), where the crew were trained on heavy bombers, including the Halifax. Once their training was completed, they were transferred to RAF Tempsford.

Nicholas (Nick) Anderson

Nicholas Anderson, known as Nick, was born in Shrewsbury in 1921, but had moved north to Durham where he was a dairy worker. He joined the RAF in 1941 and was trained as a flight engineer. It was his role to ensure that the aircraft was fit for duty and that it remained so throughout the flight. As flight engineer, he would have been seated directly behind the pilot. Anderson was not the only member of his family in the services. An article in his local newspaper in early 1944 reports that his older brother George was an army instructor who served for eighteen years, including time in India and Egypt. Another brother, Fred, served in Italy, while a fourth, Robert, was working on the home front in a coal mine. Their sister worked in a munitions factory. Their father had served with the Green Howards in the First World War before being invalided out.

Figure 4. Nicholas Anderson. (Nigel Atkins)

Brian (Tommy) Atkins

Brian Atkins was born in Crewe in May 1922 and was educated at the John Lyon School in Harrow, near his family home in Wembley. This was an independent day school and part of a group which included Harrow School, one of the most prestigious of the English public schools. He jokingly referred to his school as the poor relation to Harrow, but it was an excellent school and remains so to this day. His education would have been considered quite privileged and no doubt stood him in good stead for his war service. He left school in 1938 at the age of 16 and joined the London, Midland, and Scottish Railway Company (LMS) as a clerk, having passed the entrance exam.[4] He was based initially at Euston, but was evacuated to Watford at the outbreak of war, most likely to the Grove, which was the headquarters of the LMS at that time. He joined the Railway Home Guard in June 1940, under the command of a First World War veteran, Major Ford. During Atkins's later interviews with the Imperial War Museum (IWM), he remembered using broomsticks instead of rifles during drills, a wry reference to the television series *Dad's Army*.[5] He volunteered for the RAF in May 1941 – to the disappointment of his father, who had been a distinguished army officer in the First World War – and joined up in September 1941, with his initial training taking place in the St John's Wood area of London. He recalled marching to London Zoo for meals and to Lord's Cricket Ground for lectures.[6] After this it was a period of training in Scarborough, though still no flying at that point. He then found himself nearer home in Hatfield, where finally flight training started, alongside the de Havilland aircraft factory. Heaton Park in Manchester was his next stop before Scotland, and then on to New York on the Arnold Scheme.[7] Arriving in New York was quite an experience for this 19-year-old; he ate steaks and saw a Joe Louis

Figure 5. Brian Atkins. (Nigel Atkins)

fight – Louis was heavyweight boxing champion of the world at that time. It must have been quite the adventure.

His education and abilities had marked him out as pilot material and he underwent some pilot training in Albany, Georgia, in the United States under the Arnold Scheme, where he found the discipline difficult but enjoyed the training. A bout of measles hospitalised him for a few days and derailed his training; on such an intensive course even a few days off meant that he lost his place. In his IWM interview he mentions his disappointment at this turn of events. He was then sent to Ontario in Canada to remuster as a bomb aimer at Trenton. This was the largest training centre for the British Commonwealth Air Training Plan, and was a hub for aircrew training from across the Commonwealth; Trenton remains a Canadian Air Force Base today. Atkins spent three weeks at the RAF Air Navigation School No.1 in Trenton, followed by three weeks at the RAF Air Navigation School No.31 in Port Albert, with further training at the RAF Bombing and Gunnery School in Picton. Despite this change of orientation, he enjoyed the intensive training, had some good times and found the people very supportive. In Canada, Atkins was known as 'Tommy Atkins', presumably in reference to the slang normally directed at soldiers and often shortened to 'Tommy', which was particularly prevalent during the First World War. With the surname Atkins it was an obvious nickname. Promoted to Sergeant he travelled to Nova Scotia (which he recalled being very cold) while he waited for transport back to England.

In December 1942, Atkins was posted to RAF Driffield in Yorkshire, for advanced training within the 1658 Heavy Conversion Unit. These HCUs were introduced by the RAF towards the end of 1941, to retrain crews to operate the new four-engine heavy bombers, including the Handley Page Halifax. Once retrained, crews would then be posted to squadrons. While at Driffield, Atkins suffered sinus issues, which restricted his flying to below 10,000ft. Initially viewed as a restriction, this would later prove to be valuable experience. In March 1943 he arrived at RAF Abingdon, where he met up with Bartter, Fry, Howell and Riggs. His albeit limited pilot training in Albany combined with his training in Ontario positioned him as bomb aimer and second pilot in the crew. He could assist the pilot if necessary on take-off and landing, but would then move to a prone position in the nose of the aircraft. In this position, which also contained a machine gun, he could aid the navigator with visual checks. His role in Special Duties operations involved ensuring that the aircraft was in the correct location for a drop. This is where his additional low-level training at Driffield would prove vital for the role the crew would find themselves in.

Clarence (Joe) Fry

Clarence William Fry, known as Joe, was born in 1918 and was the Canadian member of the crew. Many volunteers from the Commonwealth came to Britain to serve during the war. Pre-war he had been a pharmaceutical

apprentice in Ontario, we believe near Ottawa, and this would have required a good standard of education. He enlisted in the Royal Canadian Air Force (RCAF) in Toronto on 18 July 1941 to be either a pilot or an observer, which was the standard entry channel at this time.

After a short wait, he began his basic training on 9 September at No.1 Manning Station in Toronto. Such was the number of candidates that when he had completed this training on 26 October he had to wait for aviation training. He spent two months at other locations, including No.4 Bombing and Gunnery School, which was located in Fingal in south-west Ontario. Finally, on

Figure 6. Clarence Fry. The white stripe on his cap indicates that he was still in training. (Fry family)

21 December he began aviation training at No.6 Initial Training School, covering the basics of flying, mechanics, meteorology, and navigation.

Fry obviously did well and was deemed suitable for pilot training as he was posted to No.12 Elementary Flying Training School in Goderich, Ontario, on 28 February 1942. For reasons unknown he was unable to complete this training and was reclassified as an observer, which meant training as a bomb aimer and navigator. The records show that Fry was skilled at navigation, and he graduated on 11 September 1942, ranked high enough in his class to be commissioned as a Pilot Officer. He was posted overseas on 25 September and was one of 50,000 Canadians to serve in either the RCAF or the RAF during the war. Fry found himself ultimately posted to Abingdon, where he would become the navigator of the crew, positioned in front of the flight engineer.

Ernesto (Bill) Howell

Ernesto Howell was the Argentinian member of the crew, whose nickname was Bill. His surname suggests that his family had been part of the Welsh settlement in Patagonia from 1865, which retained a strong link to Wales.

Howell was born on 31 December 1917 in Marcelino Escalada in the Santa Fe province of Argentina. He worked as a cattle farmer and was also a rugby player at the Buenos Aires Curupayti Rugby Club. Howell was issued with a British visa in Buenos Aires in June 1940. As a physically fit young man with links to Wales, this would have been a formality at the time. He set sail from Argentina at the age of 22 on the *Highland Brigade* and arrived in Liverpool on 24 September 1940. On the passenger list, he gave an address in Prestatyn, North Wales, which was home to a Howell family, presumably relatives. He is listed as attached to No.10 Operational Training Unit

Figure 7. Ernesto Howell. (TNA)

(OTU) in RAF Abingdon from October 1940, so clearly wasted no time after his arrival before signing up to aid the war effort. Initially, records show Howell as Aircraftman Second Class (AC2), but within a year he had been promoted to the rank of Leading Aircraftman, before being promoted again in 1942 to Sergeant. He was the wireless operator in the crew and would have been positioned behind the navigator.

Walter Riggs

Walter Ralph Riggs, known simply as Riggs, was born in 1922 and lived in Blandford Forum, Dorset. Not much is known about his early life but he had been working as a clerk in a grocery store before volunteering for

Figure 8. Walter Riggs. (Nigel Atkins)

the RAF in December 1941. At only 21 in 1943, Riggs would become the rear gunner. He would operate four machine guns in a flexible defence tail turret. The Special Duties Halifax aircraft that the crew would fly from RAF Tempsford did not have the upper middle turret, so Riggs was the main defender of the aircraft against attacking German fighters; an enormous responsibility on such young shoulders.

Stanley (Stan) Smith

Stanley Gordon Smith was born in 1924 in Surrey and was the youngest member of the crew. He had no nickname, and was known simply as Stan. He lived in Mortlake, which today sits in south-west London, but at the outbreak of war was part of Surrey. Prior to joining the RAF in February 1943 he was a cinema projectionist. At this point in the war, demand for aircrew was high, so his journey from joining to active service was relatively short. Smith, at only 19, was trained as a gunner, but the adapted

Halifax aircraft the crew would fly for Special Duties meant that, apart from the bomb aimer who had a machine gun, there was only one main gunner, rather than the normal three defenders. The upper gun turret was removed so that a hatch could be fitted in the floor of the aircraft. The hatch had a hinged door and allowed for agents or packages to be dropped. Smith's role was therefore adjusted to despatcher. He underwent retraining for this new role, with some of that training taking place at RAF Ringway Parachute

Figure 9. Stanley Smith. (Nigel Atkins)

Training School, at the end of which he would have had a full understanding of the equipment and would likely have made several jumps as well. Smith would be in the body of the aircraft coordinating the dropping of packages and agents with the pilot, navigator, and bomb aimer.

The despatcher's role had several aspects. He would ensure the appropriate weight distribution of packages and agents, which with multiple drops would require ongoing work. He would also coordinate with the agents, ensuring that they were ready for their drop, assisting, and checking parachutes and lines. He would also coordinate the dropping of packages and propaganda leaflets. He would then be responsible for retrieving static lines and securing them safely. There was far more to the role than simply opening the hatch and putting people and items through it. As a trained gunner he could also take over from the rear gunner if necessary.

The crew

Because of their different origins this was a group of men who would never have met under normal circumstances. Socially and professionally they came from diverse backgrounds, yet they came together and clearly got on as a crew. It was vital for a crew to know, like, and understand each other in order to work together effectively. The way in which the crew formed was seen as something akin to matchmaking. Aircrew would gather, wander, and have a chat. A crew would gradually form as a pilot would invite others to join him. It might seem an odd way to put crews together but allowing them the opportunity to meet and chat informally was a good measure for them to assess their compatibility. While Bartter was the oldest member of the crew, he was only thirty-one in 1943, with the youngest only nineteen, and over the following pages the youth of this crew should always be borne in mind.

The crew were clearly highly regarded, having been selected for both Pathfinder and Special Duties and given the choice, as Fry wrote years later. Pathfinder was a special role where the Pathfinder aircraft would lead bombing raids, dropping coloured flares onto targets for the bombing crews following them. However, the Bartter crew instead went to Special Duties at Tempsford, which would provide them with experiences they could never have anticipated.

While Fry said that they had been given a choice, their transfer to Tempsford seems to have been unexpected, according to Atkins. At the time crews were despatched to the base with no knowledge of what went on there. Special Duties were by their nature shrouded in secrecy, but they were the essential link between occupied Europe and the Allies, providing supplies and agents into occupied areas.

Every individual had a role to play, with each one pivotal to the success of an operation. Trust was vital and this crew clearly arrived at RAF Tempsford with a strong bond which allowed them to operate in a confident manner; some crews arrived at Tempsford but left soon afterwards, as they were unable to operate within the unique field that was Special Duties.

The roles of the crew in the aircraft

It is worth reflecting on the role of the pilot during these flights. While it seems easy to understand what a pilot does, consideration must also be given to the pressures on these individuals. Despite the noise, the crew would need to keep in touch throughout, confirming conditions and their position, and checking for enemy activity. The pilot would also operate the S-phone, after its introduction in 1942. This was a short-range radio system that allowed for communication between the ground and the aircraft. Although operated by the pilot, it was audible to the whole crew. Everyone on board had a role to play and it was the pilot's role to mesh the team together so as to be as efficient as possible. He was responsible for everyone on board and had to command absolute respect. It was the pilot's responsibility to be the last one to leave should an emergency arise. Every flight carried the very real risk of being shot down or suffering some other fate, and the pressure of being responsible for the aircraft, crew, and cargo – whether equipment or agents – would have weighed heavily.

Special Duties flights required not just skilled pilots but also great accuracy in navigation. Fry, the navigator, had to ensure that the aircraft maintained its course and timing throughout the return flight. Timing was particularly vital on Special Duties flights, as reception committees took great risks in placing themselves in drop zones to collect supplies and then quickly disappear. It was vital that the aircraft arrived at the predetermined time. Any delays during the flight could mean that the reception committee would leave the drop zone due to the risk of discovery, and the drop would be aborted. The navigator also handled the Rebecca/Eureka radio system, introduced in 1942. This was a system that bounced signals between a ground receiver and antennae on the aircraft. It was an excellent system as it allowed for confirmation of the drop zone without the use of lights, and the navigator could then report their position to the pilot.

The second pilot, Atkins, was also the bomb aimer. On Special Duties flights his role was to ensure, along with the pilot and the navigator, that supplies were dropped accurately and in a timely manner. After take-off, and once over the coast, he would lie prone in the nose section at the front of the aircraft, but instead of taking control and directing the pilot for a bombing run, on the Special Duties flights he would direct the final runs for the drops of supplies and agents. In effect, he would become the eyes of the navigator, picking out ground details and relaying them to the navigator as they approached the drop zone. This was vital as the navigator sat in a blacked-out area of the aircraft. The bomb aimer would coordinate with the pilot, the navigator, and the despatcher in the body of the aircraft to ensure that drops were made as accurately as possible, and also to ensure that supply drops were as concentrated as possible and not spread over too wide an area. Where in the traditional role he would release bombs, on Special Duties he released the containers and advised the despatcher when to drop extra packages or to instruct an agent to jump. It was also his role to step in to either assist or take over from the pilot should it become necessary.

Every member of the crew was vital to the success of an operation, and the flight engineer, Anderson, was integral to the safe operation of the aircraft. Anderson would liaise with the ground crew to ensure that the aircraft was fit and ready for the operation and would report back any issues when they returned. This role had only emerged with the heavy bombers in 1942, when seven-man crews were introduced. While being responsible for the mechanical systems on board, including the hydraulic and electrical systems, he also looked after the fuel system. The fuel system was obviously vital as he needed to ensure that there was enough fuel to complete the operation and return to base. This would mean continually making calculations, and extra time spent over the drop zone waiting for confirmation from the ground would impact fuel reserves, as could unexpected diversions to avoid enemy action. The role also involved being reserve bomb aimer should the bomb aimer either be injured or required to pilot the aircraft. Sometimes an aircraft would return to a different airfield due to the weather conditions or damage from attack.

The role of the wireless operator was filled by Howell. While operations were generally carried out in radio silence, he still had to be able to communicate with base and with the rest of the crew on board. In an emergency he was required to stay at his post to radio the aircraft's position to allow for potential rescue. He would also step in to assist with other roles within the aircraft as necessary.

The rear gunner, Riggs, was isolated and cold in his gun turret. While there was heating it often either failed or was inadequate. The crew all wore thick white jumpers with leather jackets, along with lined flying boots, which afforded them some protection from the elements, but they certainly felt the cold during flights. In this isolated spot, Riggs had to keep watch throughout the flight, looking for enemy aircraft. The defence of the Halifax was primarily in the hands of the rear gunner.

With the mid-upper turret removed on Special Duties Halifax aircraft, the despatcher, Smith, would sit with the packages – and on occasion, agents prior to their delivery into the drop zone. It was the despatcher who would receive the green light to make the drop, which would be directed by the pilot on confirmation from the bomb aimer.

Having come together as a crew in a manner sometimes referred to as matchmaking, it was a perfect example of self-selection. Five of the crew who met at Abingdon – Bartter, the pilot; Atkins, the bomb aimer; Fry, the navigator; Howell, the wireless operator; and Riggs, the gunner – trained on twin-engine Whitleys, flying low-level across country. In August 1943 they transferred to RAF Riccall, to the 1658 Heavy Conversion Unit to train on the Halifax Mark II. Anderson as engineer and Smith, another gunner, also joined the crew at this point. Once the Bartter crew was finally formed and had completed their training in Yorkshire, they awaited news of their first posting to an operational squadron.

According to Atkins, they thought they were being posted to a regular bombing squadron; instead they arrived at Tempsford, home to the Special Duties squadrons. They would soon learn that this was going to be a very different posting, requiring exceptional skill from the entire crew. Even though they would not be fully aware of the work they were carrying out, in the following pages we will explore the extraordinary experience that this one crew lived through.

Crews deployed to Special Duties were initially very experienced as the demands on both piloting and navigation skills were immense. These operations involved flying at very low altitudes, which went against everything the pilots had been taught, and required a level of navigational skill that often relied on visual pinpointing of landmarks such as rivers and lakes. Additionally, the bomb aimer and despatcher had to work together to ensure that the containers and packages were dropped as close to the landing site as possible. Releasing items which were going to float down on parachutes was quite different from dropping bombs. They relied on the pilot flying as low as possible to ensure that the supplies were not spread over too great an area. The bomb aimer held full responsibility as the aircraft approached its target; he would also regularly assist the navigator by giving regular pinpoints throughout the flight. The whole crew had to adapt and to develop new skills.

Chapter 2

Special Operations Executive and secret air bases

In the aftermath of Dunkirk, it was determined by a small group in government that there needed to be an organised guerrilla-style war in the enemy-occupied territories. The aim was to disrupt the enemy through sabotage, by training and arming those on the ground, whether they were civilians or the military opposed to the Nazi regime. Even before war broke out, the idea of irregular warfare was being considered. Within the Foreign Office, Section D, under Laurence Grand, 'looked to investigate every possibility of attacking potential enemies by means other than the operations of military forces'.[8] This would include helping those sympathetic to the Allied cause in times of war and propaganda. This section slightly overlapped a second section known as EH (or CS) headed by Sir Campbell Stuart, whose brief was to look into the use of propaganda to influence domestic German opinion.

There was a third body which section D also overlapped with, this was GS (R), a research arm of the general staff. In late 1938 this section was staffed by just one man, Major J.C.F. Holland, who chose to research the use of guerrilla warfare. His work, along with Grand's in section D, led to a paper being presented to the Chief of the Imperial General Staff (CIGS) on 20 March 1939. A meeting a few days later between Gort (CIGS), Foreign Secretary Halifax, Permanent Under-Secretary Cadogan, and one other Foreign Office representative agreed to move forward in secrecy to attempt to counter Nazi influence in countries where it was threatening or had already gained influence. This was all subject to the Prime Minister agreeing, which apparently Chamberlain did. As they moved into spring, Holland brought in Sir Colin Gubbins, an experienced army man, and this small one-man section grew and was renamed MI R. Section D was creative and vital to the ultimate formation of SOE, gaining contacts and influence, yet it had also annoyed many who could have been useful.[9] The collapse of France brought matters to a head with Churchill, who was an enthusiastic supporter of irregular warfare, who called in Maurice Hankey, the Chancellor of the Duchy of Lancaster. His role was to coordinate the various parties, which led to a meeting on 1 July 1940, where it was agreed to move forward.

The SOE was thus established on 22 July 1940, with the aim of co-ordinating and initiating sabotage and other subversive activities in enemy territory. It was one very secret section of the intelligence services, known to only a limited number of people even within the armed forces. Winston Churchill had appointed Labour MP Hugh Dalton, the Minister for Economic Warfare, to be the minister in charge of this new section on 16 July 1940.[10] The section, although new, was an amalgamation of the smaller sections which had laid the groundwork for what would become a vital part of the war effort. The instruction by Churchill to 'set Europe ablaze' is perhaps the most famous phrase associated with the SOE, but it was Chamberlain who signed the paper which brought the SOE to life.[11] Even after its official formation, more than a year was spent in bureaucratic wrangles and disagreements, which prevented any substantial effort being spent on causing damage to the enemy.

March 1943, the year that this book is focused on, saw the following directive, noted in a Chief of Staff memorandum for the SOE:

> You are the authority responsible for coordinating sabotage and other subversive activities including the organisation of Resistance Groups and for providing advice and liaison on all matters in connection with Patriot Forces up to the time of their embodiment into the regular forces.[12]

Sir Colin Gubbins, KCMG, DSO, MC, joined the SOE in November 1940, having worked with Holland in MI R. He had vast experience, having served in the First World War, then in Ireland, India, Poland, and Norway.[13] He was to become the Operations and Training Director, and had written three booklets – *The Art of Guerrilla Warfare*, *A Partisan Leader's Handbook*, and *How to Use High Explosives* – which utilised his knowledge gained in various parts of the world. His experience made him an ideal choice for the new service, although he was appointed only after an internal battle that saw Churchill intervene; Field Marshal Alan Brooke had attempted to stop Gubbins's move to this new service. Brooke, was surprised as many were, at the move to the SOE and attempted to keep him in the army, where it was thought his career prospects were better.[14] Gubbins's booklets were translated into several languages and distributed to regions where the SOE had a presence, and his influence was significant. Gubbins was also the basis of the character 'M' in Ian Fleming's James Bond books.[15] The SOE worked in many countries, but for the purposes of this book we shall focus on France, Yugoslavia, and Denmark. Each country had its own SOE section, or in some cases more than one section, working specifically on their region.

France

The SOE's work in France was exceptional. Starting from nothing on 22 July 1940, it soon grew to be a significant force. Six different SOE sections despatched clandestine agents to France during the war, and the Bartter crew flew many times for two of the French sections: the F-section and the RF-section, which was the liaison for the Free French Forces of Brigadier-General Charles de Gaulle. From 28 June 1940, de Gaulle was recognised as the leader of the Free French Forces by the British government. In August 1940, Churchill and de Gaulle had signed an agreement to work together, and the Bureau Central de Renseignements et d'Action (BCRA) was set up by the Free French. André Dewavrin and Claude Dansey from MI6 worked closely on this branch, which was in effect the French Secret Service. The RF-section of the SOE was staffed predominantly by French personnel and was initially led by Captain Piquet-Wicks, who had the role of liaising with the BCRA.

One significant figure for de Gaulle and the BCRA would be Jean Moulin. He started his career with the civil service, and rose quickly to become the youngest prefect in France when he was appointed in Chartres. The prefect (*préfet*) is the national government's representative in a department and a very important role, a link between regional and national government.

When the Germans invaded France he was arrested; his left-wing views made them suspect that he was a communist. He endured torture, attempting suicide before managing to escape, having refused to agree with a German directive which wrongly blamed Senegalese troops for a massacre of civilians. In fact, German bombs were responsible for the civilian deaths, but the occupiers did not want to damage the vision they were promoting as a benevolent force during a difficult time. Moulin's famed scarf hid the scar on his neck from his suicide attempt during this period. Towards the end of the year, the Vichy administration ordered the sacking of all left-wing officials and he was dismissed.

Figure 10. Maurice Buckmaster. (TNA)

He then devoted himself to the defeat of the German occupiers, and in September 1941 escaped France for England, with the aim of meeting de Gaulle. He was to become invaluable to the Free French Forces and to the organisation of the Resistance within France.

There were also smaller French sections within the SOE: the EU/P-section, which dealt with the Polish community in France, and the DF-section, which was responsible for establishing escape routes. During the latter part of 1942 another section, known as AMF, was established in Algiers, from where it launched operations in southern France. The sixth section for France was the Jedburgh section. This was formed from 100 teams of three men, drawn from primarily British, American and Free French forces, but also included the Belgian and Dutch military. Unlike the agents, they were dropped behind enemy lines in uniform, so were extremely vulnerable. They were tasked with aiding the Resistance, working ahead of the advancing invasion forces and communicating intelligence to the Allies in 1944.

In March 1941, Acting Major Maurice Buckmaster joined the SOE to become the head of the French section. Immediately prior to the war he had been working in France as general manager for the Ford Motor Company; this meant that he would later be well placed to determine appropriate industrial targets for sabotage.[16] Having returned to England specifically to join the army, he was posted to France and was one of the hundreds of thousands evacuated from Dunkirk in May–June 1940. Then, in March 1941, when he was about to leave for the Middle East, he was moved to the SOE under the auspices of the Department for Economic Warfare.

The F-section was under Buckmaster's control for over three years. During this time he was responsible for the organisation and for the running of the British circuits engaged in sabotage and resistance in France. Buckmaster's network covered almost the whole of France, under the local command of some seventy British officers and wireless operators, with numerous locally recruited helpers and supporters. These circuits would recruit, arm and work with local French Resistance fighters to sabotage

German trains, barges, bridges, and supply depots. In some cases, hit-and-run guerrilla attacks were staged. Danger was ever-present, with Wehrmacht soldiers, the Vichy police, the Abwehr, and the Gestapo everywhere: at control checkpoints, hotels, cafes and on trains. As every SOE agent knew, the Gestapo needed to turn only one operative to be able to infiltrate a circuit; this could cause at the very least misinformation, and at worst many deaths. This in fact occurred many times, with the Prosper Circuit being perhaps the most infamous and destructive.[17]

Buckmaster worked tirelessly, often into the early hours of the morning. He was both dedicated and aware of what he was asking of his agents, and was clearly mindful of the dangers faced not just by his own people but also by those French citizens who would risk everything to assist the Allies in freeing their country from the Germans. He was a hands-on leader and would take part in 'interrogating' recruits, trying to break them and their cover stories. These were grim rehearsals for what some would face once they were deployed in the field. Buckmaster had started with seven agents in 1941, and by D-Day, 6 June 1944, there were 220, working behind German lines carrying out acts of sabotage and feeding intelligence back to London. Over the course of the War, 470 agents went into France, and of those 118 failed to return.[18]

Yugoslavia

The SOE was also involved in Yugoslavia. This was a complex theatre of war and the Bartter crew would complete just one operation, dropping both supplies and agents into the zone. The SOE had been involved since 1941, but by the time our crew were despatched the Allies were switching their allegiance within the region. This is discussed further in Chapter 4, 'Events in the Mediterranean'. Yugoslavia was a difficult location for the SOE, made more so by conflicting issues within the country combined with the SOE still developing as an organisation, but by 1943 a more cohesive attitude was forming, although support was shifting to the side the Allies deemed more capable of causing damage to the Axis.

An SOE office in Cairo, which had struggled with various crises, and another outpost in Istanbul, meant that communications and a clear policy from London was fraught. Differing factions within Yugoslavia with fractured communications from SOE operatives mixed with changing agendas both within the SOE and the British government made for a confused policy.

There was a Balkan and Middle East desk at SOE headquarters in Baker Street, but the Cairo office often attempted to carve its own path and policy regardless of instructions from London. Problems with security within the SOE in Cairo saw the real risk of the military taking over the SOE office in summer 1943.

Denmark

As early as September 1940, the SOE began recruiting Danish expatriates in London to join the Danish section as agents. These agents would become part of the Royal East Kent Regiment (also known as 'the Buffs'), to which King Christian X of Denmark had been appointed Colonel-in-Chief. During the autumn of 1940, the Danish section was set up under the command of English naval officer Ralph C. Hollingworth, who spoke Danish and had spent some time in Denmark before the German occupation in April 1940.

In the early days of the war the SOE had difficulty recruiting Danish citizens, as very few of them had fled Denmark at that time. Hollingworth, in an interview with the Danish national broadcaster Denmark Radio in 1966, reflected on his time in the Second World War and explained that Germany already had major interests in Denmark, including in the food supply chain, the shipping industry, and manufacturing. Following the German invasion there was collaboration between many Danes and the Germans, and this contributed to the rise of the Resistance movement.[19]

Hollingworth was responsible for the recruitment of the many SOE agents who were dropped to help the Resistance in Denmark. Following a

tough selection process in Britain, candidates were informed that their chance of survival in the field was probably around twenty-five per cent, this was the same for all countries served by the SOE. At the same time, they had to sign documents, including the Official Secrets Act, that meant that they could never reveal the work that they were involved with. Not even their families knew what they were doing, and for many it would be

Figure 11. Ralph Hollingworth. (TNA)

decades before they could tell their stories. Many, of course, never had that opportunity.

If a candidate agreed to these conditions and became an SOE agent, they would embark on training that covered security, interrogation techniques, bluffing techniques, parachuting, burglary, sabotage, hold-ups, map reading, shooting, the use of explosives, and silent killing. The training also included a knowledge of German uniforms and ranks, the radio service, and coding systems. A total of 53 agents were dropped by the SOE in Denmark between 1941 and 1945, twenty of them in 1943.

From 1941 the recruitment of Danes from all over the world sped up and the selection of candidates for the various positions to be filled could finally start. Sabotage instructors were to train the members of the Danish Resistance groups in the field, while the wireless operators would be in charge of all communications between England and Denmark. In addition, chief agents would be trained to organise and manage underground Resistance activities. The SOE had just one section for Denmark, given the size and scope of the work to be carried out. This was known as the Danish Section, or SD-section.

The role of the Royal Air Force within Special Operations

The successes of the SOE would not have been possible without the support provided by the RAF and crews such as Bartter's. It is well documented that the RAF had been reluctant to get involved in the SOE and other Special Duties.[20] The idea of taking aircraft and crews out of the fighting and bombing missions went against the whole historical ethos of the RAF. The Director of Plans addressed these concerns in October 1941 by saying that the results from sabotage might outweigh any operational loss.[21] However, these tensions would continue and by 1943 Bomber Command had both operational and administrative responsibility for Special Duty operations. The Commander-in-Chief of Bomber Command, Air Vice-Marshal Arthur 'Bomber' Harris, repeated his opposition to its involvement in Special Duties, and this was noted at a meeting in December 1943.[22] A month later, Harris was more amenable, but still insisted that air staff be involved in the planning stages of operations, as he felt that this would offer a better chance of success.

The RAF had set up Flight 419 in August 1940 with four Lysanders, and this grew over the following years to include several squadrons flying

Whitleys and Halifaxes, along with Stirlings, Lancasters, and Albemarles.[23] The SOE required the cooperation of the RAF more than any other service, simply in order to transport agents and equipment into occupied areas. The very secret nature under which the SOE worked contributed to their difficulties in liaising with the RAF; only those directly involved even knew of the existence of the organisation. The number of aircraft allocated was an ongoing cause of friction between the two establishments; the SOE wanted aircraft ready and available for operations, while the RAF did not want to lose aircraft for missions of which it was sceptical. It was a question of value: Was it worth giving up bombing runs for potential acts of sabotage? Added to that was the fact that Special Duty flights occurred only on moonlit nights, and this meant that aircraft and crews deployed to Special Duties were working at only a fraction of their capability.

It is said that Harris chose RAF Tempsford for SOE duties as it was the foggiest airfield under his command, although boggiest would also have been a fair description.[24] Harris felt that providing aircraft for Special Duties was a waste of resources, as they would fly for only ten or twelve days a month. While he remained sceptical on the merits of Special Duties

Figure 12. Containers being dropped to Resistance fighters. (The Museum of Danish Resistance 1944–1945)

operations for the entirety of the war, it is clear that without these sorties the Resistance forces in the occupied countries would not have been as successful.

Another organisation which was to prove to be essential to the working of the SOE was the BBC. The BBC European services were used by SOE staff to send coded messages to Resistance groups, advising them of supply drops across occupied Europe. Innocuous phrases were inserted into the programmes, which would advise those on the ground of an impending drop; another message a few hours later would confirm that the flight was on its way, while a missing second message would alert the Resistance that the operation was off, due to bad weather or some other issue.

The cargo: containers and agents

The Bartter crew's work consisted of dropping both agents and equipment into enemy territory. There was a wide variety of equipment, including Sten guns, pistols, bazookas, ammunition, and explosives through to cash and grenades, and the crew would know only the number of packages or containers and their weight. The equipment was packed in either packets or containers, depending on its size and weight. There were two types of container used, the 'C' type, which were cylindrical, five feet eight inches in length with a fifteen-inch diameter, and which could hold 220 lbs (100 kg) of equipment across three inner cells, with a gross weight of 330 lbs (150 kg). When these containers were released from the aircraft they descended at a rate of 28 feet per second (8.5 m per second). Slowed by parachutes, they also had buffers to absorb some of the shock on landing. The containers were packed for RAF Tempsford at Gaynes Hall, just a few miles north in St Neots. For operations out of North Africa the containers were packed in Algeria. A smaller container, the 'H' container, was developed by Polish pilots during 1943 and tested by 138 Squadron.

Smaller packages were used for items either too delicate or unsuitable for the containers because of their size. These were packed at RAF Henlow in Bedfordshire. Initially, rubber sheeting was used as it was resilient. The items would be wrapped up in the rubber and then encased in a canvas outer ready for parachuting in. However, because of a rubber shortage, hairlok was developed.[25] This was a horsehair and latex mix, produced in two-inch-thick sheets. Further advances saw the introduction of a pannier-type package consisting of a wire frame and canvas outer.

Figure 13. An example of the containers used by Special Duties. (The Museum of Danish Resistance 1940–1945)

Sizes were determined by the aircraft and its despatching hatch, and by the physical ability of the despatcher to handle the items, which sometimes included skis.[26] In the Halifax the hatch was 40 inches (100 cm) in diameter, so packages were restricted to fit through this, with a weight limit of 140 lbs (64 kg). These could be quite a challenge for the despatcher, and sometimes, if an extra-heavy package was taken, an extra despatcher would be needed to help handle it. The skill of the despatcher in deploying these packages should not be underestimated; he needed to drop them as quickly as possible so that they landed close together. Any agents being transported would not be introduced to the whole crew, and conversation with them was discouraged, with most crews referring to the agents as 'Joes'; names were not given. Atkins mentioned that on the odd occasion some conversation would be started, but it was limited; the less everyone knew the better.[27] The agents would travel to RAF Tempsford, sometimes directly from London or more often they would have stayed for a few days nearby, normally at Gaynes Hall.

Operations, already limited to moonlit nights, were often called off because of the weather conditions, so there were limited opportunities to get agents and supplies into the occupied territories. Once airborne there was no guarantee of success; navigation was extremely difficult, with some operations failing as the crews simply lost their way. Others failed due to the reception committee failing to signal to the flight for the drop, and

Figure 14. RAF Tempsford control tower during the Second World War. (Peter Haining)

some crews were lost to crashes in poor visibility, and, of course, to enemy interception. Those on the ground were always desperate for the supplies, and delays or missed drops caused difficulties for all involved.

RAF Tempsford

The main base for Special Duties flights from England was RAF Tempsford, and this was where the Bartter crew were based, apart from a short period spent in North Africa. Tempsford is a small village in Bedfordshire, near Cambridge. The area was identified as a potential airfield as early as 1936, despite a hill to one side which would cause issues for some aircrews in poor visibility. However, it was 1940 before work began, with completion in 1941. Situated relatively close to London with the A1 main north–south road, access from the SOE's Baker Street headquarters and safe houses was uncomplicated and allowed agents to be transported directly to the airfield. Agent accommodation was also available near the base at Hazells (Hassells) Hall, with an agent holding centre a few miles north at Gaynes Hall near St Neots. While having a major road along with the

25

major north–south railway line close by might not seem the ideal location for a secret air base, it was nevertheless hidden in plain sight, and this airfield would be crucial in aiding Resistance networks across Europe.

While the Tempsford airfield was being constructed, Flight 419 was set up in August 1940 as a resource for both the SOE and the Secret Intelligence Service (SIS), initially with Lysanders, which had the advantage of short-distance take-off and landing abilities, but within months a Whitley had been added.[28] The Flight was moved from RAF North Weald to RAF Stradishall in Suffolk. However, this was not a location suited to the Lysanders, which moved to RAF Tangmere near the coast in West Sussex.[29] The Lysanders were ultimately located both at RAF Tempsford and at RAF Tangmere. They were vulnerable aircraft with little in the way of defences, but they had the ability to hop over the English Channel for drop-off and pick-up operations, and with additional fuel tanks they could reach more distant locations in France. In August 1941 Halifax aircraft were added to the Whitleys and the Flight was raised to Squadron status, No.138.[30] RAF Tempsford was also home to 161 Squadron, which also flew Special Duties. Formed from No.138, as well as handling supply drops, No.161 also handled pick-up operations from Tangmere, landing briefly in occupied territories to drop off and pick up agents and important Resistance individuals.

Early arrivals at RAF Tempsford describe it as a quagmire, seemingly unsuited to air operations. Nonetheless, following the move there by 138 Squadron, along with the packing station in St Neots which provided the equipment the crews would deliver to Resistance groups in Europe, Tempsford established itself as the primary departure point for Special Duties. Despite being a secret base, by December 1942 there were 1,938 personnel stationed there.[31] As operations grew throughout 1943 this number swelled even further. The squadrons based here would primarily carry out operations to France, Belgium, the Netherlands, Denmark, Poland, Germany, Norway and Czechoslovakia.

The airmen of 138 Squadron came from various backgrounds and countries, with most having been trained in the USA, Canada, or England. Additionally, there were many Polish airmen who had fled their country after its invasion by the Germans in 1939.

The Whitley aircraft was phased out by 1943 as the Halifax was particularly suited to the demands of Special Duties, with Stirlings joining later in the year. The Halifax was a popular aircraft with the crews who flew it, but it carried a smaller payload than the Lancaster. It was also felt that the Merlin engines were underpowered, which meant that the Halifax could not fly at higher altitudes to better avoid enemy aircraft. This was addressed in late 1943 with different engines. The Halifax aircraft had a higher survival rate than the Lancaster for crews who had to bail out.[32]

By the time the Bartter crew arrived in 1943, RAF Tempsford was a well-established if unknown airfield. However, they immediately realised that there was something different; they noticed that the upper turret on the Halifax bombers was missing, and were quickly briefed as to their new and unexpected role. There was strict discipline at the camp, under the command of Group Captain Edward 'Mouse' Fielden, and the crew were left in no doubt that the highest standards were required from all of them. They were both excited and perplexed at their deployment, as they felt that, compared to other crews stationed there, they were relatively inexperienced.

Life at RAF Tempsford was said to be comfortable, although that is a relative term. Accommodation consisted of Nissen huts, spread around the base as well as at nearby Hassells Hall, which offered senior RAF officers a mess and accommodation. Nissen huts were basic accommodation with a central coal-fired stove supplying heat. When the base was first opened, crews were billeted in local homes as the Nissen huts were, literally, under water. This truly was the boggiest station in England. There were opportunities for socialising, with regular cinema nights as well as dances and even badminton, which the aircrews could attend. These were a welcome distraction from operations, yet the crews knew that they could never discuss their work, even with colleagues at the base. Rosemund (Bobby) Straw, a member of the Women's Auxiliary Air Force (WAAF), worked as a wireless operator at Tempsford and remembers how they were billeted away from the main camp, in Nissen huts at Everton, a nearby village on the very hill that caused some aircrews problems when landing.[33] The WAAFs saw very little of the aircrews, apart from the cinema evenings on camp and darts evenings at the local pubs, which included the Black Cat, the Anchor, and the Wheatsheaf. The local population obviously knew of the base but never asked any questions. In fact, Leonard Ratcliff, who was with 161 Squadron at RAF Tempsford, recalls that if anyone asked, they were simply told it was secret and that was the end of the conversation.[34] Bobby Straw remembers the Nissen huts as not being particularly warm in the winter, with the central stove being the spot everyone sat around, listening to music by Glen Miller and chatting. She said that some of the other WAAFs did have romances with some members of the aircrews, and that there were even a couple of weddings, but generally everyone knew that they were there to do a job and they simply got on with it. She does remember the food being, in her words, 'fantastic': the first time she had beef olives was at the base![35]

The camp had heavy security around it, with barriers on the roads leading to it, and the WAAFs who were billeted at Everton had to pass through security every day. The morale at RAF Tempsford was said to be high, and both Atkins and Bobby Straw commented on this; there was never any doubt that the Allies would prevail.

The Barn at Tempsford was where agents being deployed into Europe would receive final instructions and would be checked to ensure that they had nothing about their person that linked them to England. The Barn was strictly out of bounds for most of the personnel at Tempsford, including the aircrews. Bobby Straw said that on one occasion she was walking along the road within the base when a car drove past her with curtains drawn; she later learned that it was carrying an agent out to the Barn prior to their deployment. The Barn was in effect a separate compound within the base, with an even tighter level of security than the rest of the base.

Figure 15. The Barn at the former RAF Tempsford as it stands today. (Jan Christensen)

It is clear that the station was run on the strictest security, with each individual being aware only of their own role, and while there might have been hints of what was really going on, everyone was clearly aware of the need for secrecy.

The limited interaction of aircrews and those working on the ground at RAF Tempsford, while for security reasons, also meant that any losses from the operations were not widely known. Aircraft might return bullet-ridden, or even with foliage in the undercarriage from skirting the trees, and many did not return at all. It was said that Hitler was desperate to locate the secret airfield, and there does seem to be evidence that its location might have been divulged. Translated interrogation reports from Dulag Luft, now at the National Archives in Kew, show that following the crash of Operation Spruce 20 on the night of 12/13 August 1943, one or more of the three captured airmen were coerced into giving very detailed information about RAF Tempsford.[36] Two of the crew were killed and two escaped, while those who were captured had been injured. The aircraft, a Halifax, BB334, was hit by flak and crashed near Écorcei, Orne, France.

The amount of detail extracted from the crew member or members was extensive, with not only the details of their operation but also previous operations, including precise map references. Specific details on routes, operational directives and target areas were all divulged. The captured airman described the low-altitude flying and even flying too close to an enemy airfield on one occasion. Although aircrew did not know what was within the containers they carried, he stated that it would likely be sabotage material, food, or weapons. By the time the sixth operation in July 1943 was being discussed, the prisoner was becoming confused. Beyond this he gave detailed information on the number of aircraft at Tempsford, as well as the number of operations on any given night. He noted there were twenty to twenty-five aircraft with around ten operations a night sent out during moonlit nights, but sometimes as many as seventeen or eighteen. Specific information on the role of the bomb aimer was given, although the Germans noted that they had that information from previous interrogations. The prisoner discussed the use of large-scale maps used by the bomb aimer to locate the target areas, rather than the usual air navigation maps. Information was also forthcoming on the instructions given in briefings. The prisoner, though, did categorically deny the use of any radio between the aircraft and the ground. Following interrogation at Dulag Luft in Frankfurt, the prisoner was transferred to Stalag XIB. While Tempsford is often considered the most secret of the Second World War airfields, it was by the autumn of 1943 well known to the Germans.

In total, over 1,000 personnel, 29,000 containers, and 10,000 packages were dropped by aircraft flying out from RAF Tempsford to occupied Europe during the Second World War.[37] 138 Squadron lost 101 aircraft and eighty-four crews consisting of 431 men, from various causes – including being shot down by German night-fighters or flak, problems at take-off, crashes due to bad weather conditions, and other factors.[38]

Bases in North Africa

Our crew's service also took them to North Africa, where they were stationed initially in Blida and then in Protville. From North Africa crews flew to countries including France (and Corsica), Italy, Malta, Greece, and Yugoslavia. During this time our crew was attached to 624 Squadron. This squadron, like 138, was a Special Duties squadron, deployed not on bombing raids but on the rather more irregular form of warfare: dropping supplies and agents to the various Resistance groups in southern Europe

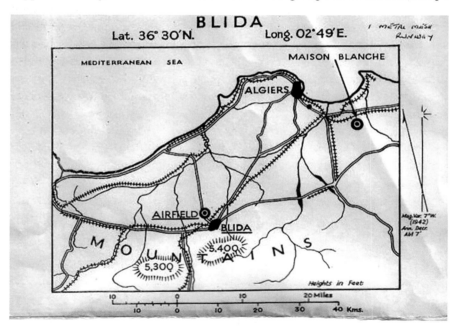

Figure 16. Map showing the location of Blida and Maison Blanche. (RAF/TNA)

and the Balkans. Blida had been taken by the Allies during Operation Torch in November 1942. For several of our crew this would be their first taste of overseas living; the sun shone and there was wine and exotic fruits to enjoy, but their visit would be relatively short.

Blida was a working airbase, with nearby Maison Blanche as a maintenance unit where the aircraft would have been serviced. The Bartter crew were also stationed at Protville, in Tunisia. This airfield was built by US Army engineers in 1943, and it was from here that the crew would fly an operation to Yugoslavia. There is little information on Protville, which was returned to agricultural use by the engineers when the Americans withdrew.

Our crew would likely have been pleased to return to Tempsford after a few weeks in North Africa. While it is known that some crews brought back crates of fruit and vegetables, there is no evidence that our crew were able to bring back such luxuries. It would not all have been a luxury jaunt, though. The crew would have been sleeping under canvas, which offered its own challenges. Scorpions were one risk to those living out of doors in North Africa. While there might have been an idea of an exotic deployment, the reality of living under canvas for several weeks would likely have made them appreciate the relative comfort of Tempsford a little bit more.

The RAF crews who flew Special Duties were all extraordinary; their activities helped Resistance operations in many countries, and undoubtedly shortened the war. Figure 17 shows the tonnage of supplies dropped across Europe by Special Duties crews; a substantial number of agents were also dropped. Resistance organisations throughout Europe were more effective because of the supplies dropped by brave and dedicated aircrews such as the Bartter crew.

Yugoslavia	16,469 tons
France	11,333 tons
Italy	5,907 tons
Greece	4,205 tons
Albania	1,205 tons
Denmark	700 tons
Poland	600 tons
Rest of Europe	2,327 tons

Figure 17 Table showing the tonnage delivered to occupied territories. (Royal Air Force Historical Society Journal 5, February 1989)

Figure 18. The Halifax II DT726 flown by the crew to North Africa. (Brian Atkins; courtesy of Nigel Atkins)

Figure 19. Riggs, Anderson, Atkins, and Smith in front of their tented accommodation in North Arica (Brian Atkins; courtesy of Nigel Atkins)

Right: Figure 20. Brian Atkins in his living quarters writing home. (Nigel Atkins)

Below: Figure 21. Fry and Atkins by a downed German aircraft in the North African desert. (Brian Atkins; courtesy of Nigel Atkins)

Chapter 3

Turmoil in France

The dropping of weapons, explosives – and agents – into France was not something that happened overnight. The idea of a guerrilla-style war alongside a traditional war had been unacceptable to many, yet it would prove not only successful but of significant importance in the liberation of France. By 1943, both the SOE and the Free French Forces were operating across France, but it had been a long hard struggle on both sides of the Channel with many sacrifices along the way. The anticipation of an Allied invasion was growing, as did the efforts to arm a resistance ready and able to help.

When France fell in 1940 many in government headed for North Africa, but one young officer, recently promoted from Colonel to Brigadier-General was the Under-Secretary of State at the War Ministry. His name

Figure 22. German soldiers marching in Paris. (Bundesarchiv, Bild 146-1994-036-09A)

was Charles de Gaulle. He travelled to London to meet Churchill on 9 June 1940, briefly returning to France before escaping to England when France fell and on 18 June, he appealed by radio from London for a French continuation of the war against Germany. He used the word *resistance* from this very first broadcast: 'every Frenchman who is still armed has the absolute duty to continue the resistance'.[39] By 28 June, de Gaulle was recognised by the British government as the leader of Free France and, from his base in London, he began to build up the *Forces Françaises Libres*, the 'Free French Forces'.

He was not, however, leader of all the French in the United Kingdom, nor the French colonies around the world. His early vision of resistance was conceived in terms of battle. It was neither detailed nor overtly political, and to many he was seen as a sphinx, though they were soon reminded that the rogue general had teeth. The idea of a sphinx was cultivated by De Gaulle who deliberately refined an aura of mystery around himself, at times adopting a sphinx like pose. He believed leaders had to possess something indefinable.

At the outbreak of the Second World War, de Gaulle was an ambitious officer; initially placed in charge of the French Fifth Army's tanks, on

Figure 23. De Gaulle making a radio address via the BBC. (WikiMedia Commons)

35

12 September 1939 he launched an attack at Bitche, in the Moselle region. He also wrote a paper, 'The Coming of the Armoured Force', which he sent to his commander, as well as to several politicians. He had a political patron in Reynaud from pre-war days, yet he had been previously passed over for promotion. Paul Reynaud was a politician and lawyer. An early supporter of de Gaulle, he backed the idea of resisting Germany. He was Prime Minister in June 1940 when France fell and was detained for the duration of the war. Although de Gaulle was building his reputation, he was a character who split opinion. Pétain's support for him was waning, and his ambitious nature was sometimes viewed poorly. Philippe Pétain was a First World War hero and had been promoted by Renaud within the cabinet. He, unlike Renaud, believed an armistice with Germany was the best solution.

In February 1940 Renaud told de Gaulle he would be given command of an armoured division when one was available. De Gaulle had written and advocated urging a tank-based defence of France. He took command on 12 May, two days after the Germans attacked, he had less than one third strength but saw some success. Despite not being at full strength and suffering significant losses, de Gaulle's actions with the division in May 1940 nonetheless slowed the German advance. His limited success earned him the temporary rank of Brigadier-General, a uniform he would continue to wear. In early June 1940, Reynaud, now Prime Minister, moved him into a government role, as Under-Secretary of State for National Defence and War, with special responsibility for coordinating with the British. A couple of brief visits to London followed, but returning from his second visit, de Gaulle found that Reynaud had resigned and Pétain was ready to seek an armistice. The next morning he boarded the same aircraft that had brought him home and headed back to London – a decision he claimed caused him anguish at having to leave his army and his country behind. The pilot who flew de Gaulle was named Fielden – the same man who would be in command of RAF Tempsford during the Bartter crew's time there.

Life under occupation

The Franco–German Armistice came into force on 22 June 1940, when Marshal Pétain agreed to effectively split France in two; a directly occupied northern sector of three-fifths governed from Paris by the Germans, and a notionally independent southern sector of two-fifths governed by the collaborationist French administration in Vichy.

The south of France under Pétain and the Vichy administration was one which rejected the French Revolutionary ideals of *Liberté, Égalité, Fraternité* – 'Liberty, Equality, Fraternity' – and instead replaced them with *Travail, Famille, Patrie* – 'Work, Family, Fatherland'. This was a clear departure from the ideals of the Third Republic, displaying both a nostalgia for the *Ancien Régime* and a reaction against the secularisation of the country. Pétain's vision, dubbed a 'National Revolution', called for the return to a simpler time, condemning the perceived decadence of the interwar Republic. Pétain viewed collaboration with the Germans as a necessity; it seems that he saw no issue with it. He saw collaborating as a way of limiting the damage of both defeat and occupation.

It is difficult for the modern reader, knowing the history of the Second World War, to understand that the French, during the early part of the occupation, neither realised nor anticipated the horrors that this war would deliver. For the first two years of occupation, most simply tried to carry on. As time went by, the promotion of Nazi ideals impinged upon French values. Slowly the realisation dawned that this was not just a military occupation, but was a force which permeated the very fabric of the country in its mission to enforce a new order.

Nevertheless, from the beginning the French showed their contempt for the Germans in many ways: in cinemas by stomping their feet during German newsreels, or leaving for a cigarette; by 'accidently' knocking over a German's drink in a bar; by misdirecting them or by pretending not to understand them. There were even instances of people dressing in blue, red, and white as a subtle reference to the French tricolour, particularly on Bastille Day, 14 July, when national colours were banned.[40] However, even these small acts of dissent could lead to arrest, deportation, and even execution.

Yet life on the surface appeared to carry on much as before: nightclubs were open for business and horse racing continued. Some have argued that this showed a collaborative acceptance of the new regime; others that it was an attempt to maintain French life in spite of the constraints: an act of defiance. It was not normal life however, as everyday items such as food and fuel were often difficult to obtain, transport became unpredictable, and even curfew hours changed.

The experiences for those in France were difficult, initially the exodus saw vast numbers flee the invaders. Generations of families took to the roads to escape the coming army, yet refuge was fleeting for many. After the armistice many had no choice but to return north to their homes and endure the misery there. The occupying force made great efforts to be seen as kindly, patting children on the head and such like. But deprivations for those under the occupying force were great, Germans were allocated three times the food coupons of the native French, and they ensured they got first choice everywhere. Eggs and fruit quickly became alien to the masses under occupation. There were punishments for those attempting to assist the occupied population, bakers were shut down for weeks if they were found to have given more bread than was allowed. The friendly face of occupation gave way to the cold reality: sudden arrests for no obvious reason and increasing violence.

Those in the country often fared better than those in towns; they regularly had more food and less interference from the authorities. The demand for French workers by factories in Germany encouraged many to simply melt away into more remote rural areas. For some this would mean becoming part of the burgeoning Resistance.

The propaganda machine from both the Nazis and the Vichy administration grew over the years of occupation and adapted to the increased level of resistance. The German presence haunted the inhabitants of France. Even if they were not dealing with the Germans on a daily basis, there was an all-pervasive mood which hung over the country. Swastikas flew over buildings, people disappeared overnight, goods of every kind were in short supply, and the Germans were always entitled to be at the front of the queue.

Paul Simon, in his 1942 publication *One Enemy Only – The Invader*, had identified the spread of the Nazi regime and wrote:

> They [the Germans] have installed themselves in the railways, public administration, police forces, banks, insurance companies, press, wireless, films, law and education. They are everywhere, even in the so-called unoccupied zone, and in the colonies under the guise of the Armistice Commissions.
>
> They are not only imposing a form of government on the French but also choosing men for that government: nominating civil servants, making laws, imposing fines, raising money, suppressing all liberty, even of thought and forcing France into one sided collaboration. A regime of tyranny has been set up … prisons are full and every day fresh executions take place.[41]

The Germans, people realised, were not simply occupying France; they were moving in and imposing their own ideas and ideals on France – something that had been occurring from the first day of occupation. The role of the SOE within France now began to grow as resistance intensified. The entry into the war by the United States in December 1941 also helped to galvanise the French population, who began to hope that salvation from German tyranny was possible. This hope encouraged and helped the Resistance movement to grow, which in turn meant that more agents and equipment were required, and the Bartter crew, with others, became the conduits for this supply.

In November 1942, after Allied Forces occupied Algeria and Morocco, Germany moved to occupy the whole of France. Any hint of independence for France was now gone. The remaining French naval fleet berthed in Toulon scuttled themselves rather than risk falling into either German or Italian hands.

During 1943 the Germans demanded even more French workers for Germany, with the *Service du Travail Obligatoire* – 'Compulsory Work Service' or STO law of September 1942, requiring all men aged 18 to 50 and all women aged 25 to 35 to be registered so that they could be transported to Germany for work.[42]

By the autumn, Hitler's *Endlösung der Judenfrage* – 'final solution to the Jewish question' – was also extended to include France. The full reality of the German occupation and intentions, including the mass deportation of Jewish people, was finally understood by the French, along with the choices they now had to make. From this point on, the roles of the Resistance, the SOE, and in turn the RAF, changed pace.

The rise of Resistance groups

There had been pockets of resistance immediately following the German invasion and occupation. These minor acts of resistance varied greatly in the early days, but increasingly, as time passed, the desire to resist grew. Whether it was cutting phone lines or defacing German propaganda, even minor acts of resistance could have serious consequences.

Many resisters had not heard de Gaulle's speech from London and there would be, over the coming years, much antagonism between de Gaulle and some members of the Resistance, with one, Henri Frenay, saying, 'It was not at the call of the General that we rose up.'[43] De Gaulle had hoped to rally the French abroad, in England and around the colonies, but he was to be disappointed. Many of the French military who were now based in England had been dismayed by the British attack on the French navy anchored at

Mers el Kébir in Algeria on 3 July 1940, due to the fear of the ships falling into German hands, and the only significant colony to join de Gaulle was French Equatorial Africa. De Gaulle's personality and past right-wing political leanings were also a bar to many of the French military joining the Free French cause. In September 1940 a failed expedition to Dakar in French West Africa by British and Free French forces left the British so concerned that de Gaulle found himself outside the trusted intelligence circle when it came to events in France.

Those who initiated the new Resistance movement within France were a varied group. Henri Frenay was from a traditional family and a career officer in the army; although captured in June 1940 he escaped and initially joined the Vichy regime. But, disillusioned by the collaborationist nature of the regime, he resigned and formed an impressive guerrilla group known as 'Combat' in northern France; he also launched an underground newspaper of the same name. Christian Pineau was a trade unionist who, with others, started the underground newspaper *Libération* in December 1940. There were businessmen such as Jean-Pierre Lévy, academics such as François de Menthon, who founded *Liberté*, and students such as Philippe Viannay, who founded the paper *Défense de la France* in August 1941.[44]

There were people across both the occupied and unoccupied zones who, like those above, represented all sections of society and who felt compelled to oppose the occupation in some way. The problem was how to organise them so that they could be effective in aiding the Allies in the ongoing war. More direct action in the form of a guerrilla war was going to be necessary. Jean Moulin, working alongside de Gaulle in London, was the man who would bring the various groups together in order to carry out this ambitious venture, always under the eye of the ever-watchful German occupiers. Moulin had been a civil servant, who escaped France in September 1941 and met with de Gaulle, who viewed him as a great man. His ambition was to unify the resistance in France and he was the first president of the National Council of Resistance – short lived, as he was captured in June 1943 while back in France, He died as a result of being tortured by Klaus Barbie.

Moulin parachuted into France for the first time in January 1942 on a BCRA operation to organise the Resistance for de Gaulle. There had been much movement between the Resistance and London, which led to potential issues for Moulin, yet he was able to make some progress. Some groups had issues with de Gaulle, others wanted to maintain their independence and distance from authority. The *Mouvements Unis de la Résistance (MUR)*, which consisted of *Zone Sud*, *Combat*, *Libération (sud)*, and *Franc-Tireur* was one merging of Resistance groups for which Moulin was responsible, with the military arm of *MUR* known as the *Armée Secréte*. Moulin managed to get himself back to London in February 1943 to report and to arrange a further return to France. This was not without difficulty. He met hostility from several Resistance groups, with Frenay accusing him of 'bureaucratising the Resistance'.[45]

By 1943, the feeling was that the tide was turning in favour of the Allies. The Allied forces were making significant gains both in the East and in North Africa, with the Germans having to fight on several fronts. The Germans had lost at Stalingrad and the Allies had taken North Africa, to name just two gains. The following quote from Jean Guéhenno, a well-known political and cultural activist who was fiercely anti-fascist, captured this feeling: 'Freedom is on the other side of a barrier of fire, but everyone is ready to cross it.'[46] This sentiment boosted the numbers joining the Resistance, as many young men, emboldened by the hopes of an Allied invasion, continued to flee the enforced work orders which had driven passive resisters to become active resisters. The number of those joining the Resistance leapt during 1943: in March the BCRA estimated a force of 126,000, yet only two months later the figure was 208,000.[47] However, while hope was rising for the French, the German forces were even more determined to strike at the heart of the Resistance.

While workers had been provided for Germany from the beginning of the occupation, registration under the STO law made avoidance more difficult. It was enacted by the Vichy administration, under Pierre Laval, with direct orders coming from Germany. The demand for 250,000 workers in the first few months of 1943 caused an immediate reaction, with young men fleeing into the countryside and protests in towns and villages. Demonstrations occurred in many places as young men were transported away. In Mazamet, 116 young men were transported while a number of protesters sang *La Marseillaise*.[48]

With an increasingly agitated population, France was beginning to fight back more effectively. Jean Guéhenno was a French essayist, writer and critic. During the occupation he refused to publish but kept a journal, which is now regarded as one of the best books on life under occupation. At the beginning of November 1943, Guéhenno tells of the jail at Fresnes where 'every day people are being executed by the Germans. The prisoners have smashed all the windows and despite a ban on singing, La Marseillaise rings out from every cell to accompany the condemned across the prison

41

yard. Threats of torture and execution fail, the singing continues.'[49] In March 1943, Moulin again returned to France and instigated the *Conseil National de la Résistance*, which brought together under one umbrella various groups and factions, apart from the communists, and they met in Paris in May 1943. Tragically, in June, Moulin was betrayed during this visit and was arrested along with other Resistance leaders at a house in Caluire, near Lyon. Initially he was transported to Lyon for interrogation by the Gestapo. There, he was tortured by the infamous Klaus Barbie, before being transferred to Paris. He died while being transported to Germany. De Gaulle described him as a 'great man in every way'. The work that Moulin was able to complete during a relatively short period enabled a cohesive Resistance to work towards the aim of a Free France. In 1964 Moulin's remains were interred in the Pantheon in Paris. François Mauriac said: 'It was not he who made the regiments, but it was he who made the army.'[50]

In addition to the groups mentioned there were many French communists and Spanish republicans, communists, anarchists and liberals who had fought in the Spanish Civil War (1936–1939), gaining experience in clandestine actions. They were to prove useful combatants.

One issue which plagued the Resistance, however, was the diversity of the groups, who often fell out with one another, and with the communists in particular viewed with suspicion; there was good reason why they were not part of the network organised by Moulin. Another group which concerned Moulin was the maquis, named after the rough brush land in Corsica. They were groups who were initially engaged in providing assistance to those escaping the STO law. Yet there was a desire for action, and Moulin had been concerned that the maquis might upset his carefully laid plans with the various Resistance groups. This was settled by the creation of a Resistance 'fortress' on the Vercors plateau, which offered the maquis a combat role.[51] Nonetheless, all of these groups, no matter their political agendas or the names under which they worked, shared a common aim: a free France.

These various groups widened over time, as overheard conversations or chance meetings allowed for a growth in the development of the Resistance. Nevertheless, the very nature of these groups meant they lacked training and equipment, and this is where the SOE became a critical factor. The RAF were a beacon for those on the ground, as noted by Guéhenno in October 1943: 'The night time flights we can hear are different from three years ago when they were heading towards England, now they are coming from England.'[52]

The Free French Forces

The major issue for all the clandestine Resistance groups was one of communication; groups had little or no knowledge of each other. While this separation was vital for survival – the less each group knew about the others the better, in case a group was infiltrated or its members captured – it caused problems both within France and for those working abroad. De Gaulle, in London, had called for action from his countrymen just days after the armistice, yet planning and organising for resistance and sabotage would take time. De Gaulle was possibly concerned that the arming of dissidents might lead to a situation like the short-lived Paris Commune of 1871; the idea seemed fraught with problems for a traditional military man like de Gaulle.

De Gaulle and his Free French colleagues in the BCRA were initially located in Carlton Gardens, with another office in Duke Street, before moving to 1 Dorset House in London. This move to Dorset House meant that there was a physical closeness with the SOE, whose offices and safe houses were located nearby, mostly in Baker Street. This concentrated area of London was a hothouse of activity, although anyone walking past would not have realised the incredible work being done behind its many closed doors. This was where the displaced French would meet and plan their missions to France. However, not all who worked for the Free French were actually French; people from all over the world worked there, but again they all wanted the same thing: a free France. Agents planned missions at these locations, picked up equipment, and – if and when they returned – were debriefed. As has been discussed, the RF-section of the SOE was the liaison department for the BCRA, and one member of the RF-section was Kay Moore. Kay was a British citizen who had been born in Canada, and was studying International Relations in Paris in 1936, prior to travelling in Europe. At the outbreak of war, she was working for the British Embassy in Paris, handling secret communications. In May 1940 she hurriedly left Paris for London and worked at both MI5 and the Canadian High Commission located at Canada House before moving to the SOE in April 1941. Her fluency in French combined with excellent organisational skills marked her out from the crowd and in early 1943 she received First Aid Nursing Yeomanry (FANY) training before moving to the RF-section. There, her role included assisting the agents with their cover stories and ensuring they were ready for deployment. This was a pivotal move because it was while attached to this department that she met Ernest Gimpel, an agent with the BCRA.

Ernest Gimpel was one of three brothers and came from a family of famed art dealers in Paris, who had counted Monet and Renoir among their friends. He fought in the French Army during the German invasion but was captured, having been wounded, at the end of June 1940. He managed to escape to Vichy where he met an old friend, Pierre Henneguier (who would later form the maquis group JULIEN), he persuaded him to work in Marseille for *Azur Transport*, a front for the Polish network F2, who fed information to MI6. One of his brothers, Jean, also worked for the company, as did their father. The Gimpel family understand that funding came via family connections. Florence, Ernest's mother, had a brother in MI6 and they seem to have provided the initial link for resistance activities. Ernest sourced information from local factories which, despite their location within the so-called Free Zone, were under German control. Intelligence was also gathered from the many places the *Azur Transport* trucks visited. On 25 October 1941, Ernest was arrested and charged with betraying national security. He was interrogated for a week but not tortured. On 27 December another prisoner arranged an ambush which allowed Ernest, with others, to escape from Fort St Nicholas in Marseille. He travelled slowly along the coast and was arrested again but managed to escape. For five months he hid near Chamonix, feeding intelligence to MI6 before his brother arranged transport from Cannes to Gibraltar. After a few weeks he was flown to RAF Hendon in England, arriving on 28 September 1942. A Polish officer who travelled with him vouched for him, and after questioning and providing very useful intelligence, he was accepted.

Gimpel was keen to continue working for the British rather than the Free French, but moved across to de Gaulle's BCRA organisation at the end of November. As his family name was well known in the art world he was given the *nom de guerre* Charles Beauchamp. Dorset House was where he would meet Kay Moore, who was to become the love of his life. According to his son, the *nom de guerre* of Beauchamp was chosen because Kay and Ernest apparently lived in Beauchamp Place, close to Harrods, during this period. After the war Ernest kept the name Charles. His is an exceptional story of bravery and endurance, and we will learn more of their story later in this chapter.

Ultimately, with the assistance of SOE and BCRA agents, the Resistance became a powerful force and overcame the complexities and differences of varying groups. The Resistance groups were still separated for their own safety, but they were also separated by ideology and politics. Support from the Allies was going to be vital to their success on the ground, which, in turn, was a key component of the action of the Allies against Nazi Germany.

Before moving on to the Special Duties operations, it is worth mentioning bombing missions. Atkins, in his oral history, recalls undertaking several bombing missions over Germany. He speaks candidly of the fear of being part of a large bombing raid. His recollection is that these raids took place in the autumn of 1943. Atkins said: 'We were professionally trained to do a specific job and carried it out to the best of our ability.'[53] While he stated that these raids took place in the autumn of 1943, he does say that they were around the time of the Firestorm raids. This is explained further in the Appendix.

The operations

All the operations which follow were carried out by the Bartter crew, and the danger of these missions should not be underestimated. They were extraordinary events, which required creative, skilled flying, navigation and coordination among the crew. These servicemen had faith in their orders, and while they understood their role, it would take years before they really appreciated the value of their contribution.

For the operations, records from the National Archives and personal recollections have been used. The aircraft used for these operations was an adapted Special Duties Halifax, a B series Mark II Special. The adapted Halifax aircraft were first delivered to Tempsford in April 1942, replacing the ageing Whitleys. They were powered by four Rolls-Royce Merlin engines and were constructed at Handley Page's facility at Cricklewood, London, and at the English Electric works in Samlesbury, Lancashire. They were originally built as bombers, so for Special Duties they were converted to carry a maximum load of fifteen containers in the bomb bay, which replaced the fifteen 500 lb bombs normally housed in the bay. The upper gun turret was removed to allow for a hatch in the floor, through which agents and packages could be dropped. It was also an escape point for the crew should it be necessary. There were also changes to the fuel vent pipes and exhaust shrouds. It had a maximum speed of 280 mph (450 kph) and could fly at up to 24,000ft (7,300 metres), although rarely did so even on bombing missions, as the cargo load impacted both speed and altitude capabilities. It had a range of around 1,800 miles (3,000 kilometres). At 15,000 ft it could cruise at 275 mph, but Special Duties aircraft flew at a low level for much of the time.

For various reasons the Bartter crew were unable to complete some of their operations, but these should not be classed as failures; the crew, aircraft, and equipment all returned safely. The crew would, no doubt, have felt great frustration at these abortive flights. Also detailed are a couple of operations where members of the Bartter crew were drafted into other crews. Given that these occurred during the crew's early days at RAF Tempsford, it is reasonable to assume that these were training opportunities for the newly arrived crew. It was quite normal for the crew members to undertake an operation with an experienced crew when they first arrived, and four of the Bartter crew were involved in such operations. Fry found himself as navigator on 'Operation Peter 6' on 22 August 1943, which successfully delivered seven containers and one sinker to a waiting reception committee. Propaganda leaflets were dropped over Le Puy.[54] The pilot, Flight Sergeant W.H. James, reported poor red lights and lights not kept on during the circuit. Just weeks later, on 14 September 1943, James was killed in action over Denmark.

The same night, 22 August, saw Bartter, as second pilot and Anderson as flight engineer, on 'Operation Dick 20', piloted by Wing Commander Richard Douglas Speare.[55] This was a successful operation, delivering eight containers, two packages and one sinker (mine) as well as twenty-five pigeons. Pigeons were used throughout the war; as homing pigeons they could be used to transport messages across borders. Propaganda leaflets were also dropped over Le Puy. The crew had set off at 22.17 and returned at 04.24. Speare would be killed in an accident on 23 November 1945. He was only 29 years old yet had an impressive record, having been awarded the DSO, DFC and Bar, and the Croix de Guerre with Palm. He crashed on Kinder Scout, the highest point in the Peak District area of England. He had been flying from High Wycombe to Norfolk. Poor weather and only a compass caused this experienced pilot to be nearly 120 miles north-west of his intended destination.[56]

Atkins served as second pilot on an operation on the same night, a flight under the command of Pilot Officer Bown. This was a two-part operation, 'Donkeyman 18'/'Publican 4', but only the first part would be completed. They took off from Tempsford at 23.25 and completed the successful drop of seven containers at 01.44 from a height of 400ft, spending only ten minutes over the drop zone west of Melun, south of Évry, between 01.35 and 01.45. Part of the Donkeyman operation was also to drop four packages of propaganda leaflets between Fontainebleau and Rambouillet, near Paris. The second portion of the operation, Publican 4, was abandoned after the

Figure 24. Map showing completed French drops by the Bartter crew. (Jan Christensen. Source: The Bartter Crew. Created by Datawrapper © OpenStreetMap contributors)

crew spent fifty-eight minutes over the confirmed drop zone, south and slightly west of Melun, but with no sign of the reception committee.

They returned to base at 05.10, following what would have been an interesting experience. The Donkeyman Circuit, a remnant of the Carte Circuit, was run by Henri Frager, who had been Giraud's staff officer.[57] The circuit would later be betrayed by a double agent and was one of a series of circuits caught up in the infamous Prosper disaster.[58] The Prosper Circuit was compromised following infiltration; its leader, Francis Suttill, was arrested and executed, along with others. There has been much debate surrounding the betrayal of the circuit; it was regarded as a series of mistakes on both sides of the Channel which led to great misfortune for many working in the field.

Before all operations, there were briefings. The navigator would attend one, which covered weather conditions; he would also spend hours studying maps relevant to the operation. The pilot and second pilot would also attend a briefing. The engineer would ensure that the allocated aircraft was ready by liaising with the ground crew.

Operation Dick 53/55: 8 September 1943, Central Loire, near Moulins

It was only a couple of weeks before the Bartter crew worked together on their first operation. On the night of 8/9 September 1943, they set out on an RF operation in aircraft BB309 to deliver weapons and equipment to the area of France codenamed 'Dick'. They would make two drops that night, which was not unusual. The Bartter crew were not the only new crew making their Special Duties debut on this evening; one of the other crews, led by Sergeant Pilot Bruce Leonard Gregory, 138 Squadron, had arrived in Tempsford just the day before the Bartter crew. Demand for Special Duties flights had increased enormously during 1943 as the Resistance, and the need for supplies, grew. Eight aircraft were sent over the Channel that night but only five were successful; the lack of a reception committee and getting lost caused the failure of three, with the other two completing only one of their planned two drops.[59]

We can only imagine the mood on board that night; no doubt one of apprehension mixed with the excitement of finally getting to fly a Special Duties operation. Both planned drops were in the Central Loire region, north of Clermont-Ferrand, centred around Moulins. The crew set off at 19.59 for their first drop zone, Dick 55, which was south of Moulins, near Gannat. The reference of Dick within the operational name links to the area of France with that codename. However, this had been refined to refer to an area known as P1, north of Paris, within the original Dick region.

The Dick area was linked to Edouard Paysant, who had joined the Resistance in 1941, initially looking for areas which could be used for dropping supplies or agents. He was originally based in the Orne region of north France, but, after helping crashed Americans flee, he attracted the attention of the Gestapo and he himself fled in July 1943. He was appointed as deputy to the head of air operations within the Free French Forces for the northern area of France. He used various aliases, including Dominique Tinchebray and Kim B. He was ultimately captured and died in Buchenwald concentration camp on 17 March 1944.

The Special Duties aircraft arrived over the drop zone at 22:59, confirming the location by ground detail and the flashing of the correct letter by the reception committee on the ground.

The crew reported that the white lights on the ground were OK but that only one red light was seen, suggesting the need for some improvement on the ground. They dropped the eight containers and two packages at 23.17 from a height of 400ft (121 metres) and immediately left the area to head for the second drop of the night. The items dropped included 480 explosives, thirty-six Sten guns, 136 Mills bombs (grenades), twenty-two pistols, twenty-four Gammon bombs (hand-thrown grenades), and thirty-two clams (small limpet mines). The alternative name for the drop was 'Congre', and a BBC message confirming that the drop was going ahead was '*La mortadelle se mange avec du pain*'. (Mortadella is eaten with bread).[60]

The crew arrived at their second drop zone, Dick 53, north of Moulins, at 23.22. Having again confirmed the location by ground detail and the reception committee flashing the correct letter to the aircraft, the drop was made at 23:43, again from a height of 400ft. This delivery included 410 explosives, thirty-six Sten guns, ninety Mills bombs, seventeen pistols, twenty-four Gammon bombs, and sixteen clams. The alternative name for this drop was 'Colin'. The BBC message confirming that the delivery was going ahead was '*L'Enfer est rouge.*' Once the seven containers, one package, and one sinker (mine) had been dropped the crew headed for home. The only issue mentioned was that at 01.05 they observed light flak directed towards another aircraft from the direction of the River Avre; they were flying at 6,500ft at the time; visibility was good for the whole flight.

What is interesting about these two drops are their locations, straddling the demarcation line between what had been the occupied north and the Vichy south. At this point in 1943 this was a line in name only; the Vichy administration was disintegrating, the German occupation was spreading, and the population were sensing a change in fortunes. Nevertheless, there were still travel restrictions as well as postal and telecommunication issues along the line.

The crew returned to base at 02.56, a few minutes short of seven hours in the air. On the night of 17 September this aircraft would crash in Denmark, with the loss of several members of the Polish crew. Because only a limited

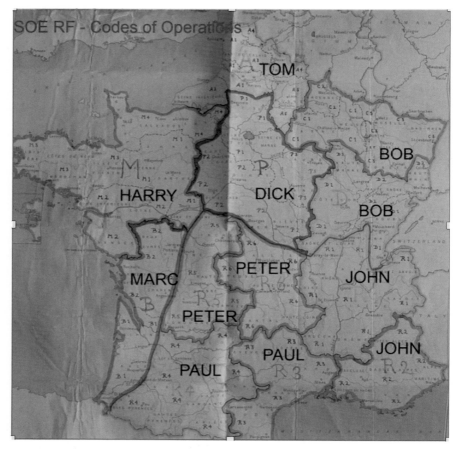

Figure 25. Map, from the National Archives, showing SOE RF codes for areas of France. (TNA)

number of aircraft were available, Special Duties squadrons did not have the luxury of allowing pilots to always operate the same aircraft.

The whole crew must have been delighted to complete their first Special Duties operation, but were no doubt mentally and physically exhausted. Exhaustion was a common problem for all flight crew, and was only partially relieved by rest. Benzadrine, an amphetamine thought to ease fatigue and boost mental alertness, had undergone testing within RAF operations, and in some cases the men were said to behave with a desirable determination and aggression. This research had been conducted during 1941 and 1942 by a former GP and ship's surgeon named Roland H. Winfield, who worked at the RAF physiological laboratories and who also flew on missions to observe the aircrews. By the end of 1942 the RAF's official policy was to issue two 5 mg pills to every crew member before each operation, but there is some anecdotal evidence that the pills were also readily available.[61] This use of drugs may seem extreme, but the crews were working under enormous pressure, and exhaustion would have been a very real issue, particularly on the return leg of an operation.

Operation Peter 19 / Detective A / Butler 10, 11 September 1943, close to Loches, Central France, Indre-et-Loire area

On 11 September 1943, the Bartter crew were back together and undertook three operations: 'Peter 19', 'Detective A', and 'Butler 10'. The crew left RAF Tempsford at 21.05 and were carrying one agent: Henri Sevenet of Detective A. The crew were also carrying a number of containers, packages, and pigeons. En route, the crew reported light flak and tracer fire below the aircraft.

Their first destination was Peter 19. The drop zone was south of Loches, which is in central France, south of Tours. The aircraft arrived at the drop zone at 23.38, and made a dry run over the river junction, but left the area at 00.16 when there was no contact with the reception committee. The crew had confirmed their location both by Gee fix and visual identity. Gee Fix was developed by the British during the Second World War. It enabled two-way radio signals to produce a location fix. It was accurate to a few hundred metres with a range of around 350 miles. There could have been a number of reasons why the reception committee did not appear that night: there might have been increased German patrols in the area, or communications could have been missed. Containers and packages which were not delivered would be returned to base, but this caused additional issues for the crew in terms of fuel consumption and simple logistics within the body of the of the aircraft. Eight packs of propaganda leaflets were dropped south-west of Saumur.

The Detective A assignment required a blind drop with no ground contact; the agent was to be landed in a field. The drop zone was identified via ground detail and Gee fixes. The aircraft arrived over the drop zone just south of Loches at 00.20, and the agent parachuted out at 00.24 from a height of 600ft. The aircraft left one minute later, continuing to the final part of the operation.

The agent dropped was Henri Sevenet (also known as Mathieu and Rodolphe). Sevenet lost his father in the First World War, and Philippe de Vomécourt, who became an important Resistance figure, was a significant

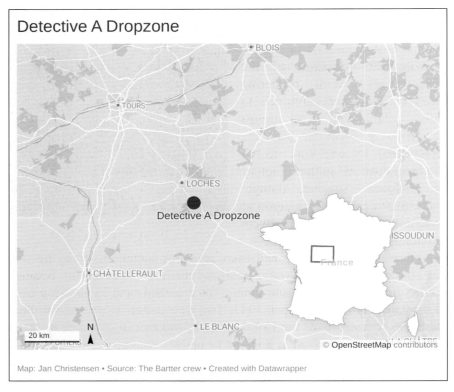

Figure 26. Map showing Detective A drop zone. (Jan Christensen)

character in his early life. Sevenet's mother was head of a reception committee which used the family's 184 hectare estate in Chedigny as a main drop zone in the Limoges region. Sevenet found employment in the Citroën car factory in Lyon as a cover for his Resistance work. Following multiple arrests his position was compromised, and so an organisation in Marseille arranged his passage to England, travelling with a Polish and a British pilot, first crossing the Pyrenees on foot and then on to Barcelona by rail. He arrived in London on 19 July 1942 and was interrogated by the SOE, who deemed him suitable for training, which lasted a month.

He was parachuted into France on 27 August 1942, dropping into the family's 184 hectare estate, to be greeted by his mother. He was tasked with sabotage on the Tours–Poitiers railway line, as part of establishing the Detective Circuit, as well as finding suitable drop zones for equipment. Additionally he was tasked with persuading de Vomécourt to head to England for training and rest, but this was rejected. Sevenet also worked with other groups, but was constantly frustrated by a lack of supplies and communication issues.

With the initiation of the Wheelwright Circuit, bordering Detective, Sevenet continued to travel, establishing small groups and training them in sabotage techniques, in one case to be used against a rubber factory in Toulouse. Sevenet, though, was warned that he was again at risk, and that the Gestapo were pursuing him.

Figure 27. Henri Sevenet. (TNA)

His extensive travelling had been attracting attention. While he was not convinced about the risks, he again made his way to the Spanish border. Sevenet would escape France for a second time by walking over the Pyrenees to Spain in April 1943. This determined 29-year-old walked for eighteen hours over the Col de Siguer, waist deep in snow, to reach Andorra. When he arrived in England he underwent a refresher course and parachute course before being reassigned. Sevenet's return to France with the Bartter crew marked a change in the SOE approach to France.

With their successes in North Africa and in Italy, the Allies felt that victory over the Germans was possible. The role of agents such as Sevenet was to prepare for the eventual Allied landing. His SOE mission instructions show that he was to revive the Detective Circuit covering a smaller area around Carcassonne. He supplied arms to Resistance group the Corps Franc de la Montagne Noire. During the first few months of his return, he concentrated on locating drop zones. Sevenet's success in arranging arms drops ensured that the local Resistance leaders soon gained confidence in him, and more volunteers were recruited. London sent one million francs a month to the Corps Franc de la Montagne Noir. With Sevenet's support they became an effective fighting force. In April 1944 the Corps attacked 300 Germans causing fifty casualties, but suffered only five themselves. In June they cut the Carcassonne–Toulouse railway line and attacked another German convoy, causing a further fifty casualties.

On 28 June 1944, the SOE London headquarters were informed that the Montagne Noire consisted of 600 well-armed men. This increase in numbers was in part due to the STO enforced work orders causing many young men to take to the maquis. On 20 July the Montagne Noire were attacked by a column of 1,500 enemy infantry, tanks, artillery, and bombers, during which they sustained heavy losses and had to leave their weapons behind. It appears that two reconnaissance planes flew over La Galaube, where Sevenet was preparing to go back to HQ by car. Sevenet had got into the car when one of the planes dropped a red marker flare. Everybody immediately got out to find cover and warn the camps by telephone. Sevenet sheltered under some large trees, the others went towards the road. A heavy gliding bomb came down, razed most of the trees, and severed Sevenet's head. His body was found by Resistance members four days later under a manure heap where the Germans had thrown his remains. His ring and rosary were removed to be sent to his mother. He is now buried in Laprade cemetery. The plaque reads:

> Resistance Village, in memory of 20 July 1944. In this grave remain for eternity four officers of CFMN (Corps Franc de la Montagne Noire), Commander Henri Sevenet, Captain Aumonier De Villeneuve, Captain De Kervenoel, Lieutenant Jourdain. In memory of recognition, fidelity and glory of all the members the Corps Franc de la Montagne Noire who under occupation assured to all the world the existence of France.

This was the danger faced by many who were dropped by RAF crews; they understood the risks and yet went anyway. Whether it was their homeland or not, they believed in the cause of freedom and were prepared to make the ultimate sacrifice, as were the RAF crews every time they flew.

The Bartter crew had continued after dropping Sevenet and arrived over the Butler Circuit drop zone, north of Tours, at 01.23. As with other drops it was identified by both ground detail and Gee fixes. Once again, there was no reception committee, this time because the whole circuit had been arrested four days earlier, on 7 September. At the time the Bartter crew were flying over the drop zone, the three members of the Butler network were being interrogated and tortured at the Gestapo headquarters at 84 Avenue Foch in Paris. These were the leader and SOE agent, François Garel (Max), Marcel Rousset (Leopold) the Mauritian wireless operator, and Marcel Fox (Ernest), who had been dropped blind in March 1943, but the containers dropped with them had been lost, including the wireless set. However, by May the circuit was again operational, with a notable success being the sabotage of the main Angers–Sable sur Sarthe railway line. On 7 September,

Figure 28. The plaque marking Sevenet's grave in Laprade. (Kevin Britchfield)

Figure 29. Gestapo headquarters in Paris. (Nigel Atkins)

Garel, Rousset, Fox, and a courier were captured during lunch at a friend's flat in Paris. The Butler circuit was then operated by the Germans for nine months; numerous containers were received by the Germans, as well as four agents falling into the enemy's hands.[62]

The Bartter crew flew over the drop zone for twenty minutes before giving up and leaving the area at 01.45, and finally returned to Tempsford at 03.42. They would have felt disappointed at failing to deliver the containers and packages, and while they did not know the exact contents, they were aware that they were dropping vital supplies to the Resistance groups. After this operation the Bartter crew were transferred to North Africa, which is detailed in Chapter 4: Events in the Mediterranean.

Operation Wheelwright 32, 16 October 1943, Gironde department, south-west France

On their return from North Africa, the crew's first operation to France was 'Wheelwright 32', on 16 October 1943. On board were fifteen containers headed for Pessac-sur-Dordogne,[63] but it was the weather which would thwart the crew on this occasion. This was an F-section operation to a well-known circuit, which will be discussed in more detail in the Wheelwright 38 operation, which the crew were able to complete.

Operation Dick 51 / Sling / Tinker 3 / Diplomat A, 18 October 1943, central France

On the night of 18 October 1943, the Bartter crew set off at 22.50 on an operation consisting of four parts, two for the SOE F-section and two for the RF-section, which liaised with the Free French Forces in London. On this occasion the regular crew were joined by H.F.W. Bampton as second pilot, with Atkins working alongside Fry at navigation. The operation consisted of 'Dick 51' and 'Sling' for the RF-section and 'Diplomat A' and 'Tinker 3' for the F-section.

Operation Dick 51 / Sling, north of Moulins, 18 October 1943, centre-west France

The drop for Dick 51/Sling was substantial, consisting of fourteen containers, six packages and eight packs of propaganda leaflets. The Sling operation was a sub-operation of 'Armada', which was an RF circuit. They had enjoyed great success with attacks on water transport via the canals. Sling had carried out attacks on electric power and pumping stations in August and September. Two members of the Resistance in particular, Marie (codename Basset) and Goujon (codename Jarrot), had an almost legendary reputation for sabotage and were credited with the operations in the autumn. We assume that this drop was carrying more supplies for them.

Operation Tinker 3 / Diplomat A, 18 October 1943 north of Troyes, north-central France

The drop for the Tinker 3 / Diplomat A F-section part of the operation consisted of one agent, one container, and packages. Originally set up by Major Ben Cowburn, Tinker was another effective sabotage unit, which scored a great success in early July by targeting the railway station at

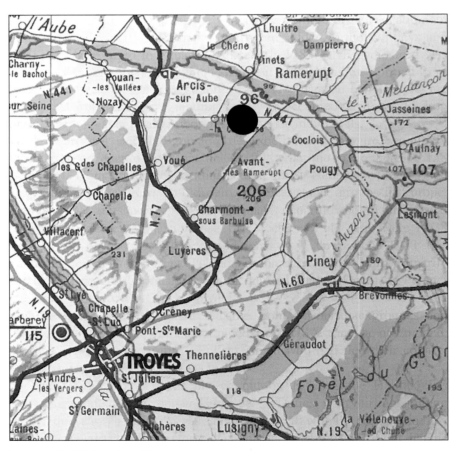

Figure 30. Tinker 3 / Diplomat A area map: approximate drop zone shown. (Tangmere Military Aviation Museum)

Troyes, causing substantial damage. Cowburn was from Lancashire, a tough oil technician. First dropped into France in September 1942, he was highly regarded; sent in on several occasions he was a stickler for security. He once said that 'Security in France was nil, ninety-five per cent of the people arrested, were caught simply because their friends could not keep their mouths shut'.[64] Cowburn gives a good account of this mission in Foot's *SOE in France*. It is clear that Cowburn ran a meticulous operation. Additionally, he is credited with arranging for itching powder to be mixed with the cloth during the manufacture of shirts for German submariners. A story circulating in Troyes suggested that at least one submarine surrendered so that the crew could get treatment for what they thought was a severe form of dermatitis. Cowburn's successes, though, also meant that he was in increasing danger and he had been withdrawn in September, handing over the Tinker Circuit to Pierre Mulsant. Tinker remained a particular target for the Germans, and Mulsant would leave with others in November, placing Tinker in suspension.

The Diplomat Circuit was headed up by Captain Maurice Dupont (also known as Abelard), a Parisian discovered by George Starr of the Wheelwright Circuit, and was initially a dormant circuit, but it would take over what it could of Tinker. The period for this drop was therefore at a time of great danger for Tinker and of activation for Diplomat. The Diplomat Circuit carried on with sabotage missions, again scoring successes with railway yards and locomotives. It was also expanded with the formation of additional services, including nursing and rationing, as well as setting up of the maquis M group. As Dupont was dropped into the Aube during October, we must wonder if the agent the Bartter crew were carrying was in fact the new leader of the Diplomat Circuit. Unfortunately, poor weather forced the crew to turn back and they landed at 02:30. Dupont had previously worked with the Wheelwright Circuit for a year before travelling to England via Spain in the summer of 1943. He would be dropped in France successfully two days later. He trained hundreds of Resistance fighters and coordinated and took part in many successful operations. He was awarded the Military Cross and was described as brave and dashing, an extremely efficient young officer.

Operation Director 57, 21 October 1943, Arles, southern France

On the night of 21 October 1943, the crew undertook 'Operation Director 57'. They were carrying twelve containers and twenty pigeons. This was an SOE F-section operation. Having taken off at 21.15, they returned unsuccessful at

02.33. Bad weather was yet again the reason for the failure of this operation, along with three others going into France on this same night.[65]

Operation Spruce 17, 7 November 1943, Rhone department, eastern France

On 7 November 1943 the crew were tasked with Operation 'Spruce 17', carrying fifteen containers and two packages. Their destination was near Beaujeu, north of Lyon, where the Spruce Circuit had been centred. This was an SOE F-section operation. The crew took off at 20.25, but the Operational Record Book (ORB) reported that reception was lost as they arrived, and so the drop was abandoned.[66]

Operation Trainer 95, Vercors, 9 November 1943, south-east France

Operation 'Trainer 95' saw the Vercors region of France receive its first substantial drop of supplies. It was an exceptional operation to an area which was growing in importance, due to the increasing numbers of maquis located in this remote region.

A total of six aircraft were to deliver ninety containers and forty-eight packages, with the Bartter crew one of the six. Four aircraft would complete their mission, with two failing to deliver their cargo, yet importantly all six aircraft arrived safely back at Tempsford. This was to be a long flight to the south-east region of France, to an area and people who had been waiting for some time for evidence that they were valued and not forgotten. The Vercors is a region of France distinguished by mountains and plateaux, a beautiful area which has Lyon to the north, Grenoble to the east, Valence to the west, and Montelimar to the south. During the Second World War the region became a centre for the maquis. These groups could take advantage of the terrain, which afforded them some protection, narrow country roads, forests, and a mountainous, challenging landscape. It would nonetheless be the site of some terrible battles as the war drew into its final years. There were numerous groups who melted into this area, and they grew in numbers, in part due to the STOs. The remoteness of the Vercors made it an excellent location to hide out in, but many wanted to do more than hide, and it became a significant area for the training of the maquis.

Figure 31. Marc Serratrice (right) with colleagues during the Second World War. (Marc Serratrice)

We have been very fortunate during our research to be able to draw on the personal experiences of Marc Serratrice, a member of the maquis who is 99 years old at the time of writing, and who retains very clear memories of this supply drop as well as his wider experiences during the war. Nigel Atkins travelled to meet Serratrice on two occasions, and what follows is the result of his interviews, as well as information from Serratrice's book, *To be 20 Years Old in the Vercors Maquis*. The SOE supplies were needed following the German takeover of the area from the Italians. But for the maquis it was a clear message that they were not forgotten and that London judged their actions to be important. It was a message that the Allies were preparing for an invasion.

There were eight maquis camps in the Vercors; Serratrice was in number three, which between June and September 1943 had grown from thirty to forty members. There was a protocol to being a camp: they had to have a militarily trained leader, and the camp had to have a roofed area, often a mountain refuge, with three camps forming a battalion. There was strict discipline, with morning duties which included obtaining water and food. The local Resistance was led by a baker and a butcher, and this helped to keep them supplied. Afternoons would be spent training and playing sport. There was also a twenty-four-hour watch on the roads in and out of the area.[67] It was also the launching point for many acts of sabotage in the surrounding area.

Having witnessed the visit of King George VI and Queen Elizabeth to Tempsford earlier in the day, the Bartter crew took off at 19.40 on the evening of 9 November 1943. From the French coast they reported 10/10 cloud cover with the base at 1,000ft until they approached Sancerre.

After this they reported clear skies with 2/10 cloud cover, and good visibility, with some mist in the valleys. Sancerre would have been a good marker on their route: on the River Loire it rises from the plains of the Loire valley.[68]

The crew arrived over their target at 23.23, remaining over the drop zone for twenty-five minutes. They confirmed the location by the sight of three bonfires, and dropped their cargo at 23.41 from a height of 700ft, a slightly higher altitude than usual because of the mountainous terrain. Just a couple of months later the mountains would claim a Halifax crew led by Flying Officer Carrol.[69]

There was to be no contact via the Rebecca/Eureka radio system. The identifying symbols for the drops were the triangle of bonfires and a flashlight identifier (one dot, two dashes) to confirm that the reception committee was in place to the lead aircraft.[70]

The situation in the region had changed over the preceding months, following the Italians being replaced by the Germans, and the situation had become more perilous for the maquisards as well as for the wider population. Serratrice stated that the maquis were under strict orders from de Gaulle to stay in their camps and not to engage in sabotage in Grenoble, which would have drawn unwanted attention to the area. This was an ongoing area of tension between the militarily trained and the civilian members of the maquis, with enthusiastic maquis members nonetheless carrying out sabotage in the area. Their role was to be in a position to prevent those Germans in the south moving north and those in the north moving south. Yet on the day of the drop, a thousand people had gathered in a park in Grenoble to mark Armistice Day, and 600 were either shot or arrested by the Nazis. Retribution was an understandable response. Sabotage also had the added advantage of encouraging people to join the maquis, but this exemplifies the perilous situation in the region during this time.

The arrival of the reception committee at the drop zone had been a close thing. The BBC had broadcast the message 'We will be visiting Marrakech' during the morning, coded specifically for the maquis in the Vercors to advise them that a drop was likely that evening. It was repeated again at noon and finally at 16.00, each time with the message repeated twice, which confirmed the drop. While the radio was monitored, bad reception meant that it was not until the 16.00 broadcast that the leaders in Méaudre realised the drop was going ahead. There followed, as described in Serratrice's book, and confirmed with him during the interview, a chaotic race to get to the remote area and to mark out the drop zone for the aircraft to identify.[71] Léon Vincent Martin, a baker from Méaudre, joined two others and rushed to the site, their trip complicated by the fact they had a car but no fuel.[72] Getting hold of petrol delayed them, and then they had to collect one more person with the supplies to light the necessary bonfires. While the road between Méaudre and Saint-Martin-en-Vercors was snow-free, they still had a climb to the Darbounouse Plateau. As discussed in Paddy Ashdown's book *The Cruel Victory*, the broadcast was heard across the region, and resulted in representatives from every camp descending on the drop zone.[73] There were men on foot, some with carts and oxen, and some even managed to get trucks onto the plateau.

The four men in Serratrice's camp first heard the hum, and then the relatively low height of the aircraft made them duck. They watched the four

Figure 32. Darbounouze Plateau. (Nigel Atkins)

aircraft drop their cargo and saw the parachutes opening and the precious cargo floating to the snow-covered ground. Descriptions of the night depict the sight of the supplies as a miracle, which was followed by frenzied activity, like excited children on Christmas morning, examining presents. The reception committee then spent the rest of the night gathering up the containers and packages which were spread over the plateau, and hiding them in a stone-built shepherd's shelter.

There was some pillaging, with Serratrice noting that 'the maquisards were far from disciplined in handing out the arms'.[74] However, the most important aspect of the drop was the confidence that the supplies brought; a recognition to those on the ground that they were not abandoned. The Bartter crew were carrying fifteen containers and eight packages, along with five packs of propaganda leaflets. These leaflets were dropped in Dijon and Valence. As the crew returned to Tempsford they reported two levels of cloud around Sancerre, with the second layer base at 4,500ft; these two cloud levels merged as they got closer to the French coast. They landed at 04.40, after another long but successful night.

Supplies to the Vercors region had long been awaited, and those on the ground had started to feel forgotten. Yet their attention to the BBC radio

Figure 33. Members of the Vercors maquis, including Marc Serratrice. (Marc Serratrice)

broadcasts brought great hope, and Serratrice said that the drop made them feel less isolated and offered them a connection to those abroad. For those on the ground though, the air-drop was just the beginning. The initial clearing of the cargo had been completed and the next teams were sent in to collect it. Two teams from Camp Three were tasked with moving the supplies to

Figure 34. Containers dropped to the Vercors maquis. (Nigel Atkins)

a safe location. Serratrice was in one of these teams and remembers that it took all morning just to get to the remote drop site; they had to travel thirty kilometres from their camp in Gève to Toutre, before beginning the climb to the plateau. He was one of twenty people who, dressed in warm clothing, climbed the 600 metres, with up to 6in of snow on the path, to the meadow

Figure 35. The terrain the supplies had to be transported over. (Nigel Atkins)

clearing. It had taken them until early afternoon to reach the site, and the winter sun lasted only a few more hours.

They could see the evidence of the previous night's activity on the snow, and the sight of the steel containers lying in the shepherd's hut were greeted with cries of delight. The serious work of moving the several tons of supplies to a secure location now began. Once the containers were opened, inside there was strapping which meant that the contents could be configured to be carried like a backpack. These were heavy though, in some cases too heavy for one person, and had to be carried by two. There were Sten guns, Colt pistols, explosives, grenades, and ammunition – all very welcome for those planning subversive action. The cargo was taken to a cave known to only a limited number of trusted maquis members; it would be February 1944 before the arms would be retrieved for use.[75]

Serratrice and his companions took twenty-four hours to move everything to the cave by foot. Moonlight assisted, but they had to use flashlights to find their way in the darkest hours of the night. They took occasional breaks either in the cave or the hut. Those on the ground were thrilled to find that within the items dropped were packages containing food, with the chocolate and cigarettes proving particularly popular. The tea was also welcomed by those carrying the packages through the snow to the cave, it warmed them during those dark hours.

While the weapons were very greatly appreciated, items such as Camel cigarettes and chocolate felt like gifts from friends, and provided a welcome personal touch; it demonstrated that those far away were thinking of them and were aware of their efforts.

Once the supplies had been safely hidden at the back of the cave, the maquis could only hope for snowfall to cover their tracks, which it did a few days later. Another maquis group, from Camp Five, then took over the guarding of the cave. The weapons would later be moved again to a more accessible location. The location of the drop and the cave were sufficiently remote that during the winter months discovery was unlikely. Yet the groups on the Vercors lived with the permanent threat of attack, they had endured several attacks in the spring from Italian forces, and while most of these troops had melted back to Italy, there remained an ever-present danger from nearby German forces. While most residing in the Vercors were sympathetic to the Resistance, there was always the risk presented by collaborators, roaming patrols, and direct attacks.

As we have seen, these were not simple supply runs, they were fraught with difficulties for the crew. Most of the time the crew were over enemy

Figure 36. Members of the Vercors maquis with Marc Serratrice (wearing glasses nearest the door). (Marc Serratrice)

territory so had to be very watchful and aware; these were long flights, so tiredness was an issue. They could easily encounter enemy aircraft and drop zones could be compromised, leaving the crew vulnerable at low altitudes as they attempted to confirm the location and ensure that the correct signs were received from the ground. For those on the ground, beyond the supplies they were signs of hope and comradeship, and the aircrews were held in the highest esteem. These were extraordinarily important moments for those who had felt isolated and were deemed enemies in their own land. There was support and assistance and it was finally arriving. The term 'air-drop' was magical to these members of the maquis; they were in awe of the aircrews who flew for hours over enemy territory to deliver supplies to help them in their fight. Even after the war, items from the drops were still being used: the parachute material made corsets, neck scarves, and even rope for washing lines.

The situation for the Vercors was difficult, with the expected Allied invasion now delayed. This delay saw a Nazi onslaught on the region, which resulted in tragedy, particularly for the civilian population. Serratrice stated that 1,800 members of the maquis had been able to hide in the mountains, but they lacked supplies and found themselves having to eat grass to survive.

Following D-Day in the north of France, those in the Vercors assumed a rapid invasion from the south, but this did not happen as soon as they had hoped. An uprising in the Vercors saw 10,000 German troops swarm into the area, with many landing by parachute and from gliders. They killed more than 600 maquis members, along with several hundred civilians. When the Americans eventually arrived, the maquis joined the French Army, but Serratrice appears to have had little respect for Roosevelt, whose lack of understanding of the area caused tension.[76] De Gaulle ensured that political appointments instigated by the Americans were not carried out, and instead placed members of the Resistance in positions of power. Unfortunately for those in the Vercors, decisions on actions for the region were indecisive, and in 1944 many paid with their lives.

Yet when the Bartter crew were part of 'Operation Trainer 95', this was a time of hope. Nigel Atkins's visits with Serratrice were emotional for both men, with Serratrice repeatedly expressing his admiration for the airmen who risked their lives to travel so far over enemy territory to find a small point in the Vercors. He commented that he was 20 years old at the time, with Brian Atkins just a year older. The operation had been a symbol of hope and an assurance that they were not forgotten.

Serratrice commented that 'they felt all their efforts and sacrifices were not in vain'. It was a historic moment for the Vercors.

Operation Trainer 41, 10 September 1943, south-east of Besançon, Doubs, south-east France

On 10 November 1943, the crew set off on 'Operation Trainer 41', carrying fifteen containers, two packages, twenty-five pigeons, and six packs of propaganda leaflets. During the war, pigeons were used by all the services to carry messages. The messages were often written on rice paper and attached either to the pigeon's leg or to a small pouch on its back. Most RAF stations had a pigeon loft, with people donating their racing pigeons to the war effort. Birds of prey were culled around the coast to help the pigeons to get home safely. Many pigeons were credited with saving the lives of downed airmen by relaying their locations back to base. The PDSA Dickin Medal was awarded to thirty-two pigeons during the Second World War for displaying conspicuous gallantry and devotion to duty.

The crew's target drop zone was south of Pierrefontaine-les-Varans. This was listed as an RF-section operation, which had been requested by de

Gaulle's Free French Forces in London. The aircraft took off at 19.40, but encountered strong winds which had an adverse effect on their fuel levels; this, together with poor visibility, led them to turn back and abandon the operation.[77] Of the seven operations that night, four were unsuccessful.

Operation Wheelwright 38, 12 November 1943, south-east of Tarbes

The Bartter crew set off at 19.42 on the night of 12 November 1943 on 'Operation Wheelwright 38'. Seven Halifaxes set off for France that evening, with four of them bound for the Wheelwright Circuit, but only the Bartter crew would complete their operation. There was only one other successful operation for 138 Squadron that night, on 'Operation Company', with weather and the lack of reception committees scuppering the rest. The Bartter crew were carrying fifteen containers, six packages, twenty-five pigeons, and six packs of propaganda leaflets.[78] Carrying fifteen containers, the maximum load for a Halifax, shows that this was a substantial air-drop, even without the drops from the other crews who failed to complete their operation. This was also the maximum that Wheelwright had ever had delivered to one drop zone, as they did not have the resources to accept and hide more than this amount at any one location. The Wheelwright Circuit, run by the formidable George Starr, is one of the best known of the SOE circuits in France. Such was his ability, Starr rose to the rank of Lieutenant-Colonel, one of only three F-section organisers to do so.[79] The Bartter crew, having safely delivered their cargo, landed back at base at 03.05, no doubt delighted with their success, given the outcome for the other crews that night.

Starr, born in London in 1904, was a mining engineer. He had been working in Belgium installing mining equipment for Mather and Coulson, a Glasgow company, when the German offensive began, and he escaped via Dunkirk with the British forces. Having joined the army, and despite his reportedly atrocious French accent, he moved over to the SOE. Following training he left for France via Liverpool in October 1942, arriving in Marseille in November. He decided to wait for various items to arrive before moving to Lyon to rendezvous with his contacts. This would prove to be a fortuitous decision, as it was at this time that Gauthier (Philippe de Vomécourt) was arrested, along with others including several of Starr's intended contacts in Lyon.

Starr was sent to France to act as advisor to Henri Sevenet (Rodolphe), yet when he did make contact with him he was unimpressed. We have previously discussed Sevenet, when the Bartter crew dropped him into France he was known to be a little cavalier and as such, attracted the attention of the Gestapo, which greatly concerned Starr, who advised Sevenet to leave the country.

As previously discussed, Sevenet was not keen on this advice. Starr later investigated Sevenet's dealings further as his concerns continued, yet Starr himself was known to be somewhat aggressive in his own dealings and was described as something of a know-all.[80] Nonetheless, the situation settled and allowed Starr to develop an extensive circuit. By August 1943, Wheelwright covered ten departments in the south of France, each with its own chief, and all were planning for the coming D-Day.

Starr was known in the field as Hilaire or Gaston, but his operational name was Hilaire. He had made a fortune in the Congo as a mining engineer. He had such charisma that the population of Castelnau-sur-l'Auvignon made him deputy mayor; this naturally further embedded him in the community and aided his true purpose.[81] His radio operator mentions that he posed as a tobacco inspector.[82]

Starr's wireless operator, Yvonne Cormeau (known as Annette), made a vital contribution to the success of Wheelwright. She was sent out to France in August 1943 and transmitted 400 messages in just twelve months.[83] Along with many in the field, she had a couple of lucky escapes; just days after arriving she saw one of her training colleagues from England; he ignored her attempts to catch his eye and she remembered, in time, the need for discretion. Another occasion saw her having to flee during the night in just her nightdress, with the Germans firing on her.[84] The story goes that her nightdress had bullet holes following this encounter, but that she was unhurt. It is vital to remember that in this war, women were also on the front line, carrying out particularly dangerous work. In an interview in 1991, Cormeau talked about Starr and the circuit, describing the rural people they dealt with as wonderful. She talks of thirty cells spread across their area, extolling Starr's ability to locate remote areas which allowed for supply drops.[85] The night-time close call described above happened in spite of the fact that she moved every three days, always finding a meal and bed from sympathisers. She presented herself as a district nurse and rode around on a bicycle.

Some sources say she stayed too long in one location yet she denied this, saying that it was Starr who often stayed in an area longer than he should. She highlights the fact that there were eight villages called Castelnau in the Gers region, and that the Germans never found Starr, although they did eventually ransack the correct village, killing three inhabitants. Starr and those around him lived by the motto *Dubito ergo sum*, 'I doubt therefore I survive'. Constant wariness and suspicion was the rule for those in the field, and those who allowed a lax approach in any of their dealings often paid with their lives.[86]

Starr built Wheelwright into a substantial circuit. During November 1943 alone they would receive 104 containers and nineteen packages across seven operations and this was during the quieter winter months.[87] Starr was, with Wheelwright, the most successful in dealing with both communist and non-communist factions of the Resistance. He managed to get both working together for the common cause. His success in this area should not be underestimated, as there was ongoing antagonism between communist and non-communists groups throughout the war years. With an extensive area, and a sizeable force, Starr would ultimately have over twenty agents, who had been trained in Britain, under his command. He was one of only a couple of circuit organisers who had the ability to stretch himself across several social groups, unlike some who kept themselves around intellectuals or the gentry. Starr was no doubt charismatic, and endeared himself across the social strata, which helped to ensure his effectiveness.

Operation John 36 / Gendarme, 25 November 1943

On the night of 25/26 November 1943, the Bartter crew were tasked with 'John 36' / 'Gendarme', an operation which required two aircraft: the second aircraft would carry out Operation John 36 / Pelle / Fleau / Mine. These were the first aircraft to carry substantial amounts of cash to the Resistance groups, making this particular operation quite momentous.[88]

This was an RF-section operation, run with the BCRA. The Bartter crew were flying the John 36 / Gendarme part of the operation and carried one agent, fifteen containers, five packages, and 30 million francs (equivalent to €4.6 million today). Within the supplies dropped were ninety Sten guns, 130 Mills bombs, forty-eight Gammon grenades, twenty pistols, and explosives.[89] The second aircraft was piloted by Warrant Officer Pick, and carried two agents specifically described as saboteurs, fifteen containers, five packages, and just over 30 million francs. The records show that it was listed as a non-moon operation with no cloud cover at the drop zone and with starlight noted.

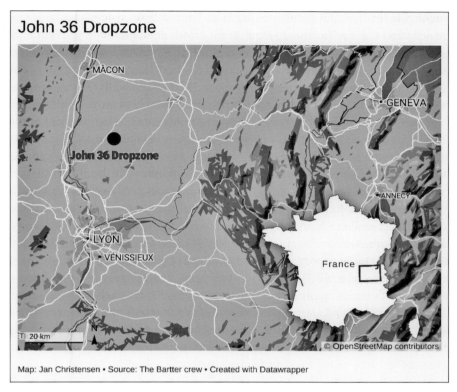

Figure 37. John 36 drop zone. (Jan Christensen)

The Bartter crew took off in aircraft LW275 at 20.35 with Ernest Gimpel aboard. His name was listed as Cercle, but he also had the alias Gendarme.

Different aliases or operation names were often given for additional security. Given the experiences that Gimpel had already endured, it gives an idea of the character of the man that he was keen to return to France to carry on the fight. Gimpel's training in England had gone well, with excellent results and reports on his suitability for fieldwork, and he was fit and agile despite his injury from the beginning of the war. He exited the Halifax and deployed his parachute to return to France with false papers declaring him to be a Vichy-residing civil servant by the name of Charles Henri Blanc. He was to be deployed to the Paris region, to work as deputy to André Boulloche. Boulloche had parachuted into France in September 1943, having arrived in England in May and undergone training with the Free French Forces. He, along with his two sisters, had joined the Resistance while living in Paris. It was necessary for Gimpel to be dropped some distance away from the capital. The Paris area was simply too densely populated to allow for the discreet dropping of personnel and a substantial number of containers.

The official records show that the aircraft arrived over its drop zone, near Châtillon-sur-Chalaronne, north of Lyon, at 23.49, and confirmed that the reception committee was in place by the Rebecca/Eureka radio system. The ground call sign was 'Monique', with the aircraft signal being 'Daphnis'; these call signs were an extra layer of security to ensure that enemy forces had not compromised the drop zone, and failure by the reception committee on the ground to give the correct call sign would mean an aborted operation.[90]

Atkins, in his Imperial War Museum interview, mentions the use of the Aldis lamp in signalling the ground to confirm call signs.[91] The only issue the crew reported was that the lights had been switched off and only put back on as they were overhead. This may have caused a momentary delay as they waited for the lights to reconfirm the drop zone. They made two runs over the area to drop both Gimpel and the containers and packages. The first drop at 23.57 was made from a height of 650ft, the second at 00.04 from 500ft. The pilot was able to confirm the safe arrival of the agent via the use of the S-phone. On confirmation of a safe drop, they departed the area at 00:09, with the Pick crew arriving just three minutes later.

Figure 38. Ernest (Charles) Gimpel.
(Ordre de la Libération)

The second aircraft, captained by W/O Pick, had taken off from Tempsford at 20.50 to complete 'John 36' / Pelle / Fleau / Mine and dropped two agents, Marcel Suarès and Pierre Briout, who were specifically trained in sabotage. They also carried containers and, like Bartter's aircraft, around 30 million francs. These were dropped between 00.12 and 00.25, south of Châtillon-sur-Chalaronne. The crew picked up the signal from the Rebecca/Eureka radio system nine miles from the target at an altitude of 2,000ft. On the first run they used the lights on the ground, but reported a slight overshoot on the second run; nonetheless, both men and equipment arrived safely.

Once Suarès and Briout landed, their initial mission was to make their way to Paris and contact André Rondenay, who was in charge of sabotage operations in and around Paris. They were tasked with industrial sabotage; while bombing could be effective, it often meant civilian casualties and factories razed to the ground, whereas sabotage could effectively stop production with little or no loss of life, and the buildings and structures were often left intact. Sabotage would target machinery which would halt production – and in some cases sabotage would not even be considered as the fault. Following D-Day in 1944, both Suarès and Briout left Paris and were involved in sabotage on the Canal de Nivernais, as requested by the Allies. Tragically, on 15 June, Briout was with a group who were ambushed and killed in a brutal, undisciplined attack. He, along with others who died that day, was awarded the Compagnons de la Libération. Suarès, who was not involved in that fateful day, continued instructing groups from the Aube, Niévre, and Yonne, and led several sabotage raids on railways and bridges. He returned to Paris on hearing of Rondenay's arrest and was captured, but escaped and survived the war. Like Briout he was awarded the Compagnons de la Libération.[92]

The ground reception committee was known as Bugeaud, from the Ain region, and the drops were being made to the Marquis Circuit, who had requested them, and while the original intention had been for a total of sixty-nine containers, twelve packets, and three agents, the drop was considered a success. Only twenty-nine containers were dropped, but the agents were successfully in place. The large sum of money was taken to Lyon, and two bags marked 'Sudsec' were handed over to Jourdain, another agent. Four waterproof bags were also sent with instructions that the wireless sets could be buried in them. Some days later a thirtieth container from the drop was located four miles (six kilometres) west of the drop zone.[93] The Bartter crew landed back at Tempsford at 03.35, after a successful operation, with the Pick aircraft following shortly afterwards, no doubt exhausted but satisfied with the night's work. The Bartter crew's role in getting Gimpel into France safely was vital. While he was active for barely eight weeks behind enemy lines, his contribution was rewarded with the King's Medal for Courage and the Croix de Guerre. Out of sixty-seven operations attempted in November 1943, only twenty-four were successful.

Gimpel, as deputy to Boulloche, was tasked with coordinating the Resistance groups and liaising between the groups on the ground and London. During his all too brief time on the ground in Paris, Gimpel liaised with groups in the southern zone and had a number of radios moved into Paris to allow communications with London. The communication and cooperation he secured with the south of the country was extremely important. There was an enormous and ever-present risk of capture, and on 12 January 1944, both Gimpel and Boulloche were captured. As often happened during this time, they were betrayed by one of their own. A young Sorbonne student by the name of Jacques was arrested and gave up the location of the apartment that Boulloche was using.[94] Any Resistance members who were captured were told to hold out for forty-eight hours before giving any information, as this would give time for people to realise they might have been arrested and to relocate. Jacques, though, buckled under the pressure of torture, which included a form of waterboarding, and gave up the location of Boulloche's secret office on Rue de la Santé on the Left Bank inside the precious forty-eight hours. The Gestapo arrived at the fifth-floor apartment with Jacques and made him give the secret knock. Boulloche, Gimpel and Geneviève, Boulloche's assistant, were not suspicious and Boulloche happily opened the door. During the ensuing scuffle he was shot and injured, while the others were arrested. Gimpel was subjected to horrifying torture but did not yield under the pressure. For two months he was a prisoner in Compiègne, where he was reunited with Boulloche, before being sent firstly to Buchenwald concentration camp, and then Auschwitz, and then on again to Flossenburg in Germany. Boulloche, initially hospitalised, endured a similar fate, quoted in official documents as 'cruel torture', and it is at Flossenburg that the two men were able to hide and avoid being moved again on what would have been a death march. Extraordinarily, both men survived the war. It was from there that both Gimpel and Boulloche were finally liberated on 24 April 1945, and returned slowly to Paris.

Gimpel's only thought at this point was to find his great love, Kay Moore, who fortunately had been deployed to France with other Allied personnel. She had been sent to Paris with the rare (for a woman) rank of Commander, to help dismantle the wireless network. She nursed the emaciated Gimpel back to health with support from her RF friends, who shared her shock and pain at the sight of such a brave man's suffering. Moore left the SOE on 22 August 1945 and married Ernest in London a week later, with Boulloche as a guest. Moore was awarded an MBE for her invaluable work during the war. After the war Ernest would always be known as Charles; the younger pre-war Ernest, conventional and centre-right in his politics, was not the same man who emerged from the war: he was less conventional and his politics had shifted towards the centre-left.

Gimpel's father and brothers were all involved in the Resistance. Sadly, Gimpel's father perished in the Neuengamme concentration camp in January 1945. His brother Jean joined the Resistance and was involved in many successful operations on the ground. He was a skilled saboteur and was awarded the Croix de Guerre, the Medaille de Resistance and the Légion d'honneur. He married a fellow Resistance member, Denise Corre, who was introduced to Jean by Moore. Denise would be known as Catherine after the war. As well as a post-war career as a diamond broker, Jean was a famed writer and historian who often held Enlightenment-style salon afternoons at his home in London.[95] Ernest's other brother, Peter, fought with the British Army, joining the 51st Highland Division and later gaining a commission with the 60th Rifles. He then joined the GHQ Liaison Regiment, known as Phantom. This was a reconnaissance unit, where his bilingual skills would have been valued. The unit's role was to feed information on battles and other pertinent details back to command, which then influenced operations. It was a front-line role and Peter was at El Alamein from the first day, involved in the Italian campaign at Monte Cassino, and ended the war inside Germany. Due to the intelligence nature of the work, Peter remained listed with the Kings Royal Rifle Corps, as was common for anyone transferred to intelligence duties. After the war, in 1946, Peter and Ernest (Charles) opened the Gimpel Fils Art Gallery in London, named in honour of their father. It became renowned for its support of artists from Britain, France and the United States, and was unrivalled for both quality and range as one of the foremost galleries for the post-war avant-garde movement.

While there is no definitive answer as to why the brothers settled in London, Ernest's son, René, suggests that the answer may lie in his father's escape in 1941 from prison in Marseille, as described earlier. In the escape he injured a guard and was charged and sentenced in his absence. He had refused to return for trial at the end of the war, having been decorated by France for his bravery with the Croix de Guerre, Chevalier de la Légion d'honneur, Compagnon de la Libération, as well as with the King's Medal for Courage from Great Britain. One imagines he might have felt some frustration at being lauded with medals yet called to answer for one small action. The sentence was presumably quashed at some point as he did visit France throughout the rest of his life.

For Boulloche the story was quite tragic. His parents, Jacques and Hélène, and older brother Robert, did not join the Resistance; both his father and brother worked for the government and felt duty-bound to serve their countrymen, even within the Vichy regime. Nevertheless, this did not save them from German attention. Their Paris home was raided in August 1944 and the three members of the family not in the Resistance were arrested and tortured, with Hélène being waterboarded, until the Germans were satisfied that they had no information. Ten days before the liberation of Paris they were put on what would be the last train to leave Paris and reach Germany. The men and women were separated, with Hélène sent to Ravenbrück, where she died on 25 October 1944. Jacques died on 18 February 1945 in Buchenwald. Robert had died in Ellrich on 20 January 1945.[96] When André returned to his parents' apartment in May, almost four weeks after he was liberated, his sisters were shocked at his appearance. When he discovered what had happened to his parents and his brother, he wished he had not returned. Nevertheless, he would go on to have a successful political career after the war. The young Jacques, who had been broken by torture and had given them up, was not given the reward he was promised by the Gestapo and he perished in a German concentration camp.

Factors impacting the operations

The brutality that the men on the ground endured is hard to imagine, but it is necessary to remember the extraordinary work they carried out as well as the suffering they both saw and endured. Many, like Gimpel, would say little of these events in the years that followed, even to close family. As we have seen, operations relied on multiple strands coming together: the weather, aircraft operating safely, avoidance of enemy fire, coordination between the ground crew and the aircrew, and, when in place, effective communications with the drop zones. Also, the appearance at the drop zone of a reception committee was often a necessity, which sometimes didn't happen due to communication issues – either errors or the signal, for example from the BBC, being jammed. If the enemy was active in the area it would be too dangerous for the reception committee to be out and about at night. The noise of an approaching aircraft was impossible to mask, so the reception committees were extraordinarily vulnerable. While these would have been frustrating events for all involved, getting back to base safely was of paramount importance. Supply runs could be attempted again, and every flight was successful if the aircraft and crew made it home.

The crew had to be flexible, switching into other crews as needed. Slotting into another crew, or having a new crew member, was not always easy; crews developed an understanding of each other and their methods, but circumstances were such that when called upon, they answered. Ultimately, what mattered was delivering supplies to those fighting for their lives and freedom on the ground. While many of the operations were successful, the Bartter crew, like many others, were thwarted in completing several.

Those operations which, for whatever reason, were not completed would have been felt most keenly on the ground. Supplies were ordered and required, and any delay caused a disruption to activities in the field of operation for these Resistance circuits. Around a quarter of operations failed due to weather conditions, although the number climbed nearer to 35 per cent during the winter months.[97]

Between 5 and 15 per cent failed due to navigation issues, with crews literally becoming lost. A few failed due to mechanical issues and some were lost after delivering their cargo, for reasons not always known. It is difficult to put a number on those which failed due to a lack of reception committees, but going through the ORBs it was a fair number; the majority failed for this reason or the weather.

In spite of the challenges, National Archive records show that, in just six months of 1943, 587 agents and more than 15,000 tons of equipment were delivered into Europe.[98] Overall, it is impressive how few aircraft were lost, seventy-five over France, and this was no doubt down to the skill of the crews. The Bartter crew would have felt a level of weariness at the wasted time spent over enemy territory when operations failed, but also an exhilaration when they were successful. Flying in Special Duties, as we have seen, required great skill, yet these men sought no special recognition; they were, in their view, simply doing their job. As we shall see in Chapter 4, these Special Duties flights were not limited to departures from England. The Bartter crew found themselves on an operation to North Africa for a short period.

Chapter 4

Events in the Mediterranean

Winston Churchill is reported to have said that the Mediterranean represented the soft underbelly of a crocodile, and he felt that a war front in the region could prove vital in defeating the Germans.[99] The Mediterranean theatre of war was able to develop once North Africa had been completely taken by the Allies in 1943. There were multiple operations ranging across the region and the Bartter crew would find themselves despatched from Tempsford before they had time to properly settle in. This region was not soft, however, it was tough, with challenging terrain and differing politics across many countries moving at an extraordinary pace.

This chapter will give a brief outline of the general situation in the Mediterranean before moving on to a specific operation in Yugoslavia. Atkins, second pilot and bomb aimer, in his oral history at the Imperial War Museum, talks of the crew's sojourn to North Africa.[100] Within this he speaks of Corsica, Greece and Yugoslavia. While there are details of two flights the crew undertook to Yugoslavia, details on other flights remain elusive; this could be because of the very nature of the fast-moving situation in the region. Circumstances were changing almost daily throughout the region, and the Bartter crew's arrival had been ordered so that there would be aircraft available to react to any demands.

North Africa

Algeria in North Africa had fallen to the Allies under General Dwight Eisenhower in November 1942, in Operation Torch. Algiers had provided little opposition to the Allies, in part due to the French Resistance staging a coup on 8 November 1942. Nonetheless, it would be May 1943 before the war in North Africa was won by the Allies. It had been a long and tortuous campaign, with the Allies and the Axis powers both enjoying gains as well as enduring losses over the three years. Throughout, the British were able to maintain a presence in Egypt and the SOE had their regional base in Cairo, from which they attempted to organise efforts in occupied countries in Europe. Over the winter of 1942/1943, a second SOE mission was established in Algiers, primarily to coordinate efforts into southern France. The airfield at Blida, located south-west of Algiers, would be the first location our crew would be sent to in North Africa: this would be the Special Duties base for 624 Squadron. During their time there, they would move between Blida and Protville in Tunisia. Atkins also mentions Maison Blanche, now known as Dar El Beïda, an airfield located close to Algiers, which was a major maintenance and transport base for the Allies.

Corsica

The Italians had occupied an area of south-eastern France from 1940, and in November 1942 they invaded the French island of Corsica. The Italians felt the need to bolster their position, with the Allies now in North Africa. Despite some initial support for the occupying forces, resistance gradually increased. The Italians were joined by German troops, particularly after the Allied bombing of Sardinia from February 1943, which caused substantial disruption. As the weeks went by, the Resistance became better organised and requested air-drops from the Allies, although the French submarine *Casabianca* is credited with delivering more significant supplies. The island was ultimately liberated in September 1943, following assistance from the Free French Forces, along with the German withdrawal and Italian surrender.

Greece

Further to the east, Greece had refused Italy's ultimatum to allow it to enter and occupy the country. Despite warnings from his own military, Benito Mussolini invaded in October 1940 – but it was not the easy victory he had hoped for. The terrain was difficult, and the Italians were humiliated. Hitler, realising that the increasing involvement by the Allies in Greece was a potential problem, went to the aid of his Italian ally. The might of the German war machine proved too much and Greece found itself occupied by June 1941, with the British and other Allied personnel falling back to Crete and Egypt, although several thousand were captured. The country was controlled by the Germans, Italians and Bulgarians, with a collaborationist government, yet there was substantial resistance which, as we shall see with Yugoslavia, survived multiple attacks – in part due to the terrain the Resistance occupied. Greece suffered on every level during the occupation, from starvation through to the destruction of most of its industry and even infrastructure. This would lead to a civil war at the end of the Second World War. While it has not been possible to locate details of any flights undertaken by our crew, Atkins does refer to Greece in his Imperial War Museum interview.

Yugoslavia

We can see that the Allies were active across the whole area of the Mediterranean, in differing scenarios, and the crew were thrust into the middle of this. Their operation during this period was to Yugoslavia, a country not unlike Greece, which had found itself carved up into many pieces. Yugoslavia was also occupied by Germany, Italy and Bulgaria. This region of the Balkans was sometimes referred to as the 'Cinderella Front', as there were some hopes that it could develop into a serious southern front against the Axis powers.[101]

Perhaps the single most important factor to consider when looking at Yugoslavia during this period is that it is controversial. This chapter does not attempt to give a definitive history, but rather an overview of the competing forces that the Allied powers, and particularly the British, were attempting to decipher and understand. As we shall see, Prime Minister Winston Churchill's primary aim was the defeat of Nazi Germany by any means, and this caused issues when the best option for local allies appeared to be a communist force, directed by Tito, rather than those more supportive of a return of the monarch, King Peter.

Yugoslavia presented a unique theatre of warfare; it was geographically distant from northern Europe and the Allied countries had limited trade connections. The Prince Regent, Paul, although opposed to Nazi Germany, agreed to join the Axis powers – albeit with several conditions aimed at keeping the country as neutral as possible. This led to a British-supported coup which put the 17-year-old King Peter on the throne in March 1941. In turn the British hoped for a new Balkan front, but on 6 April 1941 the country was invaded by German, Italian, Hungarian and Bulgarian forces as Yugoslavia refused to join the Axis powers. The country was then carved up between the invaders. In addition, the supposedly independent state of Croatia declared itself in Zagreb on 10 April, sponsored by the Italians, while the Germans sponsored the Serbian Government of National Salvation; both of these administrations were in effect under the control of the occupiers. Following this, a reign of terror was unleashed, aimed particularly at the Jewish, Roma and Serbian people. This provoked rebellions, and drove people to support either Josip Broz, 'Tito', and his People's Liberation Movement, or Dragoljub 'Draža' Mihailović's Yugoslav Army in the Fatherland. A confused British policy dating back to 1939, coupled with strategic and economic issues, and with the SOE and others appearing to work at cross-purposes, created difficulties in understanding the true situation. The major issue for the Allies at this point was attempting to understand who within the country should benefit from Allied support; because of the muddled nature of the politics this was not as straightforward as it might have been. There were different factions based on ethnicity, religion and politics which combined to present the Allies with a complex path to negotiate. When the Germans invaded, King Peter and his government fled first to Athens and then to Jerusalem, before finally landing in London. To begin with, the Allied aim was to restore the pre-war government in Yugoslavia, but concerns persisted as to whether this was a realistic aim, given the varying factions within the country.

Support, initially, was thrown behind General Mihailović. He had started out as a member of the Chetniks, groups based on First World War sabotage specialists. Mihailović, who had been a regular army general, became Minister of War, and attracted support from Belgrade industrialists, but also from some within the Serb Agrarian Party and the former Patriotic Society in Montenegro. There were other Resistance groups, including the National Liberation Partisan Detachments under the leadership of Tito, a Croat communist. The Chetniks, some of whom were under Mihailović's control or influence, became more interested in fighting the partisans than the Axis powers,[102] and it began to be reported as early as Autumn 1941 that Mihailović's force was engaged in fighting the partisans and other groups using equipment supplied by the Allies. As time went on it became clear that Mihailović would engage the Germans only when he was sure of an Allied front in the Balkans. He would not commit to opposing the Axis powers without firm Allied support.

Lieutenant Colonel David Thomas Hudson, a member of the SOE, had been a mining engineer in Yugoslavia and spoke reasonable Serbo-Croat.[103] When he was sent in to Yugoslavia on Operation Bullseye in 1941, he found that the communist guerrilla groups were organised, and recommended that supplies be provided to them. He also produced a twenty-one-page report which stated that Mihailović emerged as 'more fanatically anti-Croat, anti-Moslem, anti-Semitic, anti-Catholic and anti-Communist than he was anti-Axis'.[104] Hudson's reports also detailed events in the summer of 1943 against Tito's forces, which described the onslaught which his partisans had endured and survived. This was perhaps the real turning point in Yugoslavia.

> No fewer than six major offensives were launched at various times against the partisans by the combined might of the Axis. These reached a bloody climax in the Montenegrin campaign of summer 1943, when the main body of Tito's forces came near to being encircled and wiped out by a force including (besides seven German and four Italian divisions) Bulgarian, Ustasi and Domobran (pro-Nazi Croatian auxiliary) troops, together with Mihailović's Chetniks, backed by strong artillery and air support. The attack failed and the partisans emerged from the battle stronger and more confident than ever. The collapse of Italy swung the balance further against Germany. The joint Axis strength fell: the partisans, with masses of Italian booty, rose to a greater height of power.[105]

Having to deal with an ongoing civil war during the wider World War is just one example of the difficulties encountered by the Allies when dealing with Yugoslavia.

Other reports in 1943 from Captain F.W. Deakin, a friend of Churchill's who had travelled to Yugoslavia, contained two important notes for the Allies; one was encouraging, stating that the partisans were aggressive and courageous in their fight against the enemy. The second was more disturbing, in that the German First Mountain Division had moved successfully via rail through territory controlled by Mihailović. Allied interception of German communications appeared to confirm that the forces under the apparent control of Mihailović were at best timid and at worst collaborating with the enemy.[106] The interception of these messages was credited to a secret source: 'Ultra'. In fact, it was Bletchley Park, the secret home of the code-breakers, intercepting German communications and decrypting them, but a secret source was quoted so that the Germans would not realise that the Allies could decrypt their communications. Although Polish mathematicians had cracked the Enigma machine, it was at Bletchley that speedy decryption was possible thanks to Alan Turing and others. Mihailović would argue that he was working to save lives by limiting his aggression towards the Axis powers, yet reports from June 1943 showed that his loyalties were directed towards internal priorities, for example in Montenegro aiding the Italians against the partisans.[107]

Meanwhile Tito had grown his communist cells, which had begun in 1937, and from April 1942 his partisan force grew from 10,000 to 20,000. The turning point for the Allies in choosing who to back came from Brigadier Fitzroy Maclean. Following ongoing disturbing reports centred on the loyalty and aims of Mihailović, Maclean was parachuted into Yugoslavia and was taken to meet Tito. This was in September 1943, and by December Allied support was transferred to Tito. This caused consternation with King Peter and his court, as well as raising questions about whether there was to be political as well as military support.

Fitzroy Maclean

Maclean was an unusual mix of soldier and diplomat which, in this instance, made him a valuable asset. Born in Cairo in 1911, to Scottish landed gentry, he was educated at Eton, like his contemporary Randolph Churchill – of whom more later. Maclean read classics and history at King's College, Cambridge, followed by work in Germany before joining the diplomatic service. Initially posted to Paris, he requested a transfer to Moscow, where he was stationed for a couple of years. At the outbreak of the war diplomats were a reserved occupation and so he was not allowed to enlist in the armed forces. Nonetheless, he had determined to fight so he resigned from the diplomatic service, stating that he was going into politics, and then immediately joined his father's old regiment, the Queen's Own Cameron Highlanders, while also entering politics. He soon became a lance corporal and in 1941 he was commissioned and also became MP for Lancaster. He was recruited by David Stirling, the founder of the SAS (Special Air Service) and proved himself on operations across the North African desert. He met up with Randolph Churchill during this time, when Churchill was working as an observer on various operations. Following one such operation in Benghazi, in what is now Libya, Maclean was involved in a road accident between Alexandria and Benghazi which also included Churchill and Stirling; several weeks in hospital followed for both Maclean and Churchill.[108]

Having spent two years in Africa, the Middle East, and Crete, Maclean was summoned to Cairo and then back to London in July 1943, being advised that he would be parachuted into Yugoslavia. He knew little of Yugoslavia, and once in London he learned of the doubts surrounding Mihailović and how little was known about the partisans. Maclean was invited out to Prime

Minister Winston Churchill's official country residence, Chequers, along with others, and while there news broke that Mussolini had resigned on 25 July 1943. In Churchill's words to Maclean: 'This makes your job more important than ever. The German position in Italy is crumbling. We must now put all the pressure we can on them on the other side of the Adriatic. You must go in without delay.'[109] It would, in fact, take until September for Maclean to reach Yugoslavia, but by this point the partisans numbered in the hundreds of thousands. It was also in September that King Peter and a small number of cabinet officials made the move from London to Cairo.

Maclean returned to Cairo and set about building his team, which he details in his book *Eastern Approaches*. His team included one American, Major Lin Farish of the United States Army Corps of Engineers, who delighted Maclean by stating that he could build aerodromes; Maclean had realised that air support was going to be vital in any actions.[110]

Maclean and his team were parachuted into Yugoslavia over two nights and were taken to meet Tito. The partisan organisation impressed, as did Tito himself. Maclean felt that there was a clear command structure, which he thought vital in guerrilla warfare. Having met Tito, Maclean also travelled around to learn as much as possible. He left Yugoslavia on 5 October 1943 for Cairo, via Italy. His report, wired to London following his incursion into Yugoslavia, argued that, after the war, it would be Tito and his forces that would triumph. He also reported this to Winston Churchill when they met in Cairo in November, and gives the following account of their conversation:

> I now emphasized to Mr. Churchill the other points which I had already made in my report, namely that in my view the Partisans, whether we helped them or not, would be the decisive political factor in Yugoslavia after the war and, secondly, that Tito and the other leaders of the Movement were openly and avowedly Communist and that the system they would establish would inevitably be on the Soviet lines and, in all probability, strongly orientated towards the Soviet Union.
>
> The Prime Minister's reply resolved my doubts.
>
> 'Do you intend,' he asked, 'to make Yugoslavia your home after the war?' 'No, sir,' I replied.
>
> 'Neither do I,' he said. 'And, that being so, the less you and I worry about the form of government they set up, the better. That's for them to decide. What interests us is, which of them is doing the most harm to the Germans?'[111]

This was the overriding factor, who was doing the damage to the Germans, not a concern for long-term politics. Concerns from the very beginning had been voiced about the ability of the exiled government to provide unity, and putting all effort behind Mihailović would be further destabilising. Tito, while communist, had provided a degree of unity across the Serbs, Croats and Slovenes that was lacking from other sources.

Following Maclean and Churchill's meeting, resources were increasingly focused on aiding Tito and his partisans. While the Allies didn't want to cut Mihailović off completely, it had become clear that he was not mobilising against the Germans. It should be noted, though, that Maclean was not universally popular, with complaints registered in official papers stating that he was inhibiting activity, some of which Tito had approved.[112]

Reports produced by SOE staff in early December 1943 used both Maclean's assessment and that of Brigadier Charles Armstrong, who was embedded with Mihailović's forces.[113] Maclean had investigated Tito, and Armstrong had investigated Mihailović. A note written at the top of the report dismissed it as ill-informed, while a handwritten note at the bottom suggested that the imminent Christmas spirit may have been responsible for the conclusion, which thought that Tito might be weaned off communism and that King Peter might return.[114] What this perhaps shows is that, despite the evidence, hope in some circles remained of a communist victory which would also allow the monarchy, and even democracy, to return.

There is no doubt that this was a difficult, and at times contentious, situation for the Allies, yet they had offered support early in the war, and while the sands shifted within Yugoslavia the aim of any assistance was to cause the Germans as much damage as possible. Yugoslavia did offer the perfect geography for subversive resistance activity though: a mountainous terrain where the Resistance could hide from the German aggressors. Reports from the ground would prove pivotal in adjusting support and determining where assistance was most useful.

As we can see, the Bartter crew were in the Mediterranean region at a time of considerable activity: Maclean in Yugoslavia, the liberation of Corsica, and the crew's mission into Yugoslavia would all occur over a period of days. The taking of North Africa had initiated a chain reaction across the region, and the Bartter crew were in the middle of it. It cannot be emphasised enough just how frenetic the situation was, with circumstances changing almost daily; just days after the crew left the region, Italy switched allegiance to the Allies.

A significant event for the region occurred weeks later with the Tehran Conference in November 1943, when Winston Churchill told a surprised

Joseph Stalin and Franklin D. Roosevelt that he would be officially throwing Allied support behind Tito. Churchill subsequently gave a statement in the House of Commons on 22 February 1944, where he spoke of Deakin and of Maclean. Within his statement he said:

> General Mihailovitch, I much regret to say, drifted gradually into a position in which some of his commanders made accommodations with the Italian and German troops … I can assure the House that every effort in our power will be made to aid and sustain Marshal Tito and his gallant band … We intend to back him with all the strength we can draw.[115]

In his statement Churchill emphasised the difficulties within Yugoslavia in relation to its internal politics, but, as had been agreed at Tehran by all sides: 'There is one thing that we agreed … above all others, to which we are all bound in solemn compact, and that is to fall upon and smite the Hun by land, sea and air with all the strength that is in us.' The credit to Deakin and Maclean was not as fulsome as it seemed; intelligence from Ultra messages from Bletchley Park had been a major – if secret – factor in confirming decision-making.

The main issues for the Bartter crew in Yugoslavia would be the flying conditions. Yugoslavia offered a mountainous terrain which, while suited to guerrilla warfare, was not conducive to good, let alone safe, flying conditions. Our crew had to contend with an unfamiliar geography and the dangers that posed. Fortunately, they could leave the politics to others.

Operation Geisha 1 to the Papuk Mountains

To say that RAF crews had to be adaptable is perhaps an understatement, but the Bartter crew had to adapt to a new location. They were one of four Special Duties crews posted to North Africa in early September 1943 to aid operations on the Balkan front; they would be seconded to 624 Squadron for these operations. They had barely settled into Tempsford and had completed only two operations before this temporary relocation was ordered; but, professional as ever, they accepted the alteration to circumstances without any apparent issue. 624 Squadron was in its infancy, having only recently been formed from 1575 Flight. It was, like 138 Squadron, formed to be a Special Duties squadron which would operate over Italy, southern France, Yugoslavia and Czechoslovakia, dropping supplies and agents.

The order to Tempsford for four Halifax aircraft to be made ready for a two-week secondment to North Africa was sent through on 15 September, with cypher messages the following day ordering the aircraft to proceed.[116] Orders were that the aircraft would not be tropicalised and should proceed via Gibraltar to Blida.[117] Initial orders stated that they would be carrying spares for aircraft that were currently out of action in North Africa, as well as maintenance packs for their own aircraft. However, it seems that the situation moved swiftly, and supplies were coordinated by Transport Command, using a Liberator aircraft from 138 Squadron, although they did carry their own maintenance packs, with the note on documents stating that Air Ministry packs were not available. This was a fluid situation with the aircraft initially due to head to Portreath in Cornwall before this was changed to Hurn in Dorset.

An interesting paper within official records shows that on 17 September, orders were received that crews were to be sent, whether inoculated or not. When informed of this, Group Captain Edward 'Mouse' Fielden, in command of RAF Tempsford, stated that he thought the orders impossible but would 'get onto it'. The crew set off on 18 September at 10.00, with records explaining the delay as being due to inoculations and vaccinations for the crews, as well as the servicing of the aircraft, suggesting that Fielden wanted his crews well prepared. As well as the regular crew, they were also carrying some ground crew: Cpl Thorney, LAC Johnson (Flight Mechanic Engines), AC Philpott and AC Middleton (Flight Mechanic Airframes). They stayed in Hurn until 24 September, when they took off for Gibraltar at 03.35, a flight that took just short of five-and a-half-hours. They got a couple of hours' respite before the three-hour flight to Blida in Algeria.

According to records, the crew had just over a week at Blida to acclimatise before they flew again. This, as previously discussed, may not have been the case, as 624 Squadron were involved in drops to Corsica. Blida was being used by the RAF to run supplies and agents into southern France, Italy and Corsica at this time. While the base for the SOE was in Cairo, they managed to get fourteen Halifax aircraft assigned to North Africa in the spring of 1943 to assist with operations into Yugoslavia and Greece, ultimately having access to forty aircraft by 1944, with aircraft moving west to bases as the situation allowed. On 1 October, the Bartter crew flew from Blida to Protville via Cape Negro. This would be the station from which they would fly to Yugoslavia.

Operation Geisha 1 took place on the night of 2 October, heading for the Kalnik area of the Papuk Mountains in Yugoslavia, a flying distance of about 684 miles (1,100 kilometres) from the base. There were significant differences for the crew flying in this region as opposed to northern Europe. Because the area had limited German aircraft and most of the fighting was ground-based, the distinct lack of flak was a welcome change, but the mountainous terrain was challenging for the crew. They were carrying four agents, the most they could carry at any one time. They were: Captain Douglas Charles Owen; Company Quartermaster Sergeant Sykes; Sgt Pater (interpreter); and Cpl Follin (wireless operator). The agents were parachuted to a reception committee led by Lieutenant S.J. Gibbs (leader of the Cyanide team). As well as the agents, the crew also dropped supplies, including nine Sten guns and nine other sub-machine guns, four rifles, 3,300 rounds of ammunition, 108 grenades, and 630lbs of explosives, along with a couple of wireless sets, batteries and a generator.[118] These supplies were packed in twelve containers and nine packages. The agents also brought with them 150,000 Italian lira, 150 sovs (likely gold sovereigns or paper pounds) and 100 US dollars.

Unfortunately, the operation could not be completed that evening. The aircraft took off at 20.58, crossing over Plane Island at 2,000ft fifteen minutes after take-off. Official records show they altered course at 21.34 to avoid a storm; by this time they were at 5,000ft. At 23.10 Bartter took the decision to abandon the operation over Italy as the storm was severe and they were encountering

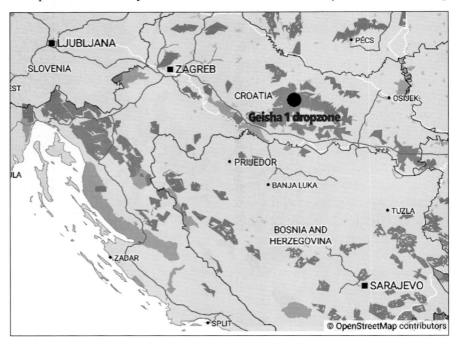

Figure 39. Map showing Geisha drop zone. (Jan Christensen)

Figure 40. Geisha memorial in the Papuk Mountains. (Nigel Atkins)

rainstorms above 13,000ft, which is above freezing height. They also reported storms on the return journey. This would have been a very uncomfortable journey and without doubt they would have been relieved to land safely back at Protville after just over five hours of flying. The operation was repeated with the identical cargo the next evening, with the aircraft leaving at 21.55.

This time the weather was more favourable, although haze was reported over Italy, which impacted their ability to pinpoint their location. They used the Italian coast and Polaris for a rough fix at 01.25 from a height of 8,000ft. Nonetheless, they arrived over the target area in the Papuk Mountains, Yugoslavia, and were able to confirm the drop zone having circled above.

The correct letter was flashed by the reception committee, and a cross formed from bonfires confirmed the location, along with a green flare. With four agents and a substantial amount of equipment to drop, delivery was completed over five runs, which took twenty-five minutes. Unlike in France, where drops were completed from just a few hundred feet, the terrain in this area of Yugoslavia meant that the drops took place at a height of 3,600ft. Riggs, the rear gunner, reported seeing all parachutes open, and the aircraft left the area at 03.38, arriving back at base at 07.40.[119]

The object of the mission was to extend liaison with partisan forces in Slavonia, Yugoslavia, to coordinate their operations with the Allied Mediterranean Strategy, and to arrange and receive additional essential supplies of weapons, ammunition, explosives, etc. There was to be no support for any group engaged in a civil war, and those being dropped were warned not to get involved in any political controversy. They were there in a purely military capacity to aid any group fighting the Axis forces. The railway system within Slavonia was the primary target, and the Cairo office was to be kept informed via regular reports. The Geisha team joined the SOE Cyanide team led by Gibbs, who were already embedded with Tito's 6 Corps.[120] There were many divisions of Tito's partisans and many British liaison teams embedded with them. Tito's 6 Corps covered the administrative district of Slavonia, to the River Drava in the north, the River Sava in the south and a line between Sotin and Racinovci in the east and Bukovica, Grubisno Polje, and the River Ilova in the west. The partisans controlled about half of this area permanently, mostly in the Papuk and Psunj mountain areas. The corps was well organised with good discipline and morale, and were good at keeping records. They had 9,000–10,000 regulars, including women, although efforts were made to draw the women from the front line into more administrative and domestic roles. Before regular drops of British and other Allied equipment and supplies they relied on old Yugoslav Army or captured Axis equipment. The corps was seen to be efficient and well trained for their circumstances, both geographically and militarily.[121]

Two days after the Geisha team were dropped, Maclean, along with Colonel Vivian Street, began the journey out of Yugoslavia, having met Tito.[122] They endured a hazardous land journey plus a fishing-boat trip from Hvar to Vis before being picked up by the Royal Navy.[123] It was this initial visit which led Maclean to recommend support for Tito.

The Geisha team

Captain Douglas Charles Owen, the lead officer being dropped, had only passed his parachute course on 9 September. Born in London in 1916 and educated at Ardingly in Sussex, Owen joined the Inns of Court Regiment in 1934 and stayed attached to them until 1939, when he moved to Bovington Camp to be an instructor. In 1942 he was posted to Canada and attached to the British Army Staff in Ottawa, again as an instructor. Owen had a range of skills that made him attractive for special operations, including a working knowledge of both French and Serbo-Croat, and he was approached by a Major Lomax. He would remain listed as a member of the Royal Armoured Corps, as was usual for those chosen for Special Duties. A large number of agents were recruited by individuals who kept an eye out for those who might be suitable for the unconventional side of warfare. Owen would stay with the partisans for some time, being withdrawn to the Cairo ops pool in July 1944 for three weeks' rest. Although attached to Cairo he went to Bari in southern Italy. Once in Bari he wrote a substantial report which covered every aspect of his interaction with the partisans, and wider information on conditions in the country. He reported that the partisans were an effective force, and he had a good view of their capabilities. This was vital intelligence and would have helped shape ongoing policy in the region. It appears that Owen returned to Yugoslavia in April 1945 as leader of a mission to the partisans, with his records showing a possible promotion to acting major. Sadly, it is unclear what happened after this, but Owen died in the Queen Alexandra Military Hospital in London on 1 January 1948, after being transferred from the Royal Victoria Military Hospital near Southampton. The other members of the team were, as already listed, Company Quartermaster Sergeant Sykes, who was of Croat origin, Sgt Pater (interpreter) and Cpl Follin (wireless operator). While interpreter and wireless operator are self-explanatory, Sykes, with his local knowledge combined with experience of the logistics of warfare, would have been invaluable in the field. They were dropped to what could have been an agent identified as Langside.

Heading home

Six days after dropping the agents and equipment the crew were on their way back to Blida, where they spent a couple of days before their return journey to England. The demand for the return of aircraft was high due to the ever-increasing demand on Special Duties flights, and official records show that the aircraft's return date was being queried on 8 October. They set off for the return journey to England on 9 October.

As well as transporting ground crew back to England, Randolph Churchill was also one of the passengers on the Bartter crew's flight back to Tempsford. They would discover that he was quite the boorish character. Atkins, in his Imperial War Museum interview, recalls that the way Churchill spoke to members of the crew was 'in a way that you would not expect an officer to speak to his men'.[124] Atkins and the rest of the crew found Churchill to have an arrogant personality, and felt that he could have been easier to get on with; he did not leave a good impression. It seems that Atkins was choosing his words carefully, but Churchill's reputation for rudeness is well documented. As on the outward journey, the flight stopped over in Gibraltar. Fog delayed their departure for a couple of days, and when the fog lifted they had short notice of their take-off but had to wait for Churchill to return from the governor's residence where he had enjoyed some hospitality with Sir Frank Noel Mason-MacFarlane. It would be fair to say that Churchill did not gain any supporters from the crew on this encounter. The crew first landed at RAF Lyneham on 12 October before returning to Tempsford on 13 October and resuming operations from there.

Chapter 5

Shot down over Denmark

Denmark at the start of the war

In this chapter we will give a brief outline of the general situation in Denmark during the Second World War before moving on to the operations code-named 'Table Jam 18' and 'Table Jam 19', which became the Bartter crew's last operations in December 1943.

On 31 May 1939, Chancellor of the Reich Adolf Hitler signed a Non-Aggression Pact with Denmark. This was supposed to ensure that Germany would not invade. In reality, the Pact proved to be worthless. Within a year, on 9 April 1940, Germany launched operations *Weserübung Süd* and *Weserübung Nord*, which were the beginning of the occupation of Denmark and Norway. Although it was a small country, Denmark possessed significant agricultural resources and held a strategic geographical position, being close to Norway and having, among other advantages, direct access to the Baltic Sea. The Germans also wanted to take over the operation of various harbours and airports in the country, and to establish business cooperation with some large Danish manufacturing companies.

The Danes surrendered on the same day without putting up any real fight, much to the dismay of the British government. The strategy of the Danish government was to collaborate with the Germans, with the aim of ensuring the safety of the Danish population, and of maintaining a level of Danish influence in the running of the country. The Danish government thought that such an approach would enable it to stay in place despite the German occupation. The King, Christian X, remained in Copenhagen and, unlike Norway, there was no government in exile.

In fact, many Danish people opposed this collaboration with Germany right from the start and, as German progress across Europe faltered, the Danish government's position came under increasing pressure. The Resistance movement, which grew from 1941 to 1943, not only targeted

95

the Germans but also opposed the very principle of collaboration and the Danish government that had chosen it. Many called for a clarification of the Danish government's position towards the occupying army, so that the role played by Denmark during the war would not raise any doubts or questions. In practice, during the first three years of the occupation, the population in general showed little support for sabotage operations targeting the Germans and for the unavoidable consequences of such operations, which would only have led to German retaliatory counter-measures and tighter controls.

The SOE in Denmark

From 1941, the rate of recruitment of Danes from all over the world increased and the selection of candidates for the various positions could finally start. Sabotage instructors were to train the members of the Danish Resistance groups in the field, while wireless operators would be in charge of all communications between England and Denmark. In addition, chief organisers would be trained to organise and manage underground Resistance activities in Denmark.

The first initiatives were launched as early as 1941. On the night of 27/28 December 1941, the British were ready to drop the first Danish agents into South Zealand. On that night, a crew from 138 Squadron took off from Stradishall airfield in England under 'Operation Chilblain'. Carl Johan Bruhn had been appointed as the first SOE chief organiser for Denmark and was to be parachuted in together with wireless operator Mogens Hammer. Both agents jumped from the aircraft at 01.55. Hammer reached the ground safely in a field near the forest of Torpeskoven in Haslev. He searched for Bruhn for several minutes before finding his body. Bruhn's parachute never opened; he had hit the ground and was killed instantly. Hammer did not retrieve the wireless transmitter, which was located 550 yards (500 metres) south of Bruhn's body, and which fell into the hands of the Germans the following day. Bruhn had also been wearing a special piece of equipment which made it possible to fire a gun even with your arms held up in the air. This unique piece of equipment also fell into German hands. As a consequence of Bruhn's unfortunate death, the Germans were aware, from the very first drop, of this attempt by British intelligence to infiltrate Denmark. Hammer, who was by then wanted by all German police forces, reached the Danish capital Copenhagen the next day, and managed to put himself out of harm's way by staying with some friends.

The SOE was to face more difficulties during the autumn and winter of the following year, 1942. Christian Michael Rottbøll had been appointed SOE chief organiser for Denmark following the death of Bruhn. Rottbøll was parachuted in on 17 April 1942 near the village of Jyderup, together

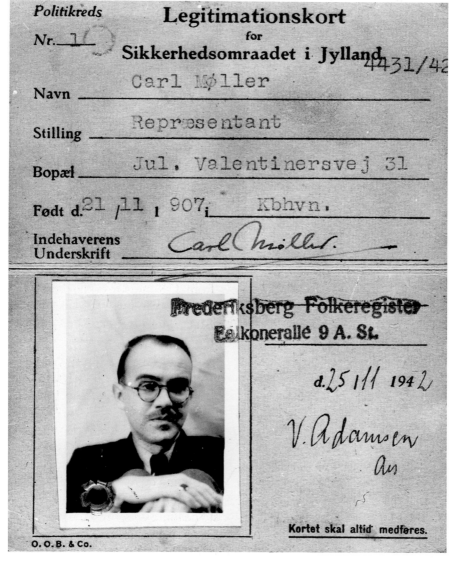

Figure 41. False ID paper for Fleming B. Muus in the name of Carl Møller (Moeller) (source: The Museum of Danish Resistance 1940–1945)

with two other agents, sabotage instructor Max Mikkelsen and wireless operator Paul Johannesen. Rottbøll managed to reach Copenhagen and hid initially at the home of Stig Jensen, in the Nyhavn district. The SOE had approached Jensen, a well-known journalist and editor with many contacts in the Danish and Swedish press, shortly after the German invasion, and he quickly became a key link with the SOE in Denmark, organising in particular the reception of weapons drops into Zealand.

Rottbøll's mission in Denmark would, however, be of short duration. In the early hours of 26 September 1942, answering a knock at the door of his hiding place in Østerbro, he was shot dead by a Danish policeman who had identified him as a wanted Allied agent. Johannesen, who was hiding in a Copenhagen apartment during the same period, also came face to face with the Danish police. Earlier that month, the Germans had informed the police that a radio transmitter had been detected in Vinkelagervej, in the Vanløse district. The police stormed the apartment on 4 September 1942. A police detective was killed, and knowing that the Germans would torture him for information, Johannesen swallowed a cyanide pill and died instantly.

After these tragic events of September 1942, the Danish section of the SOE had to be reorganised again. Hammer, who had been dropped with Bruhn in December 1941, had finally returned to England via Sweden and was now ready to be returned to Denmark. On 19 October 1942, he was dropped in the water off the beach near the village of Tisvildeleje.

Hammer took up the position as SOE chief organiser for Denmark, left vacant by the death of Rottbøll, a position he kept until the appointment of Flemming B. Muus in March 1943; the fourth SOE chief organiser for Denmark in less than two years. Hollingworth, as head of the Danish section of SOE, would be traumatised by his experiences. His daughters have spoken of him being haunted by memories; he smoked heavily and sadly died of a stroke in his fifties.[125]

Muus's first drop in Denmark

After Flemming B. Muus completed his training as an SOE agent it was decided that he would be sent into Denmark on 11 March 1943 as the SOE's chief organiser.

Pilot Alan Hunter Cachemaille Boxer and his crew from the 138 Squadron at Tempsford were chosen to carry out this operation in their Halifax P627. In addition to Muus, three other agents were to be dropped, sabotage instructors Einar Balling, Jens Paul Jensen and Verner Johansen. During the preliminary briefing before take-off, the crew were informed that they were to drop the four agents by parachute around midnight under 'Operation Table Gossip', followed by the drop of containers under 'Operation Table Top'. They were also carrying four air-drop bicycles equipped with

Figure 42. Parachute used for dropping a bike into Denmark. (The Museum of Danish Resistance 1940–1945)

parachutes, which would be dropped together with the agents. Despatchers Evans and Tice ensured that the agents were prepared to jump at the right time. Henry Aspen, the flight engineer, co-pilot Ken Batchelor, wireless operator Donald Alexander Joseph Cameron, rear gunner Clarence William Elderton, and navigator Robert Vatten MacMillan made up Boxer's crew.

On that Thursday night at 19.13 local time, the Halifax bomber took off from Tempsford and headed for the coast. The aircraft flew over Sheringham at 19.45 and crossed the North Sea in a clear, cloudless sky. At 22.09, they reached the Danish western shores at Svinkløv, where they dropped down to only 500ft (150 metres) to avoid detection by the net of German radars monitoring the area. Boxer managed to avoid being picked up by the German radar stations in North Jutland, which were right on their route. The SOE agents were dropped between 22.16 and 22.34 at an altitude of approximately 550ft (170 metres). As instructed by the pilot, the agents were to jump when the aircraft reached position 56°53'52'N, 09°45'02'E near Hornum Lake in Støvring, approximately seven miles south of the town of Nibe. On the morning following the drops, and after finding a large part of the equipment dropped in the Abildgaard fields, the Danish Attorney General issued the following message to the Danish police stations:

> On the night of the 11th to 12th March, four English agents landed in the Nibe municipality. On the dropping site the following equipment has been found: four individual parachutes, 4 helmets, 4 pairs of Mud jump boots.
>
> Approximately 4 to 5 metres away from the site were found four airborne bicycle parachutes and three men bicycles. The fourth bicycle was found approximately 1 kilometre south of the others, so it should be assumed that the wanted persons have followed this direction and have, in all likelihood, boarded the train to Copenhagen tonight.
>
> A thorough inquiry and a strengthened surveillance of all railway stations and checkpoints are requested. These persons are to be considered as armed and carrying shortwave transmitters.

Some local people had found the bicycles on the morning after the drops. The Germans had been informed at 08.00 and immediately started an extensive search, which failed to find the four agents. In Denmark, Flemming Juncker was the contact person responsible for helping the

Figure 43. Three of four bikes dropped in Denmark. (The Museum of Danish Resistance 1940–1945)

agents, and he managed to find three of them. Shortly after this, Muus started working as chief organiser, based in Copenhagen. Soon afterwards, Monica Wichfeld contacted Muus and started to participate in the planning of Resistance activities in the area of Lolland-Falster. She would occasionally shelter Danish agents in her home in Maribo, Engestofte Manor. Wichfeld's daughter Varinka also joined the Resistance and became secretary to Muus.

Varinka and her mother had joined the Resistance movement as early as 1941, and distributed illegal publications. When Muus needed an assistant in the summer of 1943, Varinka was glad to offer her services. She was mainly in charge of encoding the messages exchanged between Muus and London.

She was then 21; her family and friends called her Inkie, but her codename during the war was Kirsten. The following year she married Muus. The ceremony was celebrated by the village's mayor, Christian Pedersen, in the living room of his farm (Fruerlund) in Tystrup. At that time Varinka was hiding in nearby Jægerhuset, the summer house of prominent political figure Hermann Dedichen.

Figure 44. Varinka Muus, daughter of Monica Wichfeldt, sitting on the stairs at the entrance of Engestofte Manor, 1945 (The Museum of Danish Resistance 1940–1945)

Figure 45. Christian Pedersen's grandson on the farm Fruerlund in 2016. (Jan Christensen)

SHOT DOWN OVER DENMARK

Under Muus's effective command, the number of sabotage operations increased significantly. By November 1943, over 500 attacks had been carried out by organised Resistance groups against main railway lines, and nine enemy ships had been sunk. Industrial sabotage was also stepped up from 1943 onwards, targeting both companies and stores with arson attacks and explosions. In response, the Germans increased their retaliation against Danish companies as well as cultural organisations and schools. With the help of the Schalburg Corps (a Danish volunteer corps and a branch of the German SS), the Germans tried to infiltrate the Danish Resistance groups. At the same time, the *Wehrmacht* started to kill Danish citizens randomly in retaliation for the murders of German soldiers or informants.

In July 1943, a mine-laying ship fresh from the Odense Steel Shipyard was targeted by a Resistance sabotage operation with SOE equipment. The Germans posted guards at the shipyard, and so the Danish workers started a protest strike which then rapidly spread to other companies and factories around the town. Strikes and civil disturbances soon broke out in other main cities such as Aalborg, and there were demonstrations and strikes throughout the country. The Germans again retaliated by imposing a curfew, which then led to further demonstrations, riots, and strikes, eventually ending with a general strike paralysing the entire country. The Germans finally yielded and lifted the curfew. A new wave of strikes and sabotage operations struck several large cities in the following weeks.

Despite lifting the curfew, the Germans were quick to impose heavy counter-measures to punish sabotage, but these counter-measures were the responsibility of the Danish government. One of them was that any prison sentence exceeding eight years had to be served in Germany, which the Danish government strongly opposed. In August, the situation worsened to the point that the Germans presented the following ultimatum to the government:

> The German government demands that the Danish government undertakes the following:
> The government must immediately declare a state of emergency throughout the whole country. The state of emergency must impose the following individual measures:
> 1. Public gatherings of any group over five people are strictly prohibited.
> 2. Engaging in strikes and providing support to strikers is strictly prohibited.

3. Gatherings indoors or outdoors are strictly prohibited. A mandatory curfew is established between 8:30 pm and 5:30 am. Restaurants must close at 7:30 pm. All weapons and/or explosives held by the population must be handed over to the authorities by September 1st, 1943, at the latest.
4. It is strictly prohibited to harm or abuse citizens for reason of collaboration with the German authorities or any other connection they or their relatives may have with the Germans.
5. Censorship of the press and media should be conducted with German assistance.
6. Special emergency Danish courts should be set up to deal with all activities in breach of the measures taken for the purpose of restoring order and security.

Failure to comply with the above-mentioned obligations is punishable by the severest sanctions provided by the law currently in force, which grants the government authority to take all necessary measures for the purpose of restoring order and security.

Operations of sabotage and attacks of any nature, and participating thereto, against the *Wehrmacht* and its members, as well as possession of weapons or explosives after September 1st, 1943, will be unquestionably punished by death. The government of the Reich expects the Danish government to accept the present terms before 4 pm today.

Copenhagen, August 26th 1943.

At the same time, the Danish Prime Minister, Erik Scavenius, received a letter from the Third Reich's Gauleiter of Denmark, Werner Best, following a sabotage operation and an assault on a German officer in the town of Odense:[126]

Copenhagen, August 28th 1943.
His Excellency the Prime Minister Erik Scavenius

Your Excellency,
Following the incidents that took place in Odense and in particular following the assault on one of our officers, the government of the Reich instructed me to inform you that it demands the following:

Within 5 days, the town of Odense is ordered to pay a fine of 1 million kroner to a fund to be specified by the commanding officer of the German troops. The Danish government must take all necessary measures to identify and hand over to the occupying forces all the persons responsible for the assault on the German officer. Until denunciation of the culprits, the following punitive measures are imposed on the town of Odense:

a. Strict prohibition to walk or drive in the streets between 8 pm and 5 am.
b. All cinemas, theatres and entertainment venues must be closed until further notice.
c. All restaurants must close at 7 pm.

If the culprits are not handed over before September 4th, ten citizens of Odense selected by the administrative authority of the occupying forces will be arrested and imprisoned until the denunciation of the culprits. The government of the Reich informs the Danish government that it will face even stricter measures should such a situation happen again.

W. Best.

When the Germans demanded that the Danish government impose the death sentence for sabotage, the government refused and handed its resignation to King Christian X, although he would not accept it. What followed was the unusual situation of the country being run by the Permanent Secretaries of each Ministry. Parliament did not meet, and the Permanent Secretary of the Ministry of Foreign Affairs, Nils Svenningsen, had a leading position and acted as a link to the German occupiers.

Meanwhile, on 16 September 1943, the Freedom Council was set up during a meeting in Copenhagen. It was outside official government influence, and its purpose was to coordinate the efforts of the various Danish Resistance groups against the Germans, for instance by coordinating sabotage. It ran along the lines of a substitute government in Denmark during the occupation, drawing together and unifying the many different Resistance groups, with help from the SOE. As SOE chief organiser, Muus was also a member of the Freedom Council.

In October 1943, Muus fled to Sweden and flew back to England to receive intelligence on the various Resistance operations envisaged by the

Figure 46. Prime Minister Erik Scavenius and the Third Reich's Plenipotentiary Gauleiter in Denmark, Werner Best, on 6 February 1943. (The Museum of Danish Resistance 1940–1945)

SOE. A new Resistance organisation was to be implemented in Denmark. The occupied country was to be divided into a number of regions, each with a regional staff, and with two independent Resistance structures: one in charge of organising and running the armed Resistance, and the other in charge of organising drops by parachute and the distribution of the dropped equipment. This division would add to the security of the Resistance.

The new regional groups also had to be at the disposal of the SHAEF (Supreme Headquarters Allied Expeditionary Force) if a ground invasion should take place. On the evening of 10 December 1943, Muus was carrying the new Resistance organisation plans when he boarded the Halifax BB378 with pilot Bartter and his crew at Tempsford. They had set course for Denmark, and Muus was to be dropped near Skjoldenæsholm Manor, in the municipality of Ringsted, as part of 'Operation Table Jam 18'. The aircraft was also carrying weapons for the Danish Resistance, which were to be dropped near Lake Tissø on the way back to England as 'Operation Table Jam 19'. The flight, however, did not go as planned.

Operation Table Jam 18 and 19, 10 December 1943, central Zealand

Operation Table Jam 18 had been postponed several times; the first flight was attempted on 12 November 1943 with Pilot Officer Bown and his crew, but the flight was not completed because of bad weather.[127] Nearly a month passed until Muus was finally able to return to Denmark. The codename of the operation that was to drop Muus back into Denmark was initially 'Table Jam A', but it was changed to Table Jam 18 on 3 December. Finally, on the night of 10 December, Halifax BB378 was ready to take off for Denmark under a full moon and frosty weather. Navigator Fry gives an account of that night:

> The weather promises to be very good once we get away from the remaining lot of fog which is still hanging around [...] We are off tonight on our most important assignment to date, a job we have been standing by for, for about ten days already. Three times in the past week we have been briefed and made all preparations to go but each time the flight has been scrubbed because of fog.

Before leaving Tempsford, the crew went to the mess for supper. Howell, Bartter and Fry rode up to the officers' mess. The rest of the crew ate at the sergeants' mess. On this flight the crew would be joined by Frederick Turvil, who, in his MI9 debrief described his role as 'intelligence'. He had been transferred to 138 Squadron on 17 November 1943 as a pilot with the rank of Warrant Officer. As was normal practice, he would accompany the crew on this flight as a way of acclimatising to Special Duties flights. The flight to Denmark was to be divided into two distinct operations. Fry explains: [128]

> Take off time is 20:10. Tonight [...] we are to [...] fly to a Dead Reckoning position 90 miles west of Denmark, crossing the Danish Coast at Nissum Fjord, across Jutland and over to Zealand and over target. [...]
>
> At seven we went down to the flights, drew our parachutes and dinghies. Nick Anderson, our engineer, drew our flying rations – double rations tonight, oranges, two cans of tomato juice, chocolate bars, gum, glucose tablets and some Benzedrine tablets. Besides, each of us carried an escape kit – enough for a day or two in an emergency. [...]
>
> We got our '2330' from the duty officer (a met forecast giving the winds and weather we might expect on the trip going out and coming back). Then we met the 'Major' [Muus] and we were all set to go. So out to the aircraft, a Mark II Halifax. After the usual run-up and equipment check [...] Riggs, the tail gunner, reported that the Perspex in his gun turret was covered with ice and frost. So we had to wait while the ground crew could get it cleared. They also sprayed the wings to prevent icing. [It took about an hour to remove the ice.]
>
> Finally we were ready to go again and started to taxi around the perimeter track. The moon was just coming up and with the bit of ground fog around, it was difficult to see. All of a sudden when we were going around a corner [...] one of the wheels went off the strip.
>
> When this happens to a 27-ton Halifax, the aircraft is bogged down. [...] Out we climbed, into the transport and back to the flights to stand by in the crew room. [...]
>
> The ground crew [...] brought out a tractor and some sort of hoist equipment and finally they got H-Harry back on the perimeter track. Orders then came through. We 4 were to go back to the aircraft and have another stab at getting away. This

time we got around OK and took off at 2210, two hours late; so we'll be coming home in daylight, a thing which doesn't please us very much. We set course for our Dead Reckoning position off the coast of Denmark.

After crossing the English coast at Cromer, we came down to about 400ft above the water to cross the North Sea so that the enemy couldn't pick us up so easily with his Radio direction finder equipment.

What a wizard night! Not a cloud, and the moon was very bright, in fact a little too bright for our liking. [...]

At approximately sixty miles (100 kilometres) off the west coast of Jutland, Bartter dropped to an altitude of only 200ft (60 metres). Four minutes before reaching the coastline, Bartter rose to an altitude of 2,500ft (800 metres) in order to check the aircraft's position, then dropped back down to 300ft (90 metres). Fry continues:

On ETA [Estimated Time of Arrival] at our DR [Dead Reckoning] position, I was able to get a fix and altered course for Nissum Fjord. The pilot began to climb gently so that we would cross the Danish coast and be able to pin-point accurately. We crossed the coast and Atkins, the Bomb Aimer, identified it as Nissum Fjord.

What the crew didn't know was that they had already been picked up by radar. At 00.43, a German radar station had detected the aircraft at approximately twenty miles (thirty kilometres) north of the town of Ringkøbing, heading south-east. Radar coverage in Denmark was excellent (it is detailed in the Appendix); suffice it to say that any aircraft entering Danish air space was at high risk.

At 01:06, the Fluko (*Flugwachkommando*) was informed of the aircraft's change of course towards the south of Silkeborg. At that moment, the aircraft was flying at an altitude of 300ft (100 metres). Then the following information came through from Fluko: 'At 01:32, the aircraft skirted Samsø island from the west. At 01:35 it was spotted near the village of Asnæs, main course south-east.' That was when three JU88 German night fighters took off from Kastrup airfield. According to Fry:

[...] everything was going well. There was very little wind making it rather easy to stay on track. Visibility was perfect in the moonlight and we could easily pick out roads, rivers and

Figure 47. Danish radar. (the Museum of Danish Resistance 1940–1945)

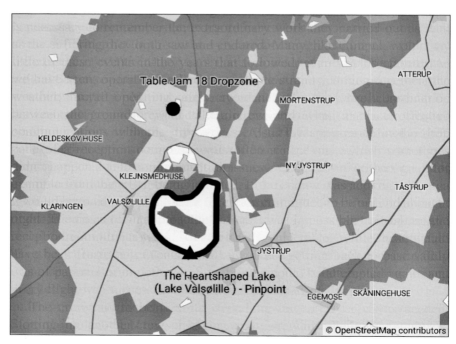

Figure 48. Valsølille, the small heart-shaped lake north of Ringsted. (Jan Christensen)

Figure 49. Nigel Atkins visiting the heart-shaped lake in September 2021. (Jan Christensen)

villages. Denmark is very flat and ideal for our type of work with low flying.

After crossing the strip of water Great Belt [Storebaelt] we hit Zealand right on track and set course for our reception point with an ETA of 0145 hours. We identified the heart shaped lake [their ground landmark].

Fry continues:

As soon as it heard the distant humming of the aircraft, the reception party lit the ground markers and flashed the letter 'G' to which the crew answered with the letter 'S'.

The agent was all set to jump but the red warning light was still on. The hatch was opened. [All he was waiting for was the green light.] But suddenly cannon shots were heard and Bartter immediately got his flaps up and dived to get away from the attack. Riggs was peppering the JU88 with his tail guns.

The battle lasted only a few minutes, and then the Halifax was on fire. Down on the ground, on the edge of Gyldenløve hill, the reception committee had been waiting in the cold winter night, the temperatures dropping to −8°C.

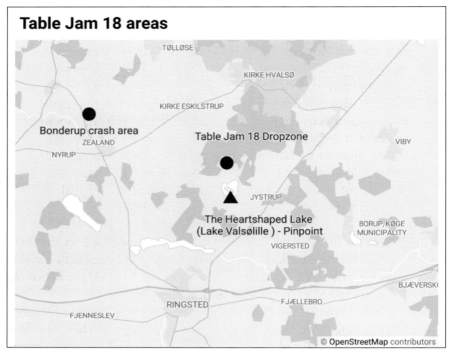

Figure 50. Intended drop zone of Operation Table Jam 18 and ultimate crash site. (Open Source / Jan Christensen)

Everything was ready for the reception, and Ib Jensen had even dug ditches in advance to hide the agents' equipment swiftly if needed. Only seconds after seeing the Halifax, they heard another aircraft, and the sound of machine-gun fire cut through the silent night. The Halifax dived in flames and disappeared from view. On the frozen field where the reception committee were waiting, they could see the steam trail left by the boiling hot bullets hitting the ground. Some jumped for shelter into a large ditch, cracking through the thin ice, others dived to one side or the other to dodge the enemy fire, before fleeing the reception site and gathering at a nearby hunter's cottage.

Fry continues his story of the burning aircraft:

> While the fight was still going on, the pilot warned us that he had to crash-land the Halifax. However the JU88 pilot was hot stuff.
>
> […] Shells screamed over our heads and Brian Atkins and I dove for the floor. If my face was as white as Atkins, we must have looked pretty scared.

Pieces of fuselage came right inside with the force of the shells. One of them hit the intercom system just above and in front of Bill Howell's face, and so we lost our only means of talking to the different members of the crew. The gunners were unable to give Bart directions as to which way to turn.

[…] Nick [Anderson] reported that one of the starboard engines or a petrol tank was hit and on fire. The flames soon spread and the whole starboard wing was on fire We were too low to bail out so Bart gave the order 'Crash Positions!' He had to yell due to the U/S intercom system and all I heard was 'Crash' but it was enough. […] The few seconds we had to wait were about the longest I've ever experienced.

Atkins's account of the landing was that '[Bartter] managed an excellent emergency landing and the hard frosty ground with no obstructions enabled us to get down safely. We were extremely lucky. […] We all got out of the aircraft and not one of us was wounded.'

It was now about 01.54. The Halifax BB378 lay still, with weapons containers hanging down from the lower ceiling of the bomb bay, in a field near the small town of Ugerløse. The bomber had crashed exactly six miles (ten kilometres) away, as the crow flies, from the intended reception site near Gyldenløve hill. Muus's account of the crash-landing included:

The pilot landed the aircraft on her belly on a field near a farm called Bonderup. We were there, fully aware that the aircraft was on fire and could blow up at any moment. The normal exit way was blocked but we managed to climb up a small hole through the top. The pilot got out through the cockpit and jumped down from the wing. The other crew members got out through the main hatch on top of the aircraft and then jumped down from its tail.

The tail gunner had trouble getting out of the rear turret because he was struggling with his battledress which was particularly thick to protect him from the cold. Atkins emphasised how lucky they had all been: 'One or two members of the crew had a very narrow escape.'

The news of the destruction of the Halifax reached the Germans. At 01.56 the Fluko was informed that aircraft were fighting south-east of Roskilde, and then at 02.07 the command received a message saying 'Enemy plane shot down.' Lehnet, a volunteer firefighter and mechanic from Ugerløse, was the first local to notice the aircraft on fire. He rung up Falck, a Danish emergency rescue and safety services company in Holbæk. The local police were called and the whole area was closed down.

The front of the aircraft was completely burned, and only the rear fuselage and tail fin were still intact after the crash. The fuselage was riddled with bullets. It seems that, before taking the photo, the Germans shot additional holes through the fuselage around the RAF roundel. Other photos show fewer holes at this same place in the fuselage. The landing gear had been ripped off, with the wheels thrown a few feet away, and the four engines were completely destroyed and scattered around. The field was soaked with fuel within a 150-ft (50-metre) radius from the aircraft. Twelve hours after the crash, the wreck of Halifax BB378 was still smoking.

At 04.45 the National Security Department of the Copenhagen police was informed by Captain Jacobsen from the German military intelligence service (*Abwehrstelle*) of the crash that took place near Bonderup. The Germans assumed that the crew was going to try and flee to Copenhagen. At the police headquarters, the chief superintendent declared it impossible for them to act on the alert raised by the Germans since the Danish police were not in charge of this type of mission. Jacobsen was informed of this

Figure 51. The wreck of Halifax BB378 in a field near Bonderup Manor. (Holbæk Museum)

Figure 52. A German soldier looking over the aircraft. (Holbæk Museum)

by phone and confirmed the stance taken by the Danish police. Meanwhile, the airmen and Muus were now on the run.

Muus was supposed to have been dropped near Gyldenløve hill; the crew of Halifax BB378 should then have continued for about twenty miles (thirty-two kilometres) east in order to drop the nine weapon containers north of Lake Tissø near the Kattrup estate, as part of Operation Table Jam 19, on their way back to England. On 12 December, however, the reception committee returned home empty-handed. Halifax BB378 never reached the Kattrup estate.

The SOE team reacted speedily to these unforeseen events in Denmark. On the morning of 12 December, wireless operator 'Table Napkin' (real name Lorens A. Duus Hansen, an engineer from Bang & Olufsen), informed London that the aircraft had been shot down but that there was no news of the crew. London then sent a message to its Danish network and to the SOE in Stockholm, so that its supporters would be informed and ready to help the airmen, who were expected to show up eventually on the other side of the Sound, the strait which separates Denmark and Sweden. It is seventy-four miles (118 kilometres) in length, with the distance between the two countries varying from 1.5 miles (2.5 km) to eighteen miles (28 kilometres). On the morning of 13 December, wireless operator 'Table Mat' (Gunnar Christiansen), informed London that 'Jam' (Muus) as well as the

Figure 53. A German official examining a wheel ripped from BB378. (Holbæk Museum)

Figure 54. Close image of the damage to the fuselage. The intensity of the fight can be seen. The shadows show German officials examining the aircraft. This photo may have been used for German propaganda. (Holbæk Museum)

other members of the crew had survived but that their whereabouts were unknown. The Germans stayed in the field near Bonderup for about two weeks to clear the crash site. They moved the wreck to the Store Merløse railway station and loaded it onto a train that would take it to a metal recycling factory in Germany.

Meanwhile, after the crash, Muus had fled on his own, towards Bonderup Manor. There was not a sound there and not a single light on. A barking dog startled him and sent him back on his way. He then headed south-west, crossing through several fields and over a stream. Twenty minutes or so later, he walked into a field owned by Karen Jensen and her husband in Vandløse, a few miles away from Bonderup. Jensen recalls: 'Muus was coming down the dirt pathway leading to our house, all dressed up in blue and papers tucked under his arm.' The family had been woken by the noise of the crash landing and could see the burning aircraft through their bedroom window. They felt that it was too dangerous to let Muus stay in the house, so Karen, her husband, and their son Niels decided to hide him in the attic of one of the annexes.

Here, Muus smoked the fifty cigarettes that he'd kept in a small tin. He hid in this attic hayloft for about sixteen hours, forcing himself to stay

Figure 55. Flemming Muus (on the left) in front of the annex in Vandløse, in whose attic he spent the night. (Ringsted-Haslev-Sorø newspapers, 2 October 1959)

awake for fear of being caught off guard by the Germans. He was exhausted but he wouldn't allow himself to sleep, and held a gun in his hand the whole night. In fact, his enemies did comb the area thoroughly, but never actually stretched the search to include the Jensens' house.

Jensen offered Muus food as well as shelter. He managed to stay awake until the time he decided to leave his hiding place, early on Sunday morning. The Jensens gave him a bike and he went to the town of Sorø, a twenty-mile (thirty-kilometre), two-hour ride. He was aiming for Dedichen's summer house, Jægerhuset, in Tystrup just outside Sorø. Due to its relatively isolated location in the countryside this house used to be the base of many famous Resistance members during the occupation. Dedichen, however, was not at home to welcome Muus, so he went back to Sorø, where a taxi took him to the Vesterport railway station. He bought a ticket to Hellerup, in the suburbs, and a newspaper which had a photo of Halifax BB378 on its front page. He arrived at 14.00, and managed to get in touch with his contacts there. Once he was safe, Muus continued with the standard protocol. He emptied the folder he had with him and transferred most of its content into his pockets. They were important copies, a few radio parts and a significant amount of money. He left instructions for his contact Niels Vilhelm Jensen to burn the folder, which he did. A few days later the SOE in London could breathe again. The Germans had not discovered that the SOE chief organiser for Denmark had landed for the second time on Danish soil.

SHOT DOWN OVER DENMARK

Meanwhile, SOE-agent Holger Henning Finn Ibsen had been parachuted into Jutland at almost the same time as Muus.[129] Ibsen recalls the night he was dropped and his first meeting with Muus in Denmark:

> In December 1943 we were finally considered suitable to be sent back, I think we were dropped on December 11th. I remember it was a bright full-moon night. On the day before, in England, we ate like princes. We knew we were to jump near Frijsenborg Castle in Hammel, and the operation went as planned.
>
> We all carried on us a syringe of morphine in case one of us broke a leg, or both, when landing, a compass and a map of Jutland. We also had 500 Danish kroner each for emergencies, a flask of ammonia to shake off the German tracking dogs, and of course an ID, a driver's licence, and ration cards. Under our flying suit we were each wearing a classical Danish suit from a famous Danish brand. Jan Junker jumped first, landed at the reception site in the fields. I fell between a tree and a haystack, and overall it all went well. Ole Geisler and his group was the reception committee. On that same night Flemming B. Muus was supposed to be sent back, but he would be dropped over Zealand.
>
> I remember being fired at, I don't know if they were aiming at the plane or at our parachutes, but guns were fired for sure, so we had to pack everything up and hide our parachutes very quickly and flee like we had the devil on our tail. Bikes had been left conveniently for us, so we rode to a pharmacist somewhere, which hid us for that first night. On the following day, we left for the town of Århus and were hidden there by the Misses Ulrich. It was our stakeout until Ole Geisler came to tell us that one of us was to accompany him to Copenhagen. We drew lots and I was chosen to go along. With Geisler we took the train to Odense and slept there at the Park Hotel. I was scared to death the whole night. I didn't really know why, but it must have been an intuition: on that very night, Junker was caught at the Ulrich sisters' flat. The Germans captured several agents that night.

Ibsen ends his account of these events: 'On the next day we reached the capital city and I met Muus. Our meeting was at the well-known Nordland Hotel – we were meeting with the Danish chief organiser after all!'

Chapter 6

On the run

Meanwhile, the officers in the crew, Bartter, Fry and Howell, set off using the stars as a guide in the hope of finding a way north to Sweden. We are fortunate that Fry gave a detailed account of this dangerous time and much of what follows is drawn directly from his own words.[130] The crew had all attended lectures detailing how to behave and what to do in the event of finding themselves in enemy territory. This covered capture, escape and evasion. MI9 was an intelligence organisation, formed after Major Holland of Military Intelligence Research (MIR) saw the potential value of PoWs who had escaped. He presented the idea of a new department to focus on this stream of intelligence and the Joint Intelligence Committee (JIC) agreed. The new department received its charter on 23 December 1939, headed by First World War veteran Major Norman Crockatt. It had five main tasks which were:

- to help British PoWs in their escapes, so they could return to combat and use up enemy resources;
- to help the escapees to avoid capture while in enemy territory; to collect and distribute information;
- to help deny the enemy information; and
- to maintain the morale of British PoWs in enemy camps.
- Interviewing escapees and evaders on their return was also a vital role in building intelligence and providing more up-to-date information on the situation on the ground in Europe.

MI9 produced an escape kit which all airmen carried. It consisted of:

- a compass, often hidden within collar studs, buttons, or badges;
- a silk map; a saw blade;
- a chocolate bar; tablets for energy;

- a rubber water bottle; Halazone to purify water;
- a razor, needle, and thread; and some currency.

Additionally, they carried photos to be used for false papers if necessary.

In addition to the above they were supplied with the 'Responsibilities of a Prisoner of War' card. However, unlike the kit, the card was never to be taken on board the aircraft, in order to eliminate the risk of the enemy knowing the instructions the crew would follow should they crash.

We know from Fry's account that it had been decided prior to take-off that if they were downed they would split into two groups, one consisting of officers and the other of NCOs, as was standard procedure. The reasoning behind this was that, if caught, the officers would be sent to one PoW camp and the NCOs to another, meaning that they might stay in their groups should they be caught. Now was the time to put all that training to good use. Fry recalls:

> I found out that I had a deep scratch on my wrist and it was bleeding, so Bartter lent me his handkerchief and tied it up for me. Then we started walking. We stuck to the shadows along hedges and kept away from any farm houses and finally came to a little creek where we had a drink. Then we sat under a big tree and with a knife cut our flying boots down to walking boots.
>
> Ernesto then suggested to throw the parts we'd cut off into the creek. We started off again walking always north by Polaris. We had formed a rather faint plan among us to try and get to the coast at the north of the island and then try somehow to get some kind of a boat and over to Sweden. Taking advantage of every bit of woods and hedges we finally arrived at the top of a hill after about 4 am. When we looked back we could still see our aircraft burning and giving off clouds of smoke. We knew that the Germans would certainly have discovered it and would be searching the neighbourhood for us. Dawn started to break about 7 o'clock to find us still walking. By now I was just staggering along. Bartter was getting slower and slower – bothered by a bad knee which he had wrenched in the crash, so that Ernesto and I had to stop and wait for him from time to time.
>
> Cover seemed to be getting harder to find and frequently we had to pass very close to farmhouses. Although it was now

Figure 56. Photo of mini compass from one of the Bartter evaders, given to the Krügermeier family. (Jan Christensen)

Figure 57. Photo of Bartter which he carried to be used in false ID papers if needed. The photos were taken in the UK, usually in the traditional style of different European countries and were carried on each flight. (TNA)

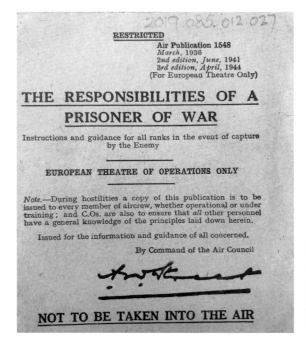

Figure 58. Responsibilities of a prisoner of war given to all airmen. (Tangmere Military Aviation Museum. Full details of this card can be seen in the Appendix)

becoming quite light, we had no alternative but to keep on going until we found a wood big enough to hide in during the day. Passing one farmhouse we decided to try and climb up into a big haystack and hide for the day but found it very wet so decided against it. Then we thought we'd take a chance and went into the barn. Here we had our first attempt at trying to make ourselves understood for the farmer had just come out to do the milking. We tried everything to make him understand, even flapped our arms like a bird to show him we were fliers and were very hungry. I think he understood but was too frightened of being caught helping flyers by the Germans. But his wife came out with five little apples and we were on our way again. I wouldn't have believed there could be so much energy in a little apple. About 8.30 am we finally came to the woods we were looking for along the shore of a huge inlet. We found a thick bunch of balsam trees and crawled under the lower branches out of sight and lay down on a makeshift bed of dead branches. Bartter then opened his escape kit and we had a piece of chocolate bar between us.

Some breakfast! But as we had no idea how long we would have to live like this, we knew what we had might have to last a long time. What a day – the longest day I've ever spent and I think the coldest. We were in our battledress and none of us had hats or gloves. The weather was below zero and although the sun was shining, we got none of it in the shade of our balsam trees. Finally our feet got so cold we took our shoes and socks off and rubbed the circulation back into one another's feet.

To add to our worries we discovered we had chosen a place in the woods where a bunch of woodcutters were at work cutting down trees and splitting them up into wood. We had to be quiet. One woodcutter passed with his horse and cart and a load of wood within 30ft of us but fortunately he didn't discover us.

At the time we didn't know if the language he was using to encourage the horse was Danish or German. We found we had only about five cigarettes between us and these were soon gone. Bartter had his pipe and a bit of tobacco and this didn't last long either. During the day we studied our map of Denmark, went over and over the distance we had walked before and tried to make some plan of action. We had walked about 20 miles but it seemed like a hundred to me. Found the woods we were in on the map and found we were on the north-west side of an inlet jutting in off the north coast. We decided then to head south again and then east and try somehow to work our way farther east and nearer Sweden. From where we were, we discovered it would be impossible to cross to Sweden under our own steam and in a small boat. About 4.30 it was beginning to get dusk and we started walking again, this time south. Again, the moon came up and we had to be very careful. About 6.30 we had our closest call. Walking about 100 yards from the shore we came over the brow of a little knoll and ran smack into a German sentry. The only thing we could do was to walk on as [nonchalantly] as possible and hope we weren't challenged. We walked on with our hands in our pockets and whistling (through pretty dry lips). How the sentry didn't recognise three British airmen in battle dress and bright moonlight I'll never know.

Every moment we expected to hear him shout halt (or the German equivalent) but he didn't although he did see us. We were lucky to get away with that. We crossed a railroad and then came to a main highway. It took us some time to get across. Several times German cars went by and we had to fall flat on our faces on the ploughed ground to avoid being seen. Finally we got across and started out again across the fields.

When we decided we were far enough south, we headed east. All the time we were getting hungrier and hungrier and made up our minds that sooner or later we'd have to take a chance and go to a farmhouse for food. Crossing one field near a farmhouse an old man yelled at us and ran after us. I think he thought we were trespassers at first. But then he seemed to understand we were allied airmen. He jabbered away in Danish.

We made foolish looking signs to show we were hungry and pointed to our mouths and rubbed our stomachs. His face beamed and we thought he had caught on. But he reached in his pocket and pulled out a piece of black tobacco of some kind. We finally gave it up as a bad job and continued on our way.

At the next farmhouse we came up to we decided we'd go and try our luck. As we came up we met two farm hands pushing bicycles and they stopped.

The two men in question were Sven Ove Frederiksen from Møllegården and Bent Olsen, a milk quality controller, on their way to a meeting. The sight of the three airmen took them by surprise. Fry continues:

> Ernesto Howell, the Argentinian, then tried to start a conversation in Spanish, and to everyone's surprise, they realised they could somewhat understand each other, since Frederiksen had learnt quite a bit of Esperanto, as president of the Tølløse Youth Association. They couldn't speak much English but [Howell] with his Spanish and Bartter with his Italian made them understand we were hungry and they took us up to the stable; a stable with about 25 Jersey cows in it. Boy that place was warm! We sat around on milk stools while one of the farmhands went up to the house and came back with some sandwiches with real Danish homemade cheese. But just as we were leaving, he ran after us and somehow made out that someone who spoke English was coming over to see us. We went back to the stable to wait while one of them went to fetch him.
>
> Olsen hopped back on his bike and cycled to the house of Wilhelm Krügermeier, who lived on the other side of the Roskilde–Holbæk road. [Krügermeier had emigrated to Canada and to the USA, and had lived there for fifteen years.] When he saw 'Canada' on my battle dress we were all set. He took us to this farmhouse just about one half mile away and from then on things were OK with us.

The next day, Olsen set off on his bike again, heading to Ryegaard Manor to fetch Count F.C.R. Scheel. The civilians who had rescued the airmen thought that the Count might have the relevant contacts within the Resistance movement to further help them. The Count was eager to do so, and he came to Krügermeier's home with two suits, two trench coats, and some shirts. Krügermeier also gave them some civilian clothes. Fry remembers that meeting in detail:

> [Bartter] got a real good fit, a dark suit and a bowler hat (made in London too), [Howell] got a brown suit and blue hat and I got a grey one but no hat and got an old brown coat.
>
> The Count told us an ambulance would call for us sometime during the afternoon. He gave us 300 kroner in Danish money each, so with what we already had, we would be all set for a

while as far as money was concerned. We said goodbye and the Count left. We didn't ask anyone their names in case we were caught.

Sunday morning [12 December] we stayed inside the house and played cards to put in the time and listened to the radio. We went out one at a time if we had to use the toilet in the barn (early in the morning). At noon we had the best meal I think I've ever had. For just the three of us, she set out two whole chickens with mashed potatoes, gravy and vegetables.

Besides that we had homemade bread and real Danish butter as white as snow. For dessert we had some kind of fruit cake covered with about an inch of whipped cream. Wow, what a cake!

On 13 December, right after the crash of Halifax BB378, the following warning appeared in the national Danish newspapers, including *Ekstra Bladet*:

The German martial law provides as follows:

The German martial law prohibits any action in favour of the soldiers who are enemies of Germany. The following message was sent tonight through the Ritzau press agency: Germany reminds the population that any help provided to soldiers of the allied enemy forces (such as, for example, enemy pilots who survived a crash) is strictly prohibited by German martial law and considered an act of support to the enemy, which is punishable by the severest sanctions, including death. Any person who is aware of the presence of an agent of the enemy military forces must immediately inform thereof the German authorities. Such actions include sheltering said individuals, providing them with clothes, money and food, as well as the communication of any kind of information and any support of a similar nature.

On the radio, the same warning could be heard over and over again: any assistance to the airmen was punishable by death. Krügermeier didn't mention this to his guests. In spite of the warnings, many Danes defied the German orders. Krügermeier, Olsen and Frederiksen were 'ordinary' people who found themselves in an extraordinary situation where they had to choose sides during the war and decided to help the Allied airmen.

The time had come to organise the next steps of their transport. The scheme was simple yet required several middlemen to cover all the tracks. Christian Pedersen, a worker at the local emergency services station, the Falck Depot, called his manager, Einar Arboe Rasmussen, who was in Copenhagen on a private hospital visit. Petersen told Arboe Rasmussen that a local Resistance worker, Mogens Scheel, a timber dealer in Roskilde, needed an ambulance to drive someone from the village of Elverdammen to a hospital in Copenhagen. Arboe Rasmussen called the Resistance worker, whom he knew, who told him about the British aircraft that crashed in Bonderup and the fact that, 'unfortunately', the Germans had not yet captured the airmen. Upon hearing this, Rasmussen immediately understood that the sick villager in question was actually the three British airmen. He rang Lindell, his employee, who was at a birthday party at the house of the caretaker, Juel Jensen. He mentioned the airmen on the loose in guarded terms and without hesitation asked if he could take care of a villager from Elverdammen. Lindell, in the middle of a celebration, declined. 'Well keep stuffing yourself then, but I hope it'll click soon!', replied Rasmussen before hanging up. Moments later Lindell called back saying that 'it had clicked', and all was finally set for the airmen's journey to Copenhagen.

Writer and journalist Lise Nørgaard, who worked at Roskilde's newspapers, *Roskilde Dagblad*, during the occupation, recalls fondly:

> In addition to being a very faithful friend, Einar was brave and
> bold, and deserves great respect. I remember how, at the end
> of the day, we would stop at the Falck Depot, which was near
> the newspaper's offices, and there were always sausage rolls
> on the table for us. Einar was the station's manager. I still can't
> believe that the Germans never figured out his, and his team's,
> secret activities at the time.[131]

Fry was clearly happy to have found a safe space and food. He recalled: 'His wife couldn't speak a word of English but she knew all about English airmen and set out to make us feel at home and brought us more to eat and also tea. Sure was great to get eating again.'

After lunch at Krügermeier's, the airmen left. They gave Krügermeier their addresses and IDs, which all crew members carried with them in case of a crash and if they needed to have forged IDs made. The battledresses were hidden by the family, who thought it was a shame to burn them. They can now be seen at Holbæk Museum in its permanent exhibition.

Those helping downed airmen ran a terrible risk to themselves and their families. The situation in Denmark meant that the Danish Police would arrest anyone found helping the Allies. This ranged from active Resistance fighters through to people such as the Krügermeier family who simply offered shelter and food. There are documented cases of people receiving up to ten years' imprisonment for helping agents; even allowing them into their home could cost a person a minimum of fifteen months in prison. The bravery of those who aided the airmen must always be remembered as they did so under the threat of substantial punishment.

Fry's detailed account of their escape continues:

> At about 1:30 the ambulance came and the driver, dressed in uniform, and a lumber dealer who was to look after us came in. We sat and talked for a while and then changed our clothes, [Bartter] shaved off his moustache, gave our wings away as souvenirs and told the farmer to destroy our clothes. Finally we said goodbye and thanked the farmer and his wife and went into the ambulance one at a time. They drew all the curtains and we set out on our way to Copenhagen. The first town we came to was Roskilde where we stopped for a while.
>
> They drove the ambulance inside some kind of a garage (or ambulance centre) and here we met the Count's brother. He gave us several packs of cigarettes (pretty awful tobacco) and I got a hat – an old sailor's hat. Most of the men could speak fairly good English, so we sat and talked for a while before setting out again. While driving through the streets we saw several German soldiers hanging around the streets watching the girls go by.

Falck's men went to get neck braces for the fugitives to wear. Each knew their part: Howell was a very sick patient, attended to by his doctor, Bartter, and a deeply grieving relative, Fry. The rest was in the hands of the Falck Depot. The three airmen were driven to Copenhagen and settled in a small flat, as Fry explains:

> Finally, about 4:30 in the afternoon, we got to Copenhagen, stopped the ambulance and then whisked us, one at a time, down the street about a block and into some kind of a club where a party was going on. We were introduced all around and

Right: Figure 59.
Kai, Wilhelm
Krügermeier's son,
wearing one of the
airmen's uniforms.
(Krügermeier
family)

Below: Figure 60.
Bartter's
battledress and hat.
(Danish Resistance
Museum)

given a drink of Schnapps each. What a drink! It burned all the way down to my toes. After about half an hour they told us we were going to go by taxi to an apartment. We were to speak not a word in the taxi. They took us to a small apartment and made us feel right at home. We were to stay here until arrangements could be made to get us across into Sweden. They left us alone, locked the door and told us not to answer the door if anyone came. About eight o'clock they returned, three couples of them. They had a birthday party arranged and weren't going to postpone it just because we were there. They brought food for us and a whole cardboard box filled with gin, rye, scotch and Pilsner beer. One of the girls (married) was the prettiest redhead I've ever seen. She spoke broken English and I think our three pairs of eyes hardly left her for the whole evening.

We ended up singing 'God Save the King' and 'Rule Britannia'. They kept asking us when the Allies were going to invade Denmark. We promised to come back and see them after the war. When the party broke up, they made beds for us on the floor. I slept on the chesterfield. At noon they sent a man up with more sandwiches (smorgasbord) and made tea for us – also a couple of Pilsner. We spent our time looking at some of their snapshots and Bartter and I played 'patience' […] Somehow they had got word to the 'Major' [Muus] and during the afternoon he came to see us. He had gotten away quite easily. The Major brought us more cigarettes and then went to see someone about taking us across the water to Sweden. They came back about seven o'clock that night. We were taken again by ambulance through the German sentries on a bridge over to a small island where we were to wait until our next part of the journey.

Our three evaders, Bartter, Fry and Howell, were lucky with the people they came across; they found themselves aided by an excellent network of resisters. There is no doubt the three crew members, and those who helped them, were in imminent danger throughout, but luck as well as planning was on their side. Their journey to this point, as previously described, was not a jolly wander through Denmark, but a fraught and dangerous escape and, as described by Fry, they were worried not just for their own safety and those helping them but also for their fellow crew.[132]

Until October 1943 the Jewish community had the protection of the collaborating Danish government, but following the resignation of the government, the Gestapo planned the mass deportation of Danish Jews to concentration camps. However, word of the plan was leaked and synagogues across Denmark told people to leave. Immediately, new escape routes via sea to Sweden opened up as news travelled and families fled, which resulted in around 95 per cent of Jewish people escaping. Around 700 Jews were captured; many had refused to take the advice and others may not have heard it. Nonetheless, it was these new routes, an extraordinary undertaking, which resulted in 7,000 people – Jews, Resistance members and downed airmen, including Bartter, Fry and Howell – being able to evade capture and to escape.

Throughout the whole of the Second World War only ninety-eight airmen were able to evade capture and escape from Denmark. Over 1,000 are buried across approximately 100 cemeteries; additionally, a number of airmen, believed to be around 500, were lost at sea. Of these losses, twelve were Special Duties aircraft with sixty airmen killed. Only seven evaded, including the three from the Bartter crew, and nineteen became PoWs, of which five were from this crew. The German radar network over Denmark made flying over the country particularly perilous. The fact that the crew survived the crash is a reflection of their skill and training, particularly, as mentioned by both Fry and Atkins, the skill of Bartter as pilot. For Bartter, Fry and Howell, their escape from Denmark was aided in no small part by the network set up to assist Jewish Danes to escape. Having been transported safely via a bridge to the island of Amager, Fry continues:

> After getting out of the ambulance, we met a sailor who was to look after us from then on; then shook hands all around. I felt very much alone after they left as they seemed so sure of themselves. The sailor took us to a cottage down by the water – a really swell little cottage which belonged evidently to a sailing man for he had pictures and model sailing boats everywhere about the room we were taken to. After about half an hour two young Danish chaps about 16 came to take us to another house. Evidently they had an idea the Germans might be coming to take over the house as living quarters. Several houses had been confiscated in that area in the last couple of days. So we set out. Again they warned us not to do any talking although once one of the boys asked if we were armed

and seemed quite surprised when we told him we weren't. Although they were so young, they had revolvers and seemed quite hardened and used to this sort of thing.

We went into the dark house and right upstairs to one of the rooms, a bedroom, lit a candle and they told us their plans. The sailor was to pick us up at 7 am the next morning and take us down to the boat. Then the three of them left and we started on the longest night I've ever spent. We sat up for a while and talked and ate a few more of our sandwiches. It was plenty cold in the room so the three of us tried to get some sleep on the chesterfield. When we got tired and cramped in one position everyone would shift and we would lay the other way for a while. Once, we heard an aircraft circling around the bay and it gave us a couple of bad moments thinking of the German aircraft again. We did a lot of talking for each time one of us would waken it would waken the others too. We kept wondering how the rest of the crew were doing and whether they had been able to escape or if they had been caught.

The night passed and the next part of their journey began, Fry continues with his detailed account:

Finally the night passed and the sailor came back again ready to take us down to the boat. We went through the back yard to a walk along the water. The thought kept running through my mind how awful it would be to be caught now we were so near to getting away. We came to the dock and the fishing boat, a small motor boat we were to go in and got down into the hold right away. It was very cramped and wet down there and smelled of fish and oil. After about 10 or 15 minutes someone opened the trap door above us (evidently an inspection of some kind) and our hearts were really in our mouths. But luckily whoever it was didn't discover us, if he had tilted his flashlight a few degrees he would have seen us. It's mighty hard to stay absolutely still and quiet when something really depends on it.

The hatch which they had used to get into the hold was hidden by coconut netting so the full hold was not visible to those searching, fortunately.[133]

We finally got underway. The boat wasn't very fast but every time the old motor chugged, it brought us that much nearer Sweden and safety for us. At about 9 am one of the deck hands told us we could come up on deck because we were inside the three mile zone around Sweden and therefore safe from any German interference. To take a big breath of fresh air, leaning against the mast and say to yourself: 'I've got away from those bloody Germans!' Boy, what a feeling! Soon the buildings began to show up in the mist and before long we were entering the harbour at Malmö on the south shore of Sweden. We docked, and the skipper (a Swedish fisherman) handed us over to the dock authorities.

There followed a certain amount of being passed around various authorities who interrogated the three airmen. They followed both advice from their training and the advice given by the Danes who had assisted them.[134] Information regarding their mission and any details on those who had assisted them was omitted from the statements they gave in Sweden. According to Fry, they declared themselves political refugees: 'Our story to the Swedish police: we were political refugees, trapped in Denmark with the war. They bought the story but I'm sure with the tongue in cheek.'

After this they were handed over to other police, where under interrogation they again repeated their story. From here they were given ration cards and taken for a meal by Lieutenant Bosse Franz, who was described by the three officers, in their official debrief by MI9, as appearing quite genuine and who made no attempt to interrogate them. From this point they were given identity cards and handed over to the British Consul, as Fry continues: 'We were then turned over to the British Legation in Malmö. Arrangements were made for us to travel by train to Stockholm.' Once in Stockholm, they were given money for civilian clothes and booked into the city centre Hotel Astoria. In 1997, Fry said he still had the dressing gown he had bought during this period. Their only obligation was to report to the British Ambassador on a daily basis.

Fry mentions that they were something of a rarity. There is also mention of captured German servicemen interned in Sweden, with a system which saw equal numbers of each side repatriated in turn. On 5 January 1944, Bartter, Fry and Howell boarded a BOAC (British Overseas Airways Corporation) flight which took them to RAF Leuchars, near Kinross in Scotland. The three officers had been extraordinarily lucky in reaching Sweden. During 1943 BOAC had set up a covert air link to Sweden from Leuchars. They used this to repatriate rescued airmen and also to import Swedish goods into the UK. We can only imagine the relief and delight of our trio on reaching, if not home, then friendly lands.

Once in London they were interviewed by MI9. These interviews are less florid than Fry's personal account; they kept to concise clear information without any descriptive enhancement. In Fry's personal account he states that he was then debriefed by Canadian Intelligence and the Canadian Air Ministry. After this he was asked if he cared for thirty days' leave, which he said he very much did care for. He, along with other Canadians, boarded the British troop ship RMS *Andes*. In a convoy it took nine days to reach New York before Fry could continue on to his home country.

Both Bartter and Howell were, like Fry, given a period of leave. After this the three escapees went in their different directions. Bartter was despatched to Howbury Hall at Waterend, near Bedford, less than ten miles from RAF Tempsford. Known as STS (Special Training School) 40, this SOE school concentrated on training on the Rebecca/Eureka radio system and the S-phone for reception committees. It has been suggested by David Hewson that the school was opened following a series of incidents involving mistakes with the equipment.[135] The school offered an intensive ten-day course, and Bartter's first-hand experience of both the equipment and the conditions under which it was used would have been invaluable. Additionally, he kept up to date with the situation at Tempsford and was able to provide up-to-date information to those he was training for the rest of the war, which was noted in official documents. He stayed in this role for the duration of the war.

Fry was repatriated to Canada on 24 January 1944. He then enjoyed some leave before being posted to No.1 Air Observer School on 16 March. It was standard that those who had evaded capture were not put back into active operations; the intelligence services preferred to avoid risking an escapee being recaptured, due to the security risk it would pose. In July he then moved on to No.7 Photographic Wing and in September was promoted to Flight Lieutenant. He was not allowed to discuss his experiences as an evader, but he could talk about the need to pay attention during the escape and evasion lectures, which were delivered in the UK.[136] He remained with the Photographic Wing until 7 March when he began his leaving procedure, finally leaving the RCAF on 16 March 1946.

Howell was despatched to the Manchester University Air Squadron on 5 February 1944, just a month after his return from Sweden. Interestingly, he is listed as 'supernumerary', which, in effect, means he was surplus to requirements and might be given a variety of roles. He was slotted into the role of a signals and armaments instructor. Despite it seeming as if Howell was simply located randomly, those with experience were highly sought after to train the new crews. He remained here until 24 April, when he was transferred back to 138 Squadron at Tempsford, where he was listed as W.Op/Air; this stood for wireless operator and air gunner, a two-pronged role on board an aircraft where the primary role of wireless operator was supplemented by manning a gun should it be necessary. As mentioned in connection with Fry, it was very unusual for someone who had escaped to be returned to a previous posting.

By 4 June 1944 he is listed as being posted to Signal Leader duties. This meant he was responsible to the Squadron Commander for signals standards and would have provided refresher courses for the squadron's wireless operators. It becomes difficult to trace exactly whether Howell was attached to a crew, as forms which used to list the whole crew changed in February 1944 to show just the lead pilot. As he provided refresher courses, it is possible that he joined various crews on operations, although it is highly unlikely that he would have flown on any flight over Denmark. Both MI9 and the RAF Director of Intelligence decided that crews would not fly over an area where they had previously been on the ground. The risk was that they might have knowledge of resistance groups, individuals and escape routes, and so if captured could pose a serious threat to those on the ground.[137]

We know that Howell took off on 8 November 1944 on 'Operation Crupper 11' in Norway in a Stirling Mk IV LJ993 with Flight Lieutenant Frederick John Ford at the helm. The aircraft was carrying two Norwegian agents, twelve containers and eleven packages. The agents were Peter Deinboll and Arne Gjestland, both specialists in railway and industrial sabotage. The weather at Tempsford was far from ideal, with low cloud and icing. Nevertheless, at the main briefing the meteorological people stated that this would lift on crossing the English coast and that the weather would be excellent over Norway.

That night twenty-four aircraft from 138 and 161 Squadrons were despatched, but only one made a successful drop. Twenty-one aircraft aborted their operations due to bad weather. Twenty-two containers were dropped for the price of 141 hours 25 minutes' flying time, two aircraft being hit by lightning and two aircraft lost when they apparently hit the sea. Fourteen crew members and two agents were lost. LJ993 was among the aircraft lost that night, and Howell, along with the rest of the crew and the two agents, crashed into the North Sea and were never found.

Figure 61. Jan Christensen preparing to lay a wreath in honour of Ernesto Howell at Tempsford Memorial Service, November 2019. (Jan Christensen)

A memorial was erected for Howell and around 20,000 other airmen with unknown graves at the Runnymede Memorial in Surrey, England. Another memorial plaque was erected with Howell's name at Manchester University, to acknowledge his time there. Having survived the crash in Denmark he was the only member of the Bartter crew to lose his life during the war. A month after his disappearance, a supplement in the *London Gazette* acknowledged him as an Acting Flight Lieutenant who was awarded the Distinguished Flying Cross.[138] This was in recognition of his contribution as a young man who was not obliged to fight, yet who travelled thousands of miles from the southern hemisphere to stand and be counted for what he believed to be right. This was his second mention in the *London Gazette*; the first one acknowledging him as part of the RAF Volunteer Reserve, promoted to Sergeant in February 1943. A year after his death a notice appeared in the newspaper local to Tempsford. It seems someone remembered Ernesto and his sacrifice, quite possibly Bartter, who had been located nearby.

> HOWELL, – In loving memory of Flight Lieut. Ernesto Howell, No.138 Squadron, R.A.F. Tempsford, Signals Leader, of Buenos Aires, Argentina, who lost his life over Norway on 9 November 1944.
>
> Youth cannot die, his veins thrilled with the spring
>
> To others fate may bring the last degree
>
> He, as he flew, passed death upon the wing
>
> Then deathless, rose to immortality

Howell was not forgotten then and remains in the thoughts of those who return to Tempsford every year to pay their respects to those who served.

Chapter 7

The war is over for you – Stalag IV B

Capture, interrogation, and imprisonment

We have seen what happened to Bartter, Fry and Howell after the crash. For the remaining members of the crew, it would be some time before they would see their homeland again and discover the fate of the others. Anderson, Atkins, Riggs, Smith and Turvil chose a different route from the crash site. For several days, they succeeded in walking a substantial distance, around forty-four miles (seventy kilometres), relying on friendly Danes for food

Figure 62. Barn with hayloft at Dronningkilde farm in the small town of Ølsted, where the airmen were captured. (Jan Christensen)

and shelter. After the crash, the five NCOs found a barn where they spent the night and the whole of the following day. They left again at nightfall, but were still exhausted and had eaten all the contents of their escape kits, so they tried their luck and knocked at a farm door along the way. There, they were fed and offered shelter for the night. In another farm, further on the course they had set, they were offered milk and bread, but the residents were too scared to let them stay the night, so they had to find shelter elsewhere.

Sadly, luck would not be on the side of our five airmen: they had survived being shot down but would not be joining the rest of the crew back in England. It was St Lucia's Day, Monday 13 December, when they arrived in Ølsted, north of Frederikssund, usually a day of light and hope. Atkins recalls that up to this point they 'received assistance from the local Danish population, mainly farming [...] were put up in barns, pigsties and such like [...] thought we were well on our way to getting back to the UK, providing we could get across the water to Sweden'.[139]

These comforting thoughts were in their minds as they settled down for another night, but there was to be no hope or guardian angel on this night. Unbeknownst to the crew, the farm's inhabitants then called the Danish police, who in turn informed the *Wehrmacht*.

The capture of members of the Bartter crew was reported in the underground Danish newspaper of Tølløse, *Dansk Daad* – 'Danish Deed' in January 1944. The paper ran from October 1943 to June 1944. It names the farmer who betrayed them, and highlights a sentiment of disapproval within the narrative, and unequivocally presents the paper's attitude towards the Nazis. The translated article stated:

> The English aircraft that crashed a few days ago near Bonderup did not carry bombs. But a lot of ammunition and weapons were found at the crash site. In the wreck, clothes and hats were also found with a Swedish label. [It was common for SOE to use fake local labels in clothing etc. for security reasons.]
>
> Five men reached St Havelse, where they asked farmer Peter Petersen for shelter and food. He showed them to his hayloft, but did not bring them food. He called the Danish police who notified the German Wehrmacht. [The police were obliged to do that.]
>
> At 02:00 the Germans surrounded the farm and caught the airmen.

>During the search of the airmen in the area around Bonderup, two of the area's occupants, farm owner P. Frederiksen and Anders Sørensen, both Ubberup, appeared as Nazi cockroaches, while guarding [giving food, drinks etc.] to several of the German soldiers participating in the search without being forced to do so. It should be remembered.[140]

This article is very insightful, not only for its open opinion on Nazi control, but also because it had no issue in naming the local farmers who had aided the occupiers: naming and shaming. According to Atkins, the farmer's actions were driven solely by money:

>The attitude he had when we contacted the farm was no different from the other farms we had help from [...] He never appeared before us when the Germans came, the only time we saw him was when we first made contact at the farm and we were shown somewhere to sleep. He was not there when the Germans came. We were taken to a building in Copenhagen. After about 3 or 4 days we were taken to Germany.[141]

Atkins explained that 'at this stage the Germans were making it very well known that there were several British aircrew on the loose, and there were rewards on our heads'.[142] He stated in his Imperial War Museum interview that the farmer received quite a large reward for his trouble in informing on the aircrew.[143] Whether a reward was given to the farmer is not documented, nor is it known if this was standard procedure, but this would have been an incentive for the Danes to become informants. When asked if he had suspected the farmer, Atkins replied, 'no, not at all, the attitude we had when we contacted the farm was no different from the other farmers we had help from. We were very well treated and very well fed, and these people took tremendous risks in helping us.'[144] In Atkins's IWM interview he explained that not only did the Danish farmers and families provide them with food and shelter, they also contributed valuable information about the location of German troops, and maps. When asked if he hated the farmer who had betrayed them, he replied 'we despised him, we found it difficult to reconcile why a man of his age was so tempted with the financial reward'.[145]

Smith briefly mentions their capture in his interview with MI9. Part of the process after repatriation and debriefing were completed was to carry out interviews with all aircrew. Smith's interview, although tellingly very brief, communicates how he felt: 'we evaded capture for three days, helped by Danes, betrayed by a Dane to Germans'.[146] Betrayed is a poignant and powerful word, especially for a member of the British services, for whom trust, integrity and loyalty were important characteristics. The fact that many Danes had aided the crew to such a great extent prior to their capture, thereby putting themselves and their families at risk of execution if they had been discovered, must have made the betrayal a very difficult pill to swallow. In Riggs's MI9 interview, although saying that his statement would be identical to that of Atkins, he wanted to add some further information. He described the farmer as a

> tall well built man of about 60 years with close cropped hair, and had with him a short slim foxy little man of 35 years who was well dressed in a blue lounge suit and wore glasses; also it was only just daylight when we knocked at the door, they were both up and fully dressed and it was the little man who took us to the hayloft where we were betrayed.[147]

This is a valuable insight into an account of the incident in which the memory had clearly been imprinted in Riggs's mind and remained precise despite his time in captivity. The two facets to this story which are prominent, and which were a common occurrence, were the level of help and sustenance that was given to the many aircrew who were shot down, and the cruel betrayals that were a recurrent theme. This is seen in many MI9 liberation report interviews in which aircrew went into great detail about the level of aid they received, and from whom they received it.

Following their capture, Atkins recalls:

> After we were taken prisoner, we were taken to a building in Copenhagen which I learnt after the war was a disused [...] Danish Army barracks [...] it was very primitive, there were cells there and we were kept in solitary confinement. Interrogated, but not in depth because it was the German Army that arrested us and took us prisoner, they weren't competent, and I think they were under instructions to get us to the Luftwaffe in Dulag Luft in Frankfurt [...] The place was the Høvelte army compound.
>
> After about three or four days we were taken to Germany. We had an escort of three or four armed guards, and we were

taken by boat from the island of Funen to German mainland. I remember changing trains in Hamburg, it was quite fascinating to be in an enemy country and seeing the enemy going about their normal duties [...] soldiers going on leave and coming back from leave and suchlike. We didn't see any damage [...] we were taken in a closed truck and we had no opportunity to study our surroundings at all. Some of the younger Germans showed hostility by shouting and spitting at us but we were never actually physically attacked. The guards, to their credit, kept us under guard. The German military mind worked in the way that if you were a military man yourself, and you behaved as a military individual then they would respect you as a military man, providing you were in the hands of the military and not one of the German civilian police organisations. The next stop was a transit camp, Dulag Luft. It was an interrogation centre for all aircrew shot down and captured by the Germans, before they were sent to a permanent PoW camp.[148]

Dulag Luft

Dulag Luft was short for *Durchgangslager der Luftwaffe*, or 'transit camp of the Luftwaffe'. It was located at Oberursel, about nine miles (fifteen kilometres) from Frankfurt-am-Main. The name Dulag Luft was one which struck fear into Allied aircrew. RAF crews were briefed at their escape and evasion lectures that if they happened to be shot down and captured, they would most likely be sent there for interrogation. Rumour and information about treatment within the camp ranged from great leniency – even to the point of normality with meals with the camp officers or excursions to the local inn – to the extreme polarity of unendurable torture and barbaric beatings. Until a man arrived and was processed, it was not clear which treatment he would experience.

Dulag Luft had been set up and managed by the Luftwaffe specifically for the purpose of interrogation, before prisoners were allocated to a permanent PoW camp. It had a capacity of 20,000, and in 1943, when the Bartter crew were held there, approximately 1,000 captured airmen per month passed through the Dulag. It was known as the largest interrogation centre in Europe.

The camp was the archetype of German controlled confinement. The boundaries of the camp were formed by two parallel fences 10ft apart which

Figure 63. IN0722, exterior view of Dulag Luft Camp. (British Red Cross)

stood 12ft tall, with trenches and barbed wire intertwined between them. Watch towers were spaced around the camp at 100-yard intervals. Trained dogs prowled the outer boundaries, and heavily armed pillboxes were scattered beyond the barbed wire. There were large white rocks that covered the length of the front lawn forming the words 'Prisoner of War Camp'.

By November 1939 it had become clear to the *Oberkommando der Wehrmacht* (OKW), the high command of the German Army who were responsible for the administration of Dulag Luft, that the most reliable and up-to-date information that they could collate and source regarding British morale and the country's war readiness would come through PoWs, who would predominantly be captured aircrew. These newly captured aircrew would become Germany's pivotal source of intelligence and data, apropos the strength and weaknesses of the RAF.[149]

The camp was enlarged over the years and was estimated to cover about 500 acres. In 1943, when the crew of Halifax BB378 passed through the Dulag, there were thirty-five to forty interrogators, which demonstrates the number of aircrew who were shot down, captured and incarcerated. There were approximately 8,000 prisoners who spent time there during that year. The perimeter and the prisoners were kept under constant surveillance during their time in Dulag Luft. A construction known as 'The Cooler' housed 103 solitary confinement cells which measured on average 9ft long, 6ft wide, and 9ft high. The walls were made of fibre-board and filled with a heavy layer of insulation material. We will see later that there was a significant reason for this. The floor was timber, with only a tiny crack under the door to allow for the flow of air, the window held a pane of frosted glass and iron bars, and the cells were fitted with electric heaters.[150] PoW accounts vary regarding the conditions, but by 1943 the state of these coolers would have probably deteriorated considerably. Many PoWs reported that there was no glass in the windows, so the bitter elements and freezing temperatures and winds cut through the cells.

According to the Geneva Convention of 27 July 1929 (of which Germany had been one of the thirty-eight signatories), Article 3 stipulated that:

> every prisoner of war is bound to give [...] his true name and rank, or else his regimental number. [...] No coercion may be used on prisoners to secure information relative to the condition of their army or country. Prisoners who refuse to answer may not be threatened, insulted or exposed to unpleasant or disadvantageous treatment of any kind whatsoever.[151]

However, many of these regulations were not always adhered to, perhaps not surprisingly given the autocratic rule of Nazi Germany. Officers pressed and interrogated the prisoners for extra information, and many spent longer in solitary conditions than they should have.

During their training, all aircrew were furnished with an information leaflet which set out the protocol if they were captured. They should give only their name, rank and number; this did not include their squadron number. The enemy were not allowed to threaten them for information, and if a prisoner systematically refused to give information then that must be respected by his captors. Guidelines about information they would try to glean was also incorporated, so they were well aware of what information to avoid discussing, and what sources and methods their captors might use to acquire information, for example by impersonating and mixing with British or Allied prisoners, and utilising agents such as medical staff or nurses to sympathise and lull them into a false sense of security. Other ploys were a friendly reception, renewed interrogation long after capture, or implying that another officer had talked and that all information was already known.[152]

Upon arrival at Dulag Luft, the PoWs would have been stripped and searched. This is described in Geoff Taylor's *A Piece of Cake*, an in-depth, invaluable, and compelling account of his experiences of capture and confinement within both Dulag Luft and Stalag IV B. Taylor was a Royal Australian Air Force (RAAF) pilot for Bomber Command, and was captive in Stalag IV B at the same time as our crew. The book also has a direct link with Atkins as two airmen, Dave Paul and Ralph Parsons, both Australians who flew for the RAAF, were prisoners at Stalag IV B. Paul and Parsons are mentioned in Taylor's book. As Atkins explains in his IWM interview:

> [The] Germans had many ways of trying to extract information from you [...] We were subjected to the hot and cold treatment as it is properly known, whereby the Germans would by one stage put the heating on to a very high degree when you were literally perspiring, and another time they would switch it all off and you would be freezing; this was done to cause you maximum discomfort and lower your morale.[153]

In many cases the hot and cold method of torture was used within the interrogation process. The interrogators would enquire if the temperature in the cell was to the prisoner's liking. This was guaranteed to rouse tempers, especially after days of solitary confinement and a lack of food.[154] The hot and cold treatment was the significant reason the cooler was insulated to such an extent; not to add comfort or luxury for the inmates, but to employ a method of torture.

This is also confirmed within Herbert Krentz's account of his stay in the Dulag. Krentz was a Royal Canadian Air Force (RCAF) pilot captured in January 1944. He describes being stripped and searched upon arrival, and then left in solitary confinement for two days without shoes to ensure he didn't escape. His joviality about the ridiculous situation was expressed through his statement: 'Escape!! with a barred window and concrete walls I believed even Superman would have stayed put.' He was then taken for interrogation by an officer who appeared to be overly pleased to see him. This rang alarm bells, as Krentz had heard about his type before. He smoked the officer's cigarettes and was invited to tea. The officer asked how he was being treated and Herbert complained about the cold, and that his wounds needed redressing. He returned to his cell, received the medical treatment almost immediately, but was rewarded with the temperature being turned up to unbearable levels.[155]

When first interrogated, the prisoners of the Dulag Luft were often asked to fill in a form for the Swiss Red Cross, in order to acquire as much information as possible. They were told that the form would help the Red Cross to locate their relatives, and would in turn let them know that they were safe. In fact, the Germans were looking to gather as many details as possible about the crew, among other things. This became known as the 'bogus Red Cross form'.[156] The form asked questions about squadrons, airfields, aircraft equipment and commanders, and sometimes also probed for previous employment details and qualifications. The purpose for this was to be able to gauge where the prisoner might be allocated for work duties after Germany had won the war.[157] Obviously the aircrew realised this was a devious ruse to glean information from them, and not a particularly subtle one. Atkins encountered this process during his confinement at Dulag Luft:

> We were also visited by the so-called Red Cross representative who maintained he was from the Swiss Red Cross and if you would give him certain information he would ensure that your next of kin would be advised that you were safe and were a prisoner of war. He asked you what squadron you were in and questions on the operation you'd been on. We had knowledge that this type of thing went on. We had been briefed in the UK as part of our training that the Germans were doing this type of thing, and previous airmen that had been shot down and got back to the UK were able to brief our own security people on this type of measures taken by the Germans so that we were on our guard. [...] I can honestly say I gave nothing except my name, rank and service number, which we were advised that we could do.

When asked how they reacted when they refused to cooperate, Atkins explained:

> The Red Cross man for example immediately lost his temper and started shouting and ranting and raving, shouting 'this will do you no good!' which gave the game away. I mean, a normal Swiss Red Cross person would not have behaved in such a manner [...] I was interrogated by two or three Luftwaffe officers, and I was treated with military respect by them.[158]

Most of the captured NCO crew of Halifax BB378 were interrogated at Dulag Luft. In his MI9 questionnaire, Anderson stated he had been kept in solitary confinement, Riggs gave the dates he was incarcerated in the Dulag, but did not elaborate any further on his experiences. Turvil did not mention Dulag Luft, and stated within his MI9 questionnaire by just penning 'No' that he had not been interrogated. Atkins also reveals that not only did he endure the 'hot box' treatment, but also that his food ration was withdrawn. Smith explained that his interrogation at Dulag Luft consisted of normal means and method.[159]

Interrogation was a constant within the camp. It varied in relation to who was being interrogated and if their character was difficult to break. Aircrew were studied by psychologists to determine their personality and traits, and this was used within the interrogation to destroy their mental resistance. Prisoners were bribed: they would receive clean clothes, some food and cigarettes in exchange for answers to the questions they were asked. Many were led into a false sense of security by overly friendly meetings with camp commandants who would chat to them about life in Britain, and their families, share their cigarettes and coffee, and sometimes not ask any questions regarding the war at all.

They would try to establish a friendship of sorts, common ground, as many had studied in Britain or visited; but those who resisted the temptation or the pressure were once again placed in solitary confinement. Many stayed

Figure 64. Brian Atkins's prisoner of war tags. (Nigel Atkins)

true to the training they were given in resisting interrogation even though they knew they would suffer for it, but many succumbed to the cruel treatment.

When asked if there was anyone at Dulag Luft who he suspected gave information to the Germans, Atkins stated:

> I didn't suspect any particular individual, but we had been warned in our training in the UK that the authorities were suspicious that there was a leakage, one or two people that were cooperating with the Germans but I had no knowledge of any particular individual, they kept you there until such times until they thought they could not get any further with you. Once they came to the conclusion that you weren't going to say very much they wanted to get rid of you, one thing that struck me during the interrogations was the amount of information they had on the special duty squadrons they seemed very versed in the names of various senior officers on the station. This was known in training as the 'show of knowledge' to undermine confidence.[160]

It was well known that many gave vital information away; archives reveal that in some cases the level of information proffered was notably in-depth, and although the Germans were significantly abreast of Allied intelligence, this would have given them the upper hand in various instances, especially within interrogation techniques. Dulag Luft interrogation reports disclose that even a member of another 138(B) Squadron from Tempsford disclosed a vast amount of information. They divulged specific details of flights, routes, courses and targets. As well as flight details, they confirmed the dropping of containers and described target marking and radio jamming. Even information on RAF airfields' administration, management and – vitally – location were given. The information given allows us to determine which crew was involved in giving the details, but it is important to understand the fear and trauma that these men experienced.[161]

The most damning area of the report was the detailed information regarding the strengths and activities of Tempsford airfield:

> two flights with 20–25 serviceable aircraft of the Halifax type [...] still carrying out the dropping of agents and sabotage materials [...] flights in which the agents are dropped are entrusted only to the most experienced crews [...] on an average about 10 a night are sent out [...] target marking is

now generally by Morse signals […] apart from the last flight
P/W never encountered either flack or fighting, a fact which
he took as proof that the low height of the flight provides
protection against the German defences.[162]

Tempsford, even now, is often described as Britain's most secret airfield,
yet, as we can see from official records, the Germans were aware of it. Their
knowledge was specific and accurate, and we can only speculate as to why
it appears that it was not targeted for bombing. There are several possible
answers: it may be that it was well protected and the bombers could not
penetrate the defences; it could also be that the intelligence was doubted and
not acted on. There is also the possibility that the Germans did not want to
let the Allies know that they knew about Tempsford and that they attempted
to monitor flights in the hope of disrupting efforts to aid the Resistance.
This interrogation report was one of many that exposed vital information to
the Germans. Many would proclaim that it showed weakness, but equally
it also portrays the stress and fear that the PoWs must have been under to
divulge such data. The information leaflet given to the RAF stated that 'the
only man you can be sure is a friend is the man you knew before capture'.[163]
As the interrogation reports show, it was sometimes the case where the
men you knew before capture were certainly not the same men you knew
after. Interrogation and incarceration took its toll on many aircrew, and was
revealed in many differing ways.

When asked if this had a demoralising effect on the individual, it is clear
from Atkins's answer that it did; this would have been the reaction and
response the German interrogators desired:

> It certainly made you think, I think the effect was to be even
> more careful with what you said, they also produced maps
> as well, showing areas in France, where they had discovered
> arms and ammunition that had been dropped they were very
> good at this and they presented that side of it extremely well.

Asked if the maps were accurate, Atkins replied:

> I couldn't really say that as most of the places I saw, you only
> saw these maps in front of you on a table, on the face of it did
> not seem any places I had been to. I think it was a ploy to try
> and break your morale and show that they knew a lot more

than they thought you knew, which they did, it did set your mind to thinking as to how they got the information. After Dulag Luft once we were taken out of solitary confinement we went into a communal hut where you met up with other aircrew, and there I met my other four NCO members of my own crew. We did not discuss anything about our RAF career or operations we had been on, we were very suspect that there were people among us who were out to listen and report back, so it was a pretty dismal time.[164]

British MI9 intelligence training documents regarding resisting interrogation and security state that discussions between aircrew were forbidden: 'a caution should be added against careless fraternisation with your own personnel. Some one may have been "broken".' It was not just informants who were divulging information from within the Dulag, it was also possible that the men could unwittingly reveal secrets without knowing it. It was reported that listening devices were installed within the buildings when the camp was expanded in 1942. Atkins stayed at Dulag Luft from 17 to 27 December 1943. He was then transferred to Stalag IV B:

Eventually after three to four days we were put on a train and I think it took us about three days to get to Stalag IV B, which was a large PoW camp at Mühlberg, between Leipzig and Dresden. This was a very large camp which had something in the region of about 25,000 occupants of all nationalities [...] all the different nationalities of occupied Europe. There was a big RAF compound there which shot down captured aircrew were in, which was full, and shortly before I arrived at this camp they were diverting RAF aircrew into the compounds with the British army which had been captured several years earlier in the North African desert campaigns [...] It was the beginning of a new experience.[165]

The new experience: Stalag IV B

The forbidding grey monolith which stood at the entrance to Mannschafts-Stammlager IV B would have been the first sight the aircrew of Halifax BB378 would have experienced. The guard tower would have loomed and overshadowed them when they entered one of the largest prisoner-of-

Figure 65. Stalag IV B entrance. (Wikimedia.org/Lutz Bruno)

war camps in Nazi Germany. The entrance represented and embodied the austere, barbaric character and foundations of the Nazi regime: oppressive, dictatorial, cruel and dispassionate.

The Bartter crew of 138 Squadron did not discuss conditions within the camp with many family members, nor is there any documentation left by them, only a small handful of letters from Anderson. What must be appreciated where life experiences within a PoW camp are concerned, whether written or narrated, is that very few spoke of their experiences, and very few put the events and memories on paper. This was for many reasons, trauma being a dominant reason for silence, with many wanting to leave the past behind them. These experiences, however, were carried with them for the rest of their lives; those accounts that we do have are invaluable and irreplaceable, no matter how small or brief they are. This chapter will draw on experience from other PoWs' accounts, and especially through Geoff Taylor's *A Piece of Cake*, which offers a valuable and vivid depiction of everyday life in the camp and of his initial contact with Stalag IV B:

> Our first impression of the camp was not of the way it spread
> across the newly harvested fields, an ugly and alien place in
> this land of farms and crops, and featureless except for the

stilted guard towers along the wire [...] we could certainly smell the place a mile before we reached it [...] it became so familiar to daily life that it was never again noticeable.[166]

Opened in 1939 and in operation until the liberation of 1945, although then under Soviet control, Stalag IV B was one of the largest prisoner-of-war camps in Germany. It was initially designed as a transit camp, and was situated about two-and-a-half miles (four kilometres) north-east of the village of Mühlberg-on-Elbe, on flat land with good visibility, sheltered, with soil which could be easily cultivated, and with a running water supply. The location had been chosen for its suitability: easily accessible, but out of view. It was far enough from the main traffic routes to not be seen, but close to a main rail line and the River Elbe for supplies. It was also selected because of its potential for expansion, which became a reality. Full capacity was estimated to be at around 16,000, but in April 1945, when Stalag IV B was liberated by the Soviet Army, they found over 30,000 prisoners, 7,250 of whom were British. Among them were the five members of the Bartter crew of 138 Squadron.

The German PoW camps were very different from the death camps of Eastern Europe, and they had a different role to play: incarceration and

Figure 66. Stalag IV B camp, main street. (Wikimedia.org/Lutz Bruno)

demoralisation. The majority of the PoWs were protected by the Geneva Convention, apart from the Soviets who suffered greatly from starvation and mistreatment. The Soviets had not signed the Geneva Convention in 1929 and therefore their prisoners of war were not covered by it. It also meant that they could not be held to account for any war crimes they themselves committed. These particular areas of the Geneva Convention highlight and stipulate some of the conditions and treatment the prisoners should live under:

> Article 2; Prisoners of war are in the power of the hostile Power, but not of the individuals or corps who have captured them.
> They must at all times be humanely treated and protected, particularly against acts of violence, insults, and public curiosity. Measures of reprisal against them are prohibited. Article 3; Prisoners of war have the right to have their person and their honour respected [...] prisoners retain their full status.

This meant that, for any direct maltreatment or persecution of any prisoner, the detaining country could be held accountable. The camps were visited and inspected by the Red Cross fairly frequently to ensure that basic needs and accommodation, as stipulated within the Geneva Convention regulations, were being adhered to; equally, the camp was administered and run by the *Wehrmacht*. Although tough and draconian, they were not on the same level as the SS, and in some cases they did not want to be. The relationship between the German Army and the SS had always been a tenuous one. The Wehrmacht were of the opinion that they were superior to the thuggish SS, who did not embody or follow any of the rules of conduct that the *Wehrmacht* did. This does not suggest by any means that the camps were easy places to live, or survive; survival perhaps being the word best to describe the lives and experiences of the crew of Halifax BB378.

The condition and sight of the existing prisoners for the new arrivals was traumatic, and would have demonstrated to them in those first few moments how uncompromising and severe life was going to be within Stalag IV B. Many PoWs have stated that they could not believe that the emaciated, bedraggled and decrepit creatures they saw upon arrival were actually soldiers.[167] The condition of the prisoners was in part due to the horrendous living conditions; Stalag IV B was despairing in the bitterly cold German winters, and tolerable only in the heat of the summer. Only tolerable though, as the relief from the freezing climate was replaced by the oppressive stench of the latrines, a constant insidious presence in the heat. Furthermore, because food was rationed severely, and offered little or no nourishment, these debilitating factors had dire repercussions on the men's health physically and mentally, and not only at the time; in some cases these would shadow them for the rest of their lives.

Upon arrival the men would have been stripped, showered, inoculated, X-rayed, deloused, had their blood tested, been weighed, their head shorn, their clothes fumigated, and their PoW tags provided. New inmates were given a disc with their PoW number stamped on it twice; if they died, then half would be filed for reference, and the other half would be buried with them. The threat of disease was one that not only the prisoners feared; it was also a constant concern of the camp commandant. An epidemic of typhus had broken out a year prior to the crew arriving at Stalag IV B; it killed thousands of Soviet PoWs and spread to the local farms and villages. When our crew arrived at the camp they were standing on ground which was hiding countless souls who had died from the epidemic. The Germans therefore had reason to be watchful of the inmates' health.

The crew were then led to their barracks. The wooden hut consisted of a brick floor, and bunks which extended up to the ceiling, which would have been fully occupied, if not overcrowded. The barracks were divided into two sections, each of which was designed to accommodate 400 persons. Space for the new PoWs was limited, with new arrivals often having to find a spot on the brick floor with just a straw-filled paillasse and a threadbare blanket to cover it. The barrack latrine was an evil-smelling hole dug just inside the door. Emitting a stench which was impossible to escape, it was also a breeding ground for illnesses – one being dysentery, from which many suffered. This then further overburdened the already struggling toilet facility. The main latrine within the camp was in no better condition than the toilet in the hut.

There were usually in every half section of the barracks two stoves connected to a central chimney, used both for heat and cooking the daily ration. Many of these did not work and needed replacing. Within this hotchpotch of life, washing would be strung up to dry, along with the meagre cooking utensils, and the remnants of the inmates' lives hanging in the air. Daily life in the camp was monotonous. Taylor described the cheerless and unremarkable experience of getting up in the morning; his description communicates the void between the PoWs and normal life at home: they knew life was beyond the wire but they were freezing, stamping their feet to stay warm:

THE WAR IS OVER FOR YOU – STALAG IV B

As the winter of 1943 sets in over Europe you watch the snow mantling the no mans land under the rusted barbed wire and the roofs of the smoky, draughty barracks and the big, stinking latrines [...] you feel you have lived here all your life [...] Death, escape, liberation, somehow the day will come.[168]

Taylor's words portray a deep sense of loss, not just loss of freedom and the constant unknown of what their fate could be, but a total loss of connection with ordinary life, a complete detachment. The normality of life an arm's length away, just over the horizon, but completely out of reach, and of never knowing if you are going to make it over that horizon; not only physically but mentally. In a relatively short period, the tedium of life in the camp became normal. From the daily roll call, to the brewing of ersatz coffee, to the boiling up of the daily rations for soup. Washing and bathing facilities at the time of the crew's incarceration within IV B consisted of each half section of the barracks having a washroom which consisted of twenty taps with cold running water. There was a boiler room where hot water was available, but a warming shower was only allowed once a fortnight. To add to these rudimentary facilities there were constant water shortages; washing was only possible from 18.00 to 06.00, as the camp commandant ordered the water to be shut off during daylight hours to save on usage. There was the promise of a new supply system, and new shower and bathing facilities were installed by 1944, but water pressure was so poor they were very often not used. Later reports by the Red Cross up until liberation stated that the washing facilities were adequate.[169]

Regarding food, from archive evidence obtained through the Red Cross, who visited the camp on a yearly basis to examine conditions, the ration scale per day, per person was:

Meat fresh or tinned 250 gm; Meat sausage/tinned 68 gm; Cooking Fat 68 gm Potatoes 2750 gm

Turnips 2000 gm

Dried vegetables 100 gm; Cereals 30 gm Peas 255 gm

Margarine 150 gm; Rye Flour 76 gm Coffee substitute 17.5 gm; Cheese 46.8 gm Bread 2125 gm

Sugar 175 gm

Jam 175 gm

Tea substitute 7 gm; Salt 105 gm[170]

Although this appears to be a fairly reasonable amount of food, it did not mean that they received even this low level of sustenance. The Geneva Convention stipulated that not only were 'prisoners of war to be confined in conditions not inferior to the standards applicable in their captor's own base camps, but were also to be supplied with food rations of similar standard'.[171] These standards were not adhered to; the truth was, the majority of the time the men survived on turnip and potato soup, although they did find other means of boosting their rations: many inmates when out on an agricultural working detail would manage to procure additional vegetables such as extra potatoes or turnips, the problem being, if discovered they would almost certainly be put in the cooler for a few days.

The typical food they received consisted of ersatz coffee, tea which was predominantly herbal, and ranged from pine needles to other unidentifiable herbs, and the black bread, Schwarzbrot, which – although it contained 50 per cent rye grain, and sliced beets – consisted of 20 per cent 'tree flour' (sawdust) and 10 per cent minced leaves and straw. This was reported to be the best method of baking black bread;[172] 'best' here undoubtedly meaning the cheapest. This was bolstered by the rotten potatoes and turnips which were made into soup, which became the PoWs' staple diet. It is documented that the rations actually received by the PoWs were a few small potatoes five to six times per week, boiled; soup which was customarily produced using whatever meagre supplies there were, but could include millet, barley, pumpkin, or tomato; and once a week pea soup. Meat was distributed possibly three days a week, and amounted to roughly two kilos per thirty men. Margarine was limited and was used for cooking. The daily 2,125 grams of bread actually fed up to seven men, and was certainly not enough to sustain any level of health. Any animal that wandered into the vicinity of the camp, for instance the healthy cat population that was resident around the camp, soon disappeared, along with a guard dog that was sent in to a barracks to quell a disturbance, showing the desperate need and extremes the men would go to for sustenance. Beyond food, heat was also an issue. The coal ration had been decreased from 75 to 25 kilos per half barrack daily, which during the winter months would have had dire consequences on the prisoners' lives. Reports in November 1944 stated that the coal ration had not been at full capacity for a while.

The only brief respite from the depressingly meagre offerings were the Red Cross parcels. These were useful not only for nutrition, but also, as Atkins explained, they were used to 'corrupt the guards': 'there was quite a traffic with the guards exchanging food for things that we wanted [...] we gave some of our food to people that were related to our escape committee to assist them with bartering and bribing the guards'.[173] The pivotal role that the Red Cross parcels played in keeping the men just above starvation was critical, especially when Christmas arrived, away from loved ones, in desperate conditions. Taylor notes that at Christmas, 'in no British barrack [was] the toast to the Red Cross forgotten'.[174] The parcels were a vital component in camp life for boosting flagging morale. The average contents of a British Red Cross parcel included not only vital vegetables and meat, they also incorporated small treats such as chocolate and pudding and custard, food which created a certain level of comfort or short-lived well-being.

Parcels and camp visits

The British Red Cross played an important role during the Second World War. They had a Prisoners of War Department that arranged parcels for prisoners, which were a link to home, but which also, in the case of food parcels, provided vital nutrition. In addition to food, there were books and sports equipment, as well as parcels from family which were sent to the prisoners. Visits by the International Red Cross to prisoners were arranged, but often prisoners were unsure as to their validity. As we have seen, the Germans would often impersonate Red Cross personnel in an attempt to gain information. However, detailed reports by genuine Red Cross personnel were made on the conditions being endured by the prisoners. A typical parcel would contain:

> 1 large Nestlé's milk, 2 ounces sugar, 2 ounces tea, 4 ounces cocoa, half a pound margarine or butter
>
> 1 tin of meat and vegetables, 1 meat roll or bacon 1 tin of salmon or pilchards
>
> 1 tin of vegetables (peas, carrots, etc.), 1 tin of egg powder or flakes
>
> 1 tin of Midlothian Oat Flour, 1 tin of service biscuits, 1 small jam or syrup
>
> 1 packet fruit (prunes, apricots, etc.), 1 bar of chocolate, 1 tin of cheese, 1 small pudding
>
> 1 packet of custard or Yorkshire pudding mix[175]

The Red Cross visited the camp most years to evaluate the living conditions, standards of food and dress, and the medical services available. The reports offer valuable insight not only into the conditions the PoWs had to endure, but also the lives they led. Atkins's brother, when asked about Brian's experiences, stated that he received food parcels in the camp from the Red Cross, and from the family: 'Brian's instinct was that he should quickly eat everything that was in the parcel. He soon learnt to spread it out.'[176] Taylor also reiterates this response towards the food parcels: upon their arrival in the camp he and his crew opened the parcels and 'ate a meal which horrified the seasoned veterans of the barrack by a prodigal consumption of the precious foods'.[177] Archive evidence shows that, between December 1944 and March 1945, 28,099 food parcels were dispatched to Stalag IV B, but it is not clear how many of these were from the Red Cross, as family members also sent them.[178] The level and degree of aid given through these parcels shows what a necessity they were; they only just kept the PoWs from starving.

The Red Cross compiled detailed reports of conditions within the camp, offering insightful descriptions as to what life was like. The reports from January 1944 onwards, when our crew would have been resident, show how the camp changed during the progression of the war. Interior barrack arrangements consisted of triple-tiered beds, with the rooms being very overcrowded, and electric lights with very weak bulbs. The roofs were leaking and were to be tarred. The huts did not have any cupboards or wardrobes, and sitting accommodation was inadequate. Latrines at this stage were in order and there was no shortage of toilet paper. There was a large central kitchen for cooking for PoWs of all nationalities, and twenty-one British cooks were at that time responsible for the food. Some British soldiers reportedly gave some of their food to the Russians, who were starving. There was a large stock of Red Cross parcels available at this time, but eating utensils were severely lacking, and this was linked to outbreaks of diarrhoea and dysentery.

Red Cross documents reveal that, towards the end of the war, conditions in the camp worsened considerably. The weather at that time made the barracks wet, and due to damp, worsening hygiene and overcrowding, diphtheria was rife. Medical supplies and equipment for the lazaret (the hospital for PoWs), especially sterilisation equipment and instruments, were not satisfactory and there was a severe shortage of dressings. This had not been the case in previous years. Although supplies in the lazaret were never fully stocked, they did at least have the bare minimum of basic medicines and were able to treat illnesses to a certain point. In October 1944 a telegram from the International Red Cross informed the British Foreign Office that there was no dentist and advised sending one from another camp which had more than one. A telegram from the Swiss Red Cross in Berne to the British Foreign Office on 5 February 1945, describing a visit to Stalag IV B, noted that there were 6,873 Britons detained at that time, and following an influx of American soldiers after the Battle of the Bulge, the camp was suffering from excessive overcrowding.[179]

By February 1945, a few months before liberation, the Red Cross report indicated that conditions had worsened further. This was not due to any marked difference in administration; it was specifically down to the progress of the war. Allied bombing had destroyed a great deal of the road and rail infrastructure, and this in turn had a direct effect upon the logistics of supplies being delivered to the camp. Equally, Germany was suffering from a severe shortage of food. German citizens were going hungry, along with its PoWs. Furthermore, American prisoners from the Battle of the Bulge had arrived in the camp, which raised the American strength from several hundred to 2,700. Another 8,500 had passed through in transit. This sudden influx escalated the overcrowding problem further, meaning that two men were often sharing one bunk, and that some were sleeping on the floor, benches, and tables. Bathing facilities had not changed, but of course were being affected by the numbers trying to use them. One of the dominant issues was the lack of food: rations had been reduced to potatoes, turnips, and dehydrated vegetables. This was alternated with three issues a week of millet, peas, or oats. Sometimes grade flour was given, but it had to be sifted to remove the maggots; it was deemed as unfit for human consumption by the Red Cross, but was perfectly acceptable in the eyes of the Germans. Equally, the dehydrated vegetables were of exceptionally poor quality. This is why many men suffered from severe malnutrition towards the end of their captivity. On top of this, coal was still in short supply. The Red Cross report described the conditions as deplorable.

Life in the camp

Along with malnutrition and diphtheria, other diseases prevalent within the camp by the end of the war were respiratory tract infections, septic conditions of the skin, pneumonia, dysentery, and malaria. The lazaret was seeing approximately 500 men per day, with 150 of those being British.

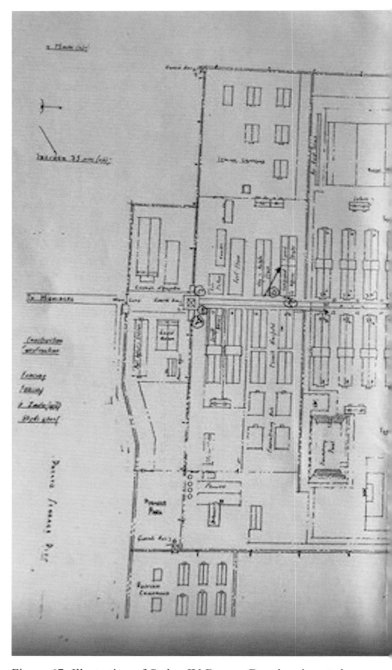

Figure 67. Illustration of Stalag IV B, near Dresden; insert shows RAF compound. (Nigel Atkins)

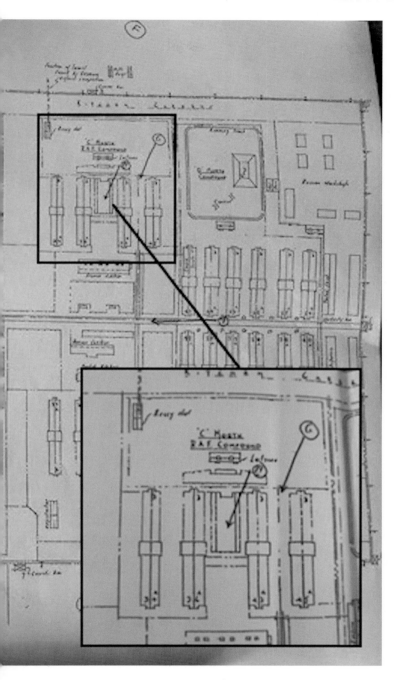

Bartering was commonplace within the camp. The German *Lagergeld* (camp money) was seen as valueless, while the pound sterling or American dollar, although used, were only for special deals. The most valued currency was cigarettes; a means to get extra food or clothing. One of the first accounts of life within the camp was written by Poul Bennit, a Danish policemen who was incarcerated there:

> the hunger for cigarettes was very big in such a PoW camp, but us Danes were lucky to receive cigarettes from home. Many English and Americans were heavy smokers. You could get a set of underwear for 50 cigarettes and wool stockings for 20 [...] the Englishmen and Americans had plenty of real tea, coffee, chocolate and cocoa in their Red Cross parcels to trade with.

Equally there was an official store within the camp where you could legally buy cigarettes, food, clothing and boots.[180]

Taylor described the end of 1943 – the time when the Bartter crew of 138 Squadron would have entered the camp – 'as unlamented, and how the flurry of snow and the howling wind from the Baltic tore at the icicles hanging from the eaves and gutters'.[181] He described the daily roll call and noted the difference in discipline between the British Army and the RAF. The Army paraded smartly to the shrill of a whistle or barked order from their barrack commander, whereas the RAF 'straggle out in our own, and if possible, the German's time'.[182] This was because they took pride in 'messing the Jerries around'.[183] He explained that the RAF were the last to have their heads counted in the compound, spending more time standing in the snow on parade, but then so did the Germans.[184] Morning roll call became a struggle of wills.

Entertainment was a necessity within the camp, with the daily grind of trying to forget the hunger that constantly plagued the mind and body, the bitter cold that ate away at morale, and the constant stench. Many servicemen found it difficult to adapt to camp life; although no one thought any worse of them for being captured it generated a burdensome sense of shame for some. They could not continue with their duty of fighting the war, and they felt they had let their fellow servicemen down.[185] Light relief came in the form of theatre, education, newspapers, clubs and sports. A specific hut was used for creating a theatre, which became known as 'The Empire', and which opened its doors in April 1944. This project created opportunities for dress-making, set construction, and looking for, or 'obtaining', materials. The productions varied, but one in particular remains prominent in camp stories. In *The Barretts of Wimpole Street*, the whole cast consisted of the men dressed up as women: the drag act of Stalag IV B. Wigs, dresses, make-up and an orchestra were all created. An inmate described it as the 'whole cast composed of women (nag-nag-gossip-divorce). It was great success and made a change from watching men for so long.'[186]

Another interest and distraction was the camp magazine *The Flywheel*. This was produced to 'depict a nostalgic look at a former life away from war and prison camps as seen by the magazine's staff'.[187] Started by Tom Swallow, along with other motor enthusiasts who were incarcerated in Stalag IV B, *The Flywheel* was a collection of motoring magazines which were circulated around the camp for the PoWs to read and pass on. Only one copy of each issue was produced, due to a lack of paper and facilities. The articles were hand-written, colour illustrations were produced from whatever could be obtained and were stuck in place with fermented millet soup. Each copy was handed around the camp and read by up to 200 prisoners. A book about the magazine was produced in 1987,[188] with Swallow donating all royalties to the British Red Cross in appreciation of their work for the prisoners. Swallow stated that many of the men had lost their 'zest for life', and succumbed to a pernicious lethargy which was typical of the conditions. His magazine endeavoured to bring like-minded men together to give them some meaning and a reason to continue.

To celebrate Christmas, concert parties were organised, pantomimes were staged, and public speaking included diverse talks and lectures by a former London undertaker, and a South African game reserve guide to name but two. The arrangements for Christmas took place over a few weeks and the barracks were decorated in appropriate homeland traditions. Decorations of garlands and streamers were made out of coloured labels from tins included in the Red Cross parcels, the colours the complete opposite of the drab and desperate living conditions; a complete antithesis to the oppressive and colourless life they led.

Atkins's interviews do not reveal a great amount of detail about life in the camp. He states that he made acquaintance with French PoWs to improve his French language skills, but he does not go any further than that. He does explain in his interview with MI9 that he could listen to news radio broadcasts on the sly, through a secret radio, and thus stay informed of how the war was progressing, which helped tremendously to keep the prisoners' morale high.

From across the horizon

Another great morale boost to the inmates were letters sent from home. This was reciprocated when the families received notification and letters either from PoWs, or others who had been in contact with them, or had information regarding their whereabouts and situation. Anderson's family wrote letters to him, and, to their great relief, he was able to write back. Howell wrote to Anderson's parents from London on 20 January 1944 after his successful escape to Sweden from German-controlled Denmark. It was written on the Swedish Astoria Hotel's letterhead paper, which gives an insight into where Howell stayed before repatriation to Britain. It was a heart-warming letter sent to reassure Anderson's parents of their son's safety, and to inform them of what occurred on the night of the crash. The opening sentence referred to an invitation they had offered him:

> At the moment I cannot possibly accept your kind invitation but I would very much like to see you, and at the first opportunity I shall [...] your wish and mine.[189]
>
> [...]
>
> As for Nick, have no anxiety he will be alright – after the crash we all met, and decided to separate into three groups. We were very happy to be alive, so that my last recollection of him is a grinning goodbye.
>
> The air ministry will unfailingly let you know as soon as news comes through from him.

Another letter which was kept by Anderson's family was from his brother George who, upon hearing of Nick's crash wrote to his parents:

> Dear Mother and Father,
> That's the best news you could have have sent me, its lifted a weight off me and I know just how you will be feeling. I think you will find that I was right and that the party split in two, but we will get to know very soon, you must not worry any more mother, even if he is a prisoner, it may be better there [...] at best he is clever and can rely on his lot in the RAF after the war. If he is a prisoner he will be OK have no fear of that. It is 10.30 at night, the RAF went over our place at 6 o'clock tonight, and we counted 100 planes and I can hear them coming back now, and I am wondering how many will not come back.

The fellow (Howell) that wrote to you will be (on) the bottom left hand corner on the snap (photo)*, you will probably have had the letter from the RAF by now, he wanted to report to them and give them all the details, if the RAF don't give you any details I would write to the fellow and ask him how it happened, but I suppose you will be getting details soon. Well I am going to try to get home for next weekend so I will knock off now. Goodnight all, I will sleep lots better now. Cheerio,

Your loving son George[190]

* However if it is the photo of the crew these authors have, it is Fry in the bottom left corner, so George was mistaken

The letters that the Andersons received also included one from RAF Tempsford, informing them of their son's crash, and the fact that he was missing in action. This very quick response was received on 11 December 1943:

Dear Mrs Anderson,

It is with deep regret that I write to confirm that your son Sergeant Anderson N. is missing as a result of air operations against the enemy on the night of the 10th/11th December, 1943.

At the time of writing no further news has been received, but immediately upon receipt of any information you will, of course, be notified. During the time that Sergeant Anderson has been with this squadron he has made many friends and was a very efficient member of his crew.

I trust that we shall hear that your son is alive and well, but in the meantime I express the sympathy of the whole Squadron in your great anxiety.

Yours Sincerely
R.D. Speare
Wing Commander[191]

This came from the same man who Anderson and Bartter had flown an operation with when they first arrived at RAF Tempsford.

A telegram was also sent by the RAF instructing that a letter should be sent to Mrs Anderson, which was of utmost priority. It included all of the letter they sent, but also instructed that, pending receipt of written notification from the Air Ministry, no further information should be given to the press, and that a letter would follow. The Air Ministry did indeed send a letter from their Casualty Branch, based in Oxford Street, London, it was dated 19 December 1943:

> Madam,
>
> I am commanded by the Air Council to express to you their great regret on learning that your son, Sergeant Nicholas Anderson, Royal Air Force, is missing as the result of air operations on the night of 10th/11th December, 1943, when a Halifax aircraft in which he was flying as flight engineer set out for action and was not heard from again.
>
> Three of the crew of the aircraft are known to have reached safety in a neutral country, but no news of your son has yet been received. This does not necessarily mean that he is killed or wounded, and if he is a prisoner of war he should be able to communicate with you in due course. Meanwhile enquiries are being made through the International Red Cross Committee, and as soon as any definite news is received you will be at once informed.
>
> If any information regarding your son is received by you from any source you are requested to be kind enough to communicate it immediately to the Air Ministry.
>
> The Air Council desire me to convey to you their sympathy in your present anxiety.
>
> I am, Madam,
Your obedient servant
J.A. Smith[192]

Mrs Anderson also received a letter from the Red Cross, which was based at St James's Palace, London. It was a reply to correspondence she had sent them and was dated 27 March 1944. The letter indicates that any parcel should be sent to Stalag Luft III, which would imply that Nick had been imprisoned there to begin with. Fred Heathfield, who was also unfortunate enough to be imprisoned in Stalag IV B, explained that this was because the number of RAF prisoners had not been expected:

> Goering told the German people that not one single RAF bomber would penetrate the defences of the Third Reich.[193]
>
> [...]
>
> RAF prisoners were dropping into Germany in such numbers the Luft camps were not big enough [...] so some of

the *Wehrmacht* camps were asked to take the surplus of NCO prisoners. Our mail was still addressed via Stalag Luft III.[194]

Anderson did not reach Stalag IV B until January 1944, the period between his stay in Dulag Luft, which as Atkins stated was only a few days, and Stalag IV B remains unclear. The letter from the Order of Saint John of Jerusalem, via the Red Cross[195] in March 1944 indicates that he may have had a short stay at Stalag Luft III:

Dear Mrs Anderson,
Thank you for your letter of March 23rd enclosing your son's postcard, which we return herewith. We are glad to see that he is in good spirits and trust that you are hearing from him frequently.
You can certainly dispatch your next of kin parcel, for which we have already sent you the labels and coupons. We think it is possible that at some future date your son may send you a different address for his parcels, but in the meantime, both letters and parcels will reach him safely addressed in the following way:–
Prisoners of War Post
Kriegsgefangenpost Sergeant N. Anderson
British Prisoner of War No.267429 Stalag Luft 3
Germany.
Please send us any alterations in camp address which you receive from your son.

Yours sincerely
K.M. Thornton Director[196]

The military letters show an urgency not only in how quickly they responded regarding informing the Andersons of their son's situation, but equally an urgency in reassuring and emotionally supporting them in their difficult and anxious time.

Finally, the letter they had been anxiously waiting for arrived. Anderson reached Stalag IVB in January 1944. For the Andersons it was the most important one among the many that had been received regarding their son; it was from Nick, dated 3 March 1944:

Dear Ma, Pa and All,
Hows everybody at home, OK I hope. I am hoping OK. If you can find Stan Bank's home address please send me it as

I would like to send him a card so that he will know what has happened. The theatre opened here last week and it was as good as some of the shows I have seen in Blighty. I've got quite a lot of the boys here who were on the course with me, they are the lucky ones I suppose as quite a few have gone down. We haven't had any snow here yet and we can still do without it. Don't forget to send me a parcel of novels and toothpaste and toothbrushes and when I get back I'll give you all a treat by cooking the Sunday dinner. Perhaps! We drink five pots of coffee a day, nearly as good as our George don't you think? Well Ma, remember don't worry as I am not taking any harm. So lots of love and cheerio, Nick.[197]

Anderson's letter, although short, conveys a great deal about camp life. Although the coffee supplied by the Germans was, as previously mentioned, often made out of nothing more than acorns, real coffee was sometimes included in the Red Cross parcels they received. They drank a great deal of it according to Nick: five pots a day, probably to while away the time. The routine and regimen of brewing a pot could have been a comfort, as well as something they would have carried out on a daily basis back home, along with the warmth of the hot brew, even though the taste may not have been the best. It also indicates that the parcels were received, and what desperately needed items were in them: novels to relieve the boredom, and most importantly dental care products. Although there was usually a dentist within the camp, suffering from toothache in such conditions would not have been an easy problem to deal with, physically or mentally.

The letter mentions the theatre within the camp, which was a great distraction from the daily drudgery. Anderson mentions the 'boys' who he was on the course with, a message to his parents that he was in good company, but not divulging any specific information about who and how he knew them. The letters that were sent home would have certainly been read by the camp *Wehrmacht* to glean any information that may have been included. He mentions the fact that there was no snow yet, and it is clear that it was something they were more than likely dreading. What is so evident from this brief communication is the upbeat tone which is conveyed through the writing, especially considering how hard and desperate life in the camp was; the mood and expression that is communicated would have been not only for his family's benefit to show them he was in good spirits, but equally it would have been for his own benefit.

Writing home would have been a direct connection to his family, and the fact that he mentions giving his family a 'treat' by 'cooking the Sunday dinner' shows he is thinking about when he would make it home, to normality, and that he still had a sense of humour – assuming that cooking was something that he never did.

This is something seen in much of the oral testimony and accounts written by PoWs. Taylor's *Piece of Cake* is very much written in this way. It portrays a stoicism and great spirit. As Tony Vercoe, a PoW himself incarcerated in Stalag IV B explains:

> despite the severity of the camp, the spartan rations, the tenacious lice, the fierce bed bugs, unhygienic conditions […] many men (prisoners) saw it would suit the Germans that poor morale and despondency were prevalent among their captives, 'let's not make things easier for them' became a developing philosophy.[198]

This is seen in Anderson's letter and is also present throughout Atkins's interview; at times it is evident that talking about it was incredibly hard. This is perhaps why much of the daily routine of camp life was not discussed, but what is apparent is the sense of endurance, loyalty and professionalism.

Although Atkins did not discuss his experiences within the camp after his return, his brother Ken remembers a few vital fragments of information, even though he had no direct contact with Brian throughout the war and his incarceration. Ken remembers that 'Joe Fry and two other men came to our house and knocked on the door shortly after the crash in Denmark. They told us that Brian was safe, but that they did not know what happened to him since the airmen split into two groups.' Ken remembers that Brian's fiancée received letters from him every month, and the family every third month. His fiancée did not share any content information with the rest of the family, but the letters they received had 'many words crossed out'. [199] Whether this was censorship by the camp administration is unclear, but it is more than likely.

Escape and sabotage

Escape from capture was a requisite of being a member of the armed forces: you were trained and expected to try to escape from prison, even if you were not successful, which of course was the case on numerous occasions.

Servicemen were also equipped with 'aids to escape' prior to going overseas, irrespective of the theatre of war to which they were going. All RAF aircrew attended lectures where they were given instruction and advice on behaviour if captured, with an emphasis on security during interrogation; the only information to be given under any circumstance was name, rank, and number. As well as their duty to escape at the earliest possible moment, additional duties to observe and collect information, to cause the enemy trouble, and to destroy all official and personal papers were also laid down. Stories of successful as well as failed escapes were discussed, as were the conditions of enemy prison camps as described by escapees.

A second lecture was entirely for the purposes of escape advice, and aids to escape were given to all combat crews. There was advice on escape both before and after capture, hints on travel through enemy-occupied land, and escape organisations within the camps. Many prisoners took this incredibly seriously, and used every opportunity to break free. 'Escape organisations were set up in most large PoW camps, with the aim of systemising the process, to give best chances of success.'[200] An important part of this second lecture was about international law on disguise, the carrying of arms by the escapee, and regulation regarding spies. A separate document explains the use of disguise and civilian clothing. They were advised to 'don civilian clothing if obtainable'[201] when escaping or evading capture, which many adopted. They were advised to retain their identity tags and to remember where they had hidden their uniforms as this would enable them to prove their identity if captured behind enemy lines – otherwise they could be accused of being spies, which could lead to regulations of the Geneva Convention not being applicable and ignored, in which case the PoW could experience incredibly harsh treatment.

Lecture three specified duties if captured, with hints on travel, and routes and conditions within specific areas in which they might find themselves. MI9 was responsible for training the airmen in escape techniques, and in particular on how to escape from PoW camps. The Geneva Convention protected PoWs to a certain extent; Article 51 states that: 'Attempted escape, even if it is a repetition of the offence shall not be considered as an aggravating circumstance in case the PoW should be given over to the courts on accounts of crimes or offences against persons or property committed in the course of that attempt.'[202] Equally, anyone who aided an escape should only incur disciplinary punishment for that offence. Many prisoners were repeat offenders, not only because they could not cope mentally with the confinement and conditions, but because they saw it as their duty.

Anderson, Atkins, Riggs, Smith and Turvil had all received the relevant training in escape techniques as a prerequisite to their mission. This was documented within their MI9 interview questionnaire when they were repatriated. Atkins received training in relation to capture in June 1943 from an intelligence officer (IO) at 10 OTU, and at Tempsford in November 1943, and also in escape and evasion from an intelligence officer in 1658 HCU in August 1943, also at Tempsford. Riggs gained his training at RAF No.10 OTU Abingdon from an IO, and also at Tempsford. Anderson received his training at Riccall, Yorkshire, 1638 Conversion Unit, and then at Tempsford in escape and evasion. Turvil received his at Hampstead Norris and RAF Croft throughout 1943.

Most escapes were engineered through working parties. The parties would go out daily to collect wood or to work in local factories or on farmland. These were ideal opportunities to either exchange identity with someone who was a member of the work party, or to become part of the work party yourself. Atkins did try to escape during his time at Stalag IV B. In his IWM interview he explained:

> Yes, I did, there were two ways of trying to escape from a PoW camp, one was by use of tunnels which is a very well known technique with regard to the Luft III camp, or you could try and get out of the camp by exchanging identity with another person who was by his rank going out on working parties. I had three attempts to escape, and on each occasion I got outside the camp by changing identity with a British army private, and on the last occasion changing identity with a French army private.
>
> There was a large contingent of French PoWs who in their own compound although we had access to it, had been prisoners in the majority of cases since June 1940 when France was occupied [...] on the face of it, it appeared they were having a better standard of treatment than we were, and then on the face of it you could take a view that they perhaps were a bit more cooperative with the Germans [...] I think this was apparent [...] but deep underneath the majority of the French were as anti-German as we were.
>
> I became friendly with several French PoWs, to start with, as a means of a pastime of trying to improve my schoolboy French. From then it developed into closer relationships, and

171

I felt that I could talk to a certain Frenchman I had met about my wishing to escape, from that time onwards. To start with […] I had no reaction from them at all, and heard nothing from them, and the subject never came up again even though I was seeing them two or three times a week.[203]

During his incarceration Atkins was informed via the Red Cross that he had been commissioned, and was told that his rank was then Pilot Officer. It seems clear that he was unaware of his promotion before this; he had not joined the officers in their mess prior to the flight and he also stayed with the NCOs when the crew split up following the crash. The Germans accepted this information, and he was told he would be moved to an officer camp, though he was not at all keen on this.

The RAF and American air forces were bombing Germany around the clock at that time, particularly the railway system, with a great loss of life. He did not want to move at that stage of the war but was keen to get out of the camp. He was asked by a Frenchman to meet one of their senior men

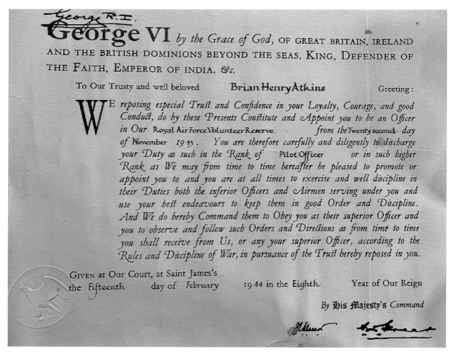

Figure 68. Brian Atkins's warrant promoting him to Pilot Officer. (Nigel Atkins)

who turned out to be on their escape committee. After a long hostile cross-questioning session, the Frenchman believed Atkins was who he said he was and agreed to help him:[204]

> I changed identity with a Frenchman and went out on a working party, there were many more Frenchman at work in Germany than there were British for obvious reasons, and I was with a French working party in a sugar beet factory, this was only a short distance perhaps fifteen miles from the camp. Sometimes they would bring the working party back into the camp each night, but, in this instance, we were billeted in a rough primitive hut environment which was certainly not a prison camp, the odd German guard but nothing like the security of a prison camp.[205]

Other members of the crew also attempted to escape. Smith broke loose but unfortunately was recaptured. He explains in his MI9 interview that he left the camp on 1 July 1944 with Anderson and a fellow PoW, Flight Sergeant H. Mott, a member of 78 Squadron who had arrived at Stalag IV B three months before Atkins and the crew; they were recaptured after three days of freedom by railway workers at Hof Station. All men returned safe and well. Anderson's account of escape also gives valuable information. He states that the first time he escaped he managed to flee from the wood collection working party which left the main camp. The second attempt was from a work party in Poppengrün with Smith and Mott. He explains that they changed identities with army privates, and were recaptured at Hof, fifty-six miles (ninety kilometres) away. Anderson's third escape attempt would be his last. He and Mott swapped identities with two US privates – Anderson with a Private Boyd Blount – and they fled from a work party travelling to Leipzig. Anderson's MI9 interview states that they were both picked up by the US 69th Division. Anderson's MI9 interview is dated 25 April 1945. It's an extraordinary achievement that one member of the crew managed to escape successfully. There were substantial risks in even attempting to escape, and Anderson's experience proves that perseverance could pay off for a small number of PoWs.

Included in the MI9 questionnaires are the descriptions of sabotage that were carried out by some members of the crew. Smith was allocated to a work party that laid gas pipes in Poppengrün from July to September 1944, and he explained that the work party, instead of laying the gas pipes, destroyed them.[206] Atkins says that he took part in the 'usual destruction and theft of German equipment to be found in a Stalag'.[207]

A liberation of sorts

Atkins discussed the liberation of the camp:

> The Russians [Soviets] came in April of '45 they actually arrived in the camp on St Georges day April 23rd [...] the majority of the Russian troops were very peasant stock, almost say Mongolian type, we treated them with great suspicion. I don't think they were briefed very much on the allied war effort and the allied personnel, they were ruthless regarding the attitude to the German guards and a lot of them were shot and strung up [...] I saw the bodies but I did not see them physically do it. I think this was their manner of warfare, they just behaved like this towards their enemy; one must also realise that the Germans treated the Russian prisoners they had very severely, because the Russians didn't recognise the Geneva convention; while the Germans recognised it as far as we were concerned because of the treatment of their own nationals, they didn't recognise it with regard to the Russians; so their behaviour was of a similar vein to what they had been carrying out in their various campaigns. We were deeply shocked because several of the German guards, who by this time were around the fifty mark, they were army personnel who were too old for fighting on the fronts and very often they were almost invalids, limping and generally not up to fighting fitness, and some of them had been PoWs in the First World War they intimated that they had been treated fairly by the British, the Americans, and the French so towards the last few months of the war they were quite cooperative.[208]

Taylor also recognised this and explained that, towards the end of the war:

> the younger more arrogant guards [had] gone to the war and in their places are tired middle aged men who last wore uniform in the trenches of France and Flanders [...] they still believe obstinately in the ultimate world victory of Nazi Germany.

Some of them are realists however, and when they come on duty after dusk their gas masks and greatcoat pockets are filled with hunks of bread which they barter for cigarettes.[209]

Both accounts relay a certain degree of respect that the PoWs had for the guards, and it would appear that it was to an extent reciprocated.

When Atkins was asked if there was any justification for killing the German guards he replied: 'personally I don't think so, by this time I had been commissioned, and there was about half a dozen of us in the British community there who had been commissioned; we then assumed our ranks and we were the senior people as far as the British were concerned.'[210]

Unfortunately the PoWs witnessed atrocities carried out by the Soviets against the German guards who had not left or escaped. Described in Vercoe's book, one particular guard, who they had named 'Blondie,' was hung upside down, had his hands and head cut off, and was spat on and defiled. A witness stated that although they would shed no tears for Blondie, seeing a bloke die like that was like being in a nightmare.[211] The liberation was certainly tainted by such memories. Although life in the camp was unbearable and the guards had shot many a PoW because of a rule infringement, Atkins insisted that none of the airmen of Halifax BB378 had been physically abused or had lacked any medical attention while in the camp.

Atkins was asked whether any of these guards were pointed out by the prisoners: 'No, I don't think so, a lot of the Germans by that time had evacuated the camp, but those who had not got away were treated like this, several of us were prepared to vouch that the German guards had treated us in accordance with the Geneva Convention.'[212] This, however, did not aid them; they were killed just the same, about a dozen or so to his knowledge, but there may have been more. Atkins continues:

> There was a tremendous language difficulty communicating with the Russians [...] until some of their interpreters came, their whole attitude to the war was so different to ours, several guards were strung up on entrance gates and outside barrack blocks [...] I have given great thought to this, and this type of thing happened without any examination of the situation they came in and they were fighting the Germans and that was it [...] we were not allowed out of the camp, we had exchanged one nationality of guards for another nationality, we weren't PoWs in that sense but we were

confined under armed guard to the camp. They did not want us running around the countryside for our own safety, their armies were operational and there was fighting going around […] they were formidable all right, large numbers of tanks, a formidable fighting force.[213]

For the four remaining PoW crew members of Halifax BB378, the arrival of the Soviets signified the end of their fifteen-month ordeal, but it was not an immediate release. The Soviets detained the prisoners within the camp for several weeks before handing them to the US Army. There were many reasons for this, but there was a great deal of unrest regarding it. It would be easy to assume that after any liberation those held captive would immediately return home, but this was very rarely the case. Logistics and warfare quite often restricted and delayed release, in some cases for many years. Thankfully for the crew, it was only a couple of weeks in their case. Documentation reveals the relationship between the Russians and the RAF, and how they communicated and worked together to resolve the difficult situation of liberation while the PoWs remained incarcerated within the camp. A report describes how conditions in the camp had descended to a deplorable level. It was clear by the morning of 25 April that steps had to be taken by men of official standing to regain complete control of the camp: 'The barrack areas were filthy, the latrines full, the water and lighting systems had broken down and generally deplorable conditions existed.'[214] This report also indicates what a dire situation the camp was in in relation to food rations. The war had taken its toll on supplies to camps, and this is why controlling the camp was decidedly more difficult in the first few days of liberation than if they had been receiving their usual ration allowance; the men had become desperate, and were starving:

> The rations had decreased to such an extent that the men were living on a very small ration of potatoes and turnip soup, while bread was issued only about four times a week, and then only in very small quantities. Red Cross supplies were very hard to get owing to the breakdown of the German railways, so that the usual regular supply of Red Cross food parcels was not forthcoming. No coal was issued to barracks for cooking and heating after the middle of February.[215]

The PoWs were in a desperate situation. Hitler was losing the war, and the well-being of prisoners was at the bottom of any list of priorities; equally, supplies had simply run out. A meeting was called and it was decided that the RAF would act as an individual unit responsible for its own men. The object of this arrangement was to restore discipline, clean the camp, and set an example to the other nationalities.[216] For a short while after liberation, groups of British and Americans were allowed out for walks; the Russians on the other hand had already broken loose due to starvation, venturing into the surrounding areas and Mühlberg to find food and clothing. Taylor explained this within his narrative:

> In a remarkably short time the first of the nature lovers and bird watchers were back [...] with smug smiles, lifeless but still warm poultry, fresh meat and eggs, real eggs that broke if you dropped them [...] by nightfall I came back with a basket of preserves, jams and fresh vegetables [...] Bill produced his first haul, fresh pork, bacon and sausage. That night we had the finest, biggest meal of our lives. Until dawn next day there was much groaning and vomiting in the barrack as shrunken stomachs firmly revolted at the sudden excess of food.[217]

This was a common reaction to over-indulging so quickly, and unfortunately many PoWs suffered and were plagued with digestive problems for the rest of their lives because of malnutrition in the camps.

By 26 April the plan to send out patrols to ensure that there was no looting was fully operational, and conditions within the camp had improved greatly; the latrines had been emptied and rations had been brought into the camp to feed the men. The reports state that all men in positions of trust worked hard, backed up by a 'healthy response by the men'. On 28 April the Russians gave the orders that no one should leave the camp. Two RAF patrols were sent out to bring back any men who had gone for a recce. From then on, Russian Army personnel were ordered to guard the exterior of the camp.[218]

This did not stop many of the newly liberated inmates from taking day excursions out of the camp however, although the majority waited for a formal exit plan. Many felt incredibly frustrated and in limbo, but the day, 6 May 1945, finally came when the Russian officers announced they were to move out of the Stalag towards Reisa:

> We were kept with the Russians for about two weeks, provided with food and eventually we were taken out of the camp under Russian escort and finally handed over to the American

forces [...] lots of photos were taken [...] we were taken to an American base, flown to Frankfurt, flown again into Brussels, then to Lyneham in the UK then we were sent on leave and to rehabilitation.[219]

While our crew did not speak in great detail about their experiences in Stalag IV B, it must be understood that this was a brutal experience, and they would have witnessed extreme cruelty. While the prisoners were housed in their national groups, they were aware that the Soviet troops suffered worse treatment, having to scavenge for potato peelings for food; equally, they noticed that the French prisoners appeared to be treated less brutally. There were occasions when the Germans killed British prisoners of war, yet then performed a gun salute at the funeral. This hints at just how dangerous it was to attempt an escape, and how fortunate Anderson was to get away, as well as others who seemed to have escaped serious punishment for attempting to escape. Although the camp already seemed to be full or even overcrowded, following the Battle of the Bulge offensive during December 1944 and January 1945, the camp was swamped with 7,500 captured American troops. Tents were erected to house the huge influx, and facilities must have been truly awful. For all those who survived this experience, it no doubt stayed with them for the rest of their lives.

Chapter 8

After the war

Much of the work the Bartter crew did during the war was secret, and remained so for decades; even they knew few details of their operations. In their different ways, it was never possible for many of our crew to completely leave their experiences behind them. On 7 May 1945 the war in Europe ended when the formal act of military surrender was signed by Germany. The news spread across the world, with the BBC announcing that the following day, 8 May, would be a UK national holiday called 'Victory in Europe (VE) Day'. Special editions of the newspapers were produced hailing the long-anticipated news.

As defeat was becoming more likely, the German pilot Klaus Möller and his wireless operator Josef Allram, who were responsible for shooting down the Bartter crew, fled Germany on 29 April 1945 on board a JU88 G-8 4R+LR bomber (manufacturer number 621800). They took off at 03.20 from Leck, close to the German/Danish border, and set course for the airport of Francisco de Sa Canreiro (formerly Pedras Rubras), which was under construction near the city of Porto, in neutral Portugal. After landing, there was some discussion about whether the aircraft contained any useful items, and there was a question of whether it could be regarded as the property of the Allies and therefore destroyed.[220] It was transported to a military base in Espinho and broken down for scrap. There is no further information on Möller and Allram, other than that they were initially held in custody by international police. They claimed to be junior officers and were vague, stating they had come from somewhere near Norway. Their post-war lives remain a mystery. They clearly did not wish to surrender and had access to an aircraft that permitted them to make their unusual escape.

Meanwhile, on VE Day 1945, of our surviving six young men, Bartter was in England and could no doubt engage in some celebration. Anderson, having escaped captivity, was also back in England, and Fry was in Canada; the remaining crew were still prisoners of war. As described in Chapter 7, Stalag IV B had been liberated on 23 April 1945, but the prisoners were not immediately released. It would be a few weeks before these members of the Bartter crew could begin their journey home. They were malnourished and weak from their captivity but, unlike some, they would survive the voyage home. We know that Atkins travelled home via Germany; his family still have the Bible given to him at Halle Aerodrome in May 1945. It carries the following inscription: 'Flying Officer B H Atkins 138 SQ RAF Presented to me by Captain Silvermann Padre USAA at Halle Aerodrome Germany May 25th 1945 on my return to England.'

We know from the Anderson family that Nick had lost a lot of weight by the time he arrived home, as had Atkins. Once home, these men spoke little of their experiences. PTSD (Post-Traumatic Stress Disorder) was not recognised at that time, and the crew were expected to simply return to normal life and carry on. They would not have wanted to inflict the horrors they experienced on their loved ones, so these were memories that they held quietly to themselves and much of which we will never truly know. Whether any of the crew suffered from PTSD is unknown, but there is no doubt that their experiences stayed with them. Bartter, Fry and Howell endured days of stress during their experiences as evaders, as well as the ultimate relief

Figure 69. Brian and Nigel Atkins. Three years after his release it is still possible to see the weight loss in Brian. (Nigel Atkins)

and joy of reaching a safe location. Those who were captured endured a very different experience, but not all their ordeals were equal; Atkins, for example, endured the hot and cold treatment, although others did not.

Post-war there were limited numbers of roles available in the services so the vast majority of service personnel were demobilised and returned to civilian life. Having been through such extraordinary experiences, they would now have to readjust to 'normality' and attempt to build a new life. The strain of adjustment must have been immense.

Arthur (Peter) Bartter (1912–1988)

Peter Bartter was the only member of the crew who was married at the outbreak of the war. He had met Francesca Castelli Gair in 1939 while working in Rome. When war threatened they moved to England and married in April 1940 in Buckinghamshire. After the war they would return to Italy with Peter now working for BOAC, the result of a merger between his previous employer Imperial Airways and British Airways. He worked globally specialising in VIP flights. The Bartters also lived for a period in Malta. They adopted Francesca's niece, Julia Castelli Gair, and she recalled her seventeen years with them in both Italy and Malta, saying that her father spoke little about his wartime experiences, other than to comment on being shot down over Denmark. Francesca often recalled the bombing of London, although she did move to Scotland for a period of time during the war.

Bartter remained in the RAF Reserve and in 1952 his rank of Flight Lieutenant in the CC class is noted in the *London Gazette*. This CC referred to civilians who would be commissioned on mobilisation without the need for training. He had held this rank in the RAF, having been promoted in September 1943. Despite not speaking openly about his experiences, Bartter kept in touch with the Krügermeier family, who had assisted the evaders, by postcard, and in 1968 he made a trip to Denmark to revisit the site of his emergency landing.

Krügermeier and Bartter were members of the Royal Air Force Escape Society. Bartter was able to see both the landing site and also his old uniform which, at great risk to themselves, the Krügermeier family had kept hidden. Within the trousers he found the third button, which was a magnetic compass, part of his escape kit. The two men relived the events of that winter in 1943 while examining the old uniform in Krügermeier's home. Figure 71 also shows an unopened escape kit in its box on the jacket.

Left: Figure 70. Peter Bartter (in the middle) with Wilhelm Krügermeier (on the left) and Svend Ove Frederiksen (on the right). (Svend Aage Mortensen)

Below: Figure 71. Krügermeier (left) and Bartter examining the uniform and checking the button compass. The box shown is Bartter's escape kit. (Svend Aage Mortensen, BT 14/12 1968)

Additionally, there are Canada badges on the table, which had obviously belonged to Fry's uniform.

Julia Castelli Gair recalls her father as an exceptional man, very honest and righteous. He was very strict with her when it came to written and spoken English, no doubt a result of his own experiences: his father was a headmaster. In fact, Bartter himself had something of a phobia around speaking and writing impeccable English. Julia remembers him as the gentle soul of her family, someone she could talk to about anything; he was open-minded with no prejudice. She recalls him reading to her and caring both for her and her aunt (his wife), whose health faded in later years. He was an exceptional man.

Sadly, in May 1988, while driving back from his local shop in Italy, he was killed in a road accident. Roadworks caused his vehicle and a bus to be on the same side of the road and, despite both drivers attempting to avoid each other, they collided head-on. For a man who survived the dangers of Special Duties flights this was the irony of fate.

Nicholas (Nick) Anderson (1921–1993)

Nicholas Anderson was the only member of the crew who stayed in the RAF. He would serve for many years, gaining the Cyprus Cross, Long Service Award, and Good Conduct Award. The Anderson family, along with the Fry and Atkins families, have very kindly provided information for inclusion in this book and have confirmed the medals that Nick was awarded. As shown in the metal detection section, his family visited Denmark to learn more about the aircraft being shot down. It is interesting to note that Anderson's family have an ongoing link with Denmark. Purely coincidentally, his son John owns a holiday home only an hour from the site where Nick's aircraft came down. Jan Christensen made contact with John and, along with his two sisters, one who lives in England and the other in Canada, they made the trip to the Holbæk Museum and provided information and letters. They met Jan Christensen and many of the letters they donated to the museum are quoted within this book.

Brian (Tommy) Atkins (1922–2000)

Brian Atkins had received a commission to Pilot Officer on 22 November 1943. When captured in December 1943 he remained with his non-commissioned colleagues, Anderson, Riggs, Smith and Turvil. It is not clear whether news of his promotion was known to Atkins or the rest of the crew prior to the crash landing. Fry, in correspondence, mentions that the crew split had been agreed prior to take-off should the worst happen.

In 1946 Atkins married Marjorie Blackburn, who he had first met during his RAF training in Yorkshire. Atkins did not return to work for the railway after the war but embarked on a new career in banking, which led him to the position of bank manager with the National Westminster Bank. One of his customers would be Bernie Taupin, most famous for his song-writing with Elton John.

Atkins was an active member of various RAF Associations, including the PoW Association and the *Amicale Action* of the French Resistance. We know from his family that he attempted to meet other members of the crew in later years. He did track down another member of the crew and hoped to meet them with his son, Nigel, but for whatever reason the meeting did not take place. It was the case for many that once the war was over they preferred to put that phase of their life behind them, and perhaps meeting a former colleague from the time would have brought up difficult memories.

Figure 72. Hugh Verity, one of the best known Lysander pilots, and Lewis Hodges, distinguished Special Duties pilot and in 1971 promoted to Air Chief Marshal, with Brian Atkins (front) and Sir Brooks Richards at the AGM of the Resistance Association, Bourg en Bresse, 24 June 1998. (Amicale Action)

AFTER THE WAR

Atkins's involvement in various groups after the war gave him the opportunity to meet and get to know some other personalities from the war, including Hugh Verity, a Lysander pilot, and Air Chief Marshal Sir Lewis Hodges. Verity is one of the best-known Lysander pilots, who flew twenty nine clandestine operations with 161 Squadron, dropping and picking up agents, Resistance members and other figures. Among those he transported were Moulin and the future French president, François Mitterrand. Verity went on to handle operational management for SOE flights in Western Europe and Scandinavia and in late 1944 was commanding SOE air operations in South-East Asia. He retired from the RAF in 1965, and his book *We Landed by Moonlight* was published in 1978. Hodges was also posted to 161 Squadron, becoming squadron leader in May 1943 – 161 Squadron was located at Tempsford, but also at Tangmere. Hodges flew operations similar to Verity's; in fact, he flew Mitterrand back to England. Like Verity, he also went out to South-East Asia and took command of 357 Squadron, a Special Duties squadron aiding Force 136 in Burma, Thailand and Malaya. His RAF career post-war saw him ultimately promoted to Air Chief Marshal in 1971. These were men who fully understood the service that Atkins and the others undertook, and it is not surprising that, in later years, they met and found a mutual bond.

After the war, Atkins named each house he lived in 'Roskilde', after the area in which the crew made their forced landing. While he spoke little of his experiences, the naming of his homes tell us that this location remained close to him for the rest of his life.

As previously mentioned, Fry and Atkins stayed in touch, and these seem to be the only two who kept in regular contact. Atkins also formed a close friendship with Muus, the agent they were carrying on that fateful night in December 1943 when they were shot down. In 1995 Atkins visited Denmark at the invitation of the Danish government, on the fiftieth anniversary of the liberation of that country; 500 people attended this commemoration. Atkins spoke at a public event about the great danger faced by the Danes who helped them, saying: 'The Danes took a very high risk, it was the lives of their whole family that was at risk. I only had the responsibility for myself, with my family safe back in England.'[221] He was able to meet the Krügermeier family who had assisted Bartter, Fry and Howell in their evasion. He thanked those who helped him and the rest of the crew during those days.

A newspaper article titled 'The spring came – like never before', tells of the visit of Atkins to Denmark and describes the veterans as those

Figure 73. Brian Atkins with his wife at the crash site, 1995, visiting to celebrate the fiftieth anniversary of the liberation of Denmark. (Nigel Atkins)

who saved 'our [Danish] honour'. Those, like Atkins, who attended, were officially thanked by Prime Minister Poul Nyrup Rasmussen, who received them at the Christianborg Palace, the seat of the Danish Parliament in Copenhagen. At a reception in the Knight's Hall, the Prime Minister said: 'We and future generations will always be grateful to you.' He welcomed them on behalf of the government, but this visit had been privately arranged and funded.

The visit by the veterans had provoked a fundraising campaign to ensure that those without the financial ability to make the trip were not left out. The event was co-organised by the oldest daily newspaper in Denmark, *Berlingske Tidende*. Their chairman Ole Scherfig pointed out that in the planning one major error was made, in not ensuring that there were funds available to invite British veterans.[222] Marie Holst, a 41-year-old religious studies student, was angered to learn that there was no money to invite those to whom Denmark owed its freedom. She set about raising funds and it was to her credit that so many veterans were able to attend the commemorations. At the reception she thanked the veterans 'who made us aware that they would like to share our joy over the liberation with us and to the hundreds of anonymous Danes who immediately sent money and who helped save our honour'.

Through the initiative started by Holst, DKK1.15 million was raised to help fund the visit by so many veterans. The Prime Minister added to Holst's comments by saying: 'There are no good and blessed wars. And there are only rarely just wars. But the battle you British fought – also for us Danes – was truly a just and necessary war.' He also addressed the veterans of the Danish Resistance saying: 'Though few in number, you also came out of nowhere to do what you felt that had to be done. And soon after, you disappeared again.' Anne Scott, who had worked for the SOE in London during the war and who moved to Copenhagen after the liberation, gave the veterans' thanks to their Danish hosts.

In addition to the official receptions, the newspaper produced an exhibition of photographs from their own archives. The veterans also visited Kronborg, where they received the salute. The castle is most famous as the setting for Shakespeare's *Hamlet*. They were also welcomed at Gentofte Town Hall and at the Skovshoved Sailing Club. From this point they saw the torch-lit procession along the Sound, attended by around 500 people. The following day they marched with the Queen's Normandy Band to the Town Hall Square to hear the Queen speak. The Rotary Club then hosted a lunch in Tivoli, where the government was represented by Hans Hækkerup, the Minister of Defence. This was an enjoyable few days for the many veterans, including Atkins, who were able to meet friends old and new and ensure that the bonds between the Danish people and those who fought for them and all of Europe were maintained.

When Atkins passed away in 2000, his service and long association with various societies was remembered, with several senior officers of the RAF attending his funeral.

Clarence (Joe) Fry (1919–2002), Canada

Joe Fry had returned to Canada in early 1944 and was demobbed in March 1946. According to his family he sold war bonds for the government but also spent some time mapping Northern Canada. Having married his wife Clare in 1946, with their son John being born in 1947, Fry returned to university to complete his training as a pharmacist, the career he had begun before the war. He worked as a pharmacist for many years before moving to be a pharmaceutical drug representative for Merck Frost.

Fry, like Bartter, would revisit Denmark to meet and thank those who helped him and his fellow crew members. In 1985, he and his wife met

Figure 74. Wilhelm Krügermeier and Joe Fry with their wives when they visited the Danish Resistance Museum. 'Frit Danmark' means 'Free Denmark'.. (press photo BT newspaper 30.08.1985)

the Krügermeier family at their home and enjoyed lunch with them. They also visited the crash site and, as shown in Figure 74, visited the Danish Museum of Resistance together. The Frys learnt that Wilhelm Krügermeier had used one pair of trousers from the uniforms left behind to work in after the war, as they were of very good quality. The Krügermeiers gifted Fry back his jacket during this visit.

Fry also met Varinka Muus, a connection to that fateful flight, but also to the assistance given to Fry during his evasion. Sadly, her husband, Flemming Muus, had died in 1982.

Beyond Fry's return visit to Denmark, there was a visit to Canada organised by the Canadian branch of the RAFES, the Royal Air Force Escape Society, in 1986. As part of this visit Kai and Ketty Krügermeier visited Joe and Clare Fry in Canada for two weeks. The Canadians ensured that their guests had no expenses, with travel provided by the Royal Canadian Air Force, while fundraising events covered other costs. While the RAF Escape Society was wound up in 1995, the Canadian branch continued until 2006.

AFTER THE WAR

Fry and Atkins stayed in close touch after the war, with Atkins visiting Canada several times. Following Atkins's death, Fry kept in touch with Brian's brother Ken. Letters between Fry and the Atkins family have been a source of information, as has information from Fry's children. Fry passed away in 2002. Fry's family kindly donated his flying jacket to the Holbæk Museum in 2016, where, following conservation work, it is now on display.

We are very grateful to the Fry family for providing information and confirming details for us during the writing of this book.

Above: Figure 75. Joe Fry, Varinka W. Muus, and Clare Fry at Copenhagen Town Hall in 1985. (Varinka W. Muus)

Right: Figure 76. Joe Fry's flying jacket. (Holbæk Museum)

Ernesto (Bill) Howell (1917–1944)

As we know, Ernesto Howell sadly perished in the North Sea, but he is, along with all the crew, remembered at the annual Tempsford Remembrance Service. He was posthumously awarded the Distinguished Flying Cross. Howell's name is inscribed on panel 202 in the Air Forces Memorial at Runnymede. This memorial, unveiled by Queen Elizabeth II in 1953, commemorates over 20,000 men and women of the air forces who perished during the Second World War during operations from the United Kingdom and northern and western Europe and who have no known grave. Howell's name is also inscribed on the Quad Memorial at the University of Manchester, acknowledging the time he spent there, as well as on a plaque at the Buenos Aires Curupayti Rugby Club.

Walter Riggs (1922–2008)

Walter Riggs returned to civilian life but we have little detail on his life post-war. We know he married Dorothy Lock in 1964 in Poole, so it seems he returned to his home area and remained there. We believe he worked for an engineering company. He sadly died in 2008.

Stanley (Stan) Smith (1924–2016)

As with Riggs, we have little information on Stan Smith after the war. It seems that, like so many of that war generation, he did his job and then returned to normal life. He spent his final years in a rest home. Sadly, we were unable to locate him before he passed away. Following his death, the story of his service appeared on the Internet and hundreds of people, who never knew him, paid their respects. It is regrettable that the deeds of these men have often been lost in the decades following the war, and it is for this reason that this book has been written.

Roger Leivers from the *Godmanchester Stirling* wrote Smith's eulogy. This was read by the Reverend Hayden Jones, army chaplain of thirty years. The following is an extract from the eulogy:

> After the war it seems that Stan, like so many of his generation went back to what could be loosely called a normal life.

AFTER THE WAR

To men like Stan it was a case of a job needed to done and they did it, it was no big deal, no great story to tell, no debt owed. Over the years the world moved on and slowly we lost these 'giants of men', this unassuming band of warriors who carried out the most dangerous and astonishing acts of courage on an almost daily basis. Who with a resigned glance acknowledged those that did not return, but who raised a glass to them in silent tribute.

Stan lived his last few years in a care home where he was loved and adored by those around him. In that place his spirit continued to live on; he never dwelt on his war-time activities, never looked for gratitude or praise, and of course there was the occasional non-PC comment about 'Germans'.

It is fitting that, as news of his passing spread across the modern idiom of the Internet, hundreds of people from across the world left their respects to a brave man, one they had never met, but who they realised they owed so much to. One person said it perfectly:

'Rest in peace Stan, flying high once again with your comrades in arms.'

Ali Lamport, who looked after Stan at the care home, remembers him:

He would potter about quite happily and chatter in his own way, dance with us on occasion too, he was absolutely delightful, a real gentleman, he never spoke about the war but would become anxious upon hearing loud bangs like fireworks and thunder. Sadly, Stan came to us too late in his illness, dementia, to be able to have any rational conversation about the war but in all honesty he may well have not wanted to talk about it all anyway.

Smith kept some RAF-related memorabilia when he moved into the care home. He had a photo of himself taken during the Second World War, his medals and a photo of a bombed Brussels/Melsbrook airfield in Belgium. Although he had no link to the photo of the bombed site, it suggests that this attack on 14 August 1944, while he was captive, stirred some feelings for him and that these memories remained with him at the end of his life.

Frederick Turvil should also be remembered. Having joined the crew on that December night in 1943, he would spend the rest of the war in

Figure 77. Stan Smith's funeral. (Ali Lamport)

Stalag IV B with other members of the crew. Post-war, Turvil stayed with the RAF; in 1953, the *London Gazette* shows him moving to the technical branch; from warrant officer he was commissioned to flying officer. In 1958 he was posted to the United States Air Force base in Santa Monica as part of a NATO team. He sailed to New York on the *Queen Mary* and from there made his way to California. In 1960 he is shown living with (presumably) his wife and two sons, but still at Mays Road in Teddington, an address which links back almost thirty years. His RAF career continued and in 1967 he was promoted to squadron leader from flight lieutenant.

Clearly his experience with the Bartter crew did not diminish his interest in the RAF and he enjoyed a full career, retiring in 1970. Records show that he died in 2000 at the age of 84.

Friendships were formed and remained strong in the decades following the war. While not all of the crew stayed in touch, there was a firm bond between some of the airmen and the Danish people who helped them during those few intense days in Denmark. These men came together from diverse backgrounds; friendships were forged during dangerous times, and of the seven young men who began the journey, six made it home and lived their lives discreetly and positively. For their families, the years after their deaths have sparked interest and a journey of discovery as they delve into the truth behind their service.

The next generation

In 2013, Nigel Atkins, Brian's son, visited the site of the emergency landing in Denmark, where he met Jan Christensen. Jan had heard only a week earlier of Nigel's planned visit to the crash site. Brian had spoken little about his war experiences and Nigel was keen to learn more. As he learnt about the aircraft being shot down and the escape of some of the crew, he determined to learn more about his father's experiences, and in turn the rest of the crew. He and Jan then embarked on a journey that would take them across countries and unearth the story told within this book. From the seeds sown during that first meeting in 2013, this book has grown beyond a son's interest in his father, to a story encompassing the whole crew and their story through the war.

In 2015, on the seventieth anniversary of the Danish liberation, Nigel returned to Denmark for the opening of an exhibition relating the story of the aircraft and crew. In preparing the exhibition there was an excavation of the crash site, details of which are contained within the Appendices.

To mark the official opening of the exhibition a programme of events was organised by the Holbæk Museum over the weekend 2–5 May. There were talks, including by Nigel Atkins and Mark Seaman – a historian who specialises in the SOE and Intelligence. Beyond this, there were workshops and tours as well as official functions, with the Mayor of Holbæk hosting a reception and dinner.

There was a Remembrance Service in Copenhagen attended by the Danish Queen and Prime Minister, to which Nigel was invited. The final day of events included a remembrance service at Copenhagen Cathedral.

Figure 78. Nigel Atkins with Karen Sivebæk Munk of the Holbæk Museum. Nigel is seen here holding a piece of the Bartter aircraft during his first visit to Denmark in 2013. (Jan Christensen)

Figure 79. Nigel Atkins (second from right) and Mark Seaman, renowned SOE historian taking part in one of the many events around the opening of the exhibition. (Jan Christensen)

Figure 80. The opening ceremony for the BB378 exhibition at the Holbæk Museum, Saturday 2 May 2015. (Jan Christensen)

Figure 81. Jan Christensen (left) with Pauline Evans, John Anderson, and Beverley Whittington, three members of the Anderson family at the crash site of BB378. (Jan Christensen)

Beverley Whittington, John Anderson and Pauline Evans, all members of the Anderson family, visited the Holbæk Museum for the first time in 2019, almost seventy-six years after their father's crash. They have provided many papers to illuminate this story and they enjoyed visiting the exhibition and learning more about the flight. They saw the respect and honour that is still afforded to the crew today. The exhibition continues to draw visitors intrigued by this crew who were shot down while bringing a great leader of the Danish Resistance home. The story of their survival continues to capture the imagination, and the museum is well worth a visit.

TVARA events at Tempsford

The Tempsford Veterans and Relatives Association works to ensure that the work and sacrifices of those who served at Tempsford remain in the public domain. To the dismay of veterans, reunions for the Tempsford

Figure 82. Tempsford as it is today. (Nigel Atkins)

squadrons ended in 1997. Bob Body, the nephew of pilot J.W. Menzies, has worked since 2000 to ensure that events continue to be held. Lady Errol, who owns the land that Tempsford lies within, generously allows families of veterans to attend events. There is an annual remembrance service held at Tempsford, where family and supporters gather at the Barn, the final spot for agents before they boarded the aircraft. Wreaths are laid, prayers are said, and those who make the journey take some time to contemplate the work of aircrews, agents, ground crews and all who made Tempsford such a vital part of the war effort. A social event with lunch and a talk afterwards is enjoyed by the families. While the number of veterans continues to diminish, it is an opportunity for many families to learn more about their relatives' role in the Second World War.

Figure 83 includes the daughters of Ralph C. Hollingworth, who was head of the Danish section of the SOE. Hollingworth had been in the Naval Reserve at the outbreak of war, but his talent for languages saw him quickly appointed to head up the new SOE in Denmark in 1940. His war record remains sealed until 2031, but his work with the SOE saw him receive the Medal of Freedom with Bronze Palm from President Harry S. Truman, the

Figure 83. Tempsford Remembrance Day 2017. From left, Margaret Fradin (Bartter's niece), Nigel Atkins (Brian Atkins's son), Ann Hollingworth (Ralph C. Hollingworth's daughter) Gillian Smith (Ralph C. Hollingworth's daughter), and Jan Christensen. (Jan Christensen)

Figure 84. Relatives and friends at the 2018 Tempsford Remembrance Service, photographed in the Barn. The Barn was the last stop for agents before boarding the aircraft. (Jan Christensen)

OBE from Queen Elizabeth II, and the Knight of the Order of the Dannebrog from the King of Denmark. Like so many, once the war was over he was not interested in revisiting it, actually asking for the medal from the King of Denmark to be posted to him, as he didn't want the fuss. He was, however, a haunted man; he smoked heavily, commenting to his daughters that if they knew what he'd been through during the war, they would understand why he smoked. He had been very much at the front of events, evading German capture by boldly engaging with them; he travelled Denmark recruiting for the SOE and organising resistance and sabotage. While after the war he would have preferred to stay in the Navy, family circumstances meant he had to return home to run the family business. He sadly died at the age of 59, a man who had done so much for the freedom of Denmark but also for many individuals.

A newsletter for the association in 2015 detailed Nigel Atkins's first visit to Denmark and his first meeting with Jan Christensen, which took place in December 2013. It details a local archivist alerting Jan to Nigel's forthcoming visit and how a small delegation then met Nigel at the crash site.

Nigel Atkins's travels

Nigel Atkins has spent considerable time visiting and meeting people linked to the Bartter crew. As well as returning to Denmark on several occasions, he has met René Gimpel, son of Ernest (Charles), in London several times, where René has continued the family business. René was pleased to meet Nigel and learn of the crew who had flown his father into France in 1943. René and Nigel enjoy a firm friendship born of the experiences shared by their fathers. During the Covid crisis Nigel, who lives in France, was asked by the Gimpel family to represent them at the annual national Remembrance Day ceremonies on 18 June in France (the anniversary of de Gaulle's speech to the French nation in 1940). This remembrance is for the 1,038 Resistance members recognised by the nation with the honour of Companion of the Resistance. Ernest Gimpel was awarded this distinction. The ceremony is held just outside Paris on the hill called Mont Valerien, where 1,000 members of the Resistance were executed. The ceremony is attended by the French President. As with Nigel's father, René's father did not say much about his experiences in the war, and so the two men have taken the opportunity to learn more.

Above left: Figure 85. (left) Nigel Atkins (left) with René Gimpel at one of their meetings in London. (Nigel Atkins)

Above right: Figure 86. (right) Nigel Atkins (left) and Marc Serratrice. (Nigel Atkins)

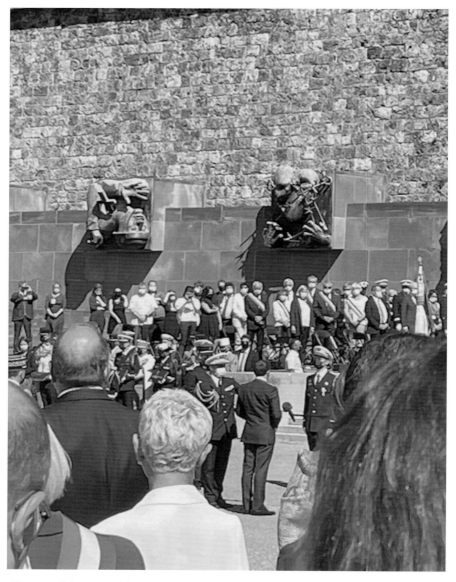

Above and opposite: Figure 87. Remembrance ceremony in Paris on 18 June 2021. (Nigel Atkins)

Nigel also visited the Vercors area of France to see where the Trainer 95 drop had taken place and was pleased to meet Marc Serratrice, a surviving member of the Resistance who clearly remembered the drop and how important it was for all. Nigel travelled to the area in August 2020 to locate

the drop zone of Trainer 95. It entailed a long trek to the plateau south of the Corrençon mountain range called Darbounouze. Stopping at a refuge for refreshments, Nigel came across a book written by Serratrice, a member of the maquis, and discovered that there was a chapter dedicated to Trainer 95. Nigel then set about finding Serratrice, who was living near Grenoble. Serratrice was then a sprightly 98-year-old who explained that he was part of the reception committee which received the consignment of Trainer 95.

He said that he joined the maquis as he was conscripted to the STO. He was helped by his sister, who was in the Resistance in Grenoble. Nigel returned to Grenoble in August 2021 and made an hour-long recorded interview with Serratrice. Nigel asked about the importance of Trainer 95 to the maquis. Serratrice replied that they had been waiting several months for arms and, as previously discussed, it was a sign of support and hope.

Perhaps most poignantly, in November 2009 Nigel also visited the site of Stalag IV B, located near the city of Dresden. While nothing but markings remain, it was a powerful experience to stand where his father had been imprisoned. Nigel managed to identify the RAF compound of the camp.

The prison camp was the size of a town. Prisoner numbers vary according to sources, but tens of thousands were held there. It was one of the largest PoW camps. The area is now a well-kept park, with the British section essentially woodland.

Nigel felt that with the peaceful nature of the land today it is very difficult to capture the atmosphere of what it must have been like in 1944.

Additionally, Nigel has visited the drop zone in the former Yugoslavia where the Bartter crew dropped a team of four in Operation Geisha. During a visit to Belgrade he had a meeting with the Patriarch of the Serbian

Figure 88. Stalag IV B memorial. (Nigel Atkins)

Above left and above right: Figure 89. His Grace Bishop Jovan of Ulpiana, on the right ready to parachute, and left, as Nigel met him. (Bishop Jovan of Ulpiana)

Orthodox Church. With him was Bishop Jovan of Ulpiana. Towards the end of the meeting Bishop Jovan said he must go as he was scheduled to do a parachute jump. Nigel said he was trying to identify where his father's crew had dropped the SOE agents and equipment in October 1943. Bishop Jovan said to send him the location details and come back in three weeks' time to celebrate his birthday. Nigel duly returned to Bishop Jovan's diocese.

Serbian hospitality is renowned for food and especially alcohol. Before finishing the celebrations in the early hours, the Bishop said that they would be leaving early in the morning. Accordingly, the Bishop drove his Land Rover for over an hour on narrow winding roads in the Papuk mountains. Stopping on a high plateau, pointing to the sky he said to Nigel, 'this is where your father dropped the agents and equipment'. On the site there is an old rusted monument representing a parachute, as shown in Chapter 4.

Additionally, Nigel has maintained contact with the Fry family in Canada, and through research for the book located Bartter's adopted daughter, Julia, who lives on a secluded farm in Costa Rica. He has also had contact with the Anderson family and the Krügermeier family through contacts of Jan Christensen.

Figure 90. Nigel Atkins and Bishop Jovan beside the Geisha monument. (Nigel Atkins)

In November 2021, Nigel was invited to the British Ambassador's residence in Paris and presented with the certificate shown in Figure 91, which acknowledges his father's suffering. Through Jan, Nigel had made contact with Philip Baker of the Prisoners of War online Memorial and Museum. It was through this contact that Nigel found himself invited to what he described as a very moving ceremony.

Medals

As with all who served, the crew were awarded medals including the 1939–1945 star. Recipients of the star were also eligible for the Bomber Command clasp. However, this was not instituted until 2013, too late for most of our crew. They were also awarded the Europe Star and the Aircrew Europe Star, along with the Defence Medal and the War Medal. Ernesto Howell was awarded the DFC (Distinguished Flying Cross) posthumously. A medal privately issued in the 1980s was available on request to those who served in Bomber Command. Nick Anderson had no interest in this, but Brian Atkins did obtain one.

There has been much controversy surrounding British government policy as enacted by Bomber Command, much directed to the heavy bombing raids in Germany and the tactics of 'Bomber' Harris. Nonetheless this was just a part of the air war. Thousands of men took part in the air war in many different roles and theatres of war, following orders and serving their country with dedication.

Many decades later, on 28 June 2012, a memorial to those who served in Bomber Command was finally unveiled by Queen Elizabeth II in Green Park, London. The roof design incorporates aluminium from a Halifax aircraft which was shot down over Belgium on 12 May 1944. When the aircraft was excavated in 1997 three of the crew were still at their stations. The entire crew were buried in Belgium with full military honours. The memorial acknowledges the 55,573 men who lost their lives during the Second World War.

France

France received 11,333 tons of equipment and supplies from the SOE during the Second World War. French society struggled for many years to reconcile resistance and collaboration. The trials, and in some cases

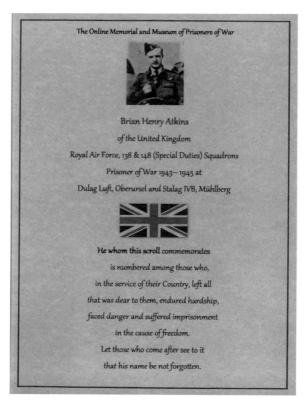

Left and below: Figure 91. Presentation for the online Memorial and Museum of PoWs, November 2021, at the residence of the British Ambassador, Menna Rawlings. (Royal Air Forces Association)

execution, of the leading actors of the Vichy regime did not lay the schism to rest. Before formal trials could be set up, some elements of the Resistance took lethal revenge on alleged collaborators. The devastation wrought on the country saw France being the largest recipient under the Marshall Plan instigated by the United States to aid post-war reconstruction. It remains an uncomfortable period for France to reflect on, but those who fought for freedom are held in the highest esteem and many Allied service personnel have over recent years been presented with the Légion d'honneur in recognition of the contribution that they made to the freedom of France.

Yugoslavia

Yugoslavia had received 16,469 tons of equipment, mostly weapons and explosives, but also food, by the SOE during the Second World War, but the end of the war would not be the end of their troubles. A Yugoslav State Commission for the Determination of Crimes of the Occupiers and their Collaborators was formed in 1945 and by 1947 had identified over 64,000 war criminals.[223] However, this was also used as a way of dealing with political enemies. Tens of thousands were murdered or exiled during the immediate post-war years.[224] A federal government of six republics was established under Tito. After Tito died in 1980, the republics suffered economic and political issues culminating in the collapse of Yugoslavia during 1991–1992. Thousands died during very difficult years for the region. Churchill had been warned about potential communist rule after the war, but had concentrated his efforts on defeating the Nazis rather than concerning himself with what a post-war Yugoslavia might be like.

Denmark

While the SOE supplied some 700 tons of equipment to Denmark during the Second World War, the Danes were extremely efficient at making their own equipment so this figure belies the efforts of this nation. Denmark, which had succumbed to German might without a fight, proved itself a worthy ally as the war progressed, and its Resistance forces were organised and proactive. From making their own very efficient radio sets to carrying out substantial sabotage, Denmark was recognised as an ally.

It was the Danish–Swedish organisation for the support of refugees (*Dansk–Svensk Flygtningetjeneste*) who had organised the transport of the Halifax BB378 crew members to Sweden. The seat of this organisation was located at 7 Forchhammersvej in the district of Frederiksberg in Copenhagen, and the head of this organisation was Robert Jensen who went by the name 'Tom'.

The *Dansk–Svensk Flygtningetjeneste* was created in October 1943. Approximately 1,650 people travelled from Denmark to Sweden thanks to its safe corridor, and around 250 people were transported the other way. On the morning of 24 July 1944, Gestapo agents stormed the offices of Jensen in Forchhammersvej. He was examining his daily post at that moment with two assistants and agent Geisler. Geisler managed to escape together with one employee, but Jensen and his close friend Thorkild Tronbjerg were both killed.

After the war, many Danish local helpers and Resistance fighters received acknowledgements, in the form of awards such as the one shown in Figure 91, from both the British and the Americans. The British had awards specifically for helpers of British service personnel during their evasion and escape.[225] The following Danes who helped the crew of Halifax BB378 received awards:

Niels Vilhelm Jensen, from Vandløse near Store Merløse
Karen Jensen, from Vandløse near Store Merløse
Frederik Jensen, from Vandløse near Store Merløse
Einar Arboe Rasmussen, from Roskilde
Wilhelm Krügermeier, from Marup
Sven Ove Frederiksen, from Marup
Bent Olsen, from Tølløse
F.C.R. Scheel, from Kirke Saaby
Mogens Scheel, from Roskilde

We understand awards were also given to local Danish citizens who aided the crew.

Denmark was a pivotal location for our crew; it was where they were shot down, but it is where some of them made friendships which lasted decades and have continued with the next generation. One flight which could have been like so many others would leave an indelible mark on both the crew and those who assisted them.

Afterword

On a frozen field near Roskilde, Denmark in December 2013, Nigel Atkins and his son Jean Marc, reflected on the Bartter crew and their SOE flights, Table Jam 18 and 19. On the fateful night of 10 December 1943, Peter Bartter was skilfully able to make an emergency landing by following the furrows of the field.

Figure 92. Nigel Atkins at the crash site 2013. (Jean Marc Atkins)

Nigel and Jean Marc wanted to shed light on these missions, which lay hidden under a veil of secrecy. The nature of the work carried out by a Special Duties crew meant that the families of these men during and after the war knew little or nothing about their assignments. The crew were unaware of all they had accomplished. They understood only that they were aiding the war effort, and for them that sufficed.

Secrecy was ingrained into the crew, and they were sworn to the Official Secrets Act during their lifetime. The crash was undoubtedly the most significant life-changing moment for the crew. As we have seen, for several of them this meant deprivation and suffering in a prisoner-of-war camp. Decades on we can only imagine the turmoil and trauma that this caused them.

Each member of the crew knew that they depended on one another, each with their specific skills. They realised that every time they flew, it could well be their last.

I am indebted to my dear college friend John Evans, whose publishing knowledge and advice have been a great support throughout the process of putting the book together. He sadly passed away just before publication, but here are some words he left, having read the manuscript:

> In World War Two, the average age of RAF bomber crews was 23. To read now about the operations undertaken by the Bartter crew facing a world so different from our own is a very moving experience.
>
> Those serving in Bomber Command knew the odds were against them. At times, some 80 per cent were failing to complete their tours of thirty operations unscathed, and those that survived being shot down faced the miseries of becoming prisoners of war.
>
> The well-researched accounts by Jan Christensen of the Bartter crew's war-time experiences are dedicated with respect and admiration to a small group of men who did their duty in very dangerous times.
>
> It is my hope that what has been a very personal journey does justice and informs the readers about ordinary men called to do extraordinary things.
>
> John Evans

AFTERWORD

A few final, fitting words are those in the dedication to the Special Duties Squadron Memorial in St Clement Danes on 18 October 2013 by Mark Seaman:

> What we have is a permanent memorial to some of the best and bravest aircrew of the Second World War and whose endeavours were in support of some of the most noblest aspirations – let us not forget their squadron crests and mottos – 'For Freedom'. What finer aspirations can there be?

Nigel S. Atkins November 2023

Figure 93. Crest of 138 Squadron. (Nigel Atkins)

APPENDICES

Appendix I

Bartter crew Special Duty flights in 1943

BARTTER FLIGHTS AND OPERATIONS FROM 21 AUGUST-10 DECEMBER 1943								
DATE	DESTINATION	SEC.	DEPARTING BASE	CODE	STATUS	TAKE OFF	LANDING	AIRCRAFT
21.08.1943			TEMPSFORD	POSTED TO TEMPSFORD				
29.08.1943			TEMPSFORD	EXERCISE HENLOW				
31.08.1943			TEMPSFORD	EXERCISE HENLOW				
31.08.1943			TEMPSFORD	N.F.T. (NIGHT FLYING TEST)				
02.09.1943			TEMPSFORD	EXERCISE POTTAM				
08.09.1943	FRANCE	RF	TEMPSFORD	DICK 53/55	C	19.54	02.56	HAL T304
15.09.1943	FRANCE	F/RF	TEMPSFORD	BUTLER 10/ PETER19/ DETECTIVE A	PC	21.05	02.56	HAL W156

214

BARTTER CREW SPECIAL DUTY FLIGHTS IN 1943

Date	From		To	Mission				Aircraft
18.09.1943	HURN, UK		TEMPSFORD	GROUND CREW ON FLIGHT	C	12.00	12.50	HAL DT 276
24.09.1943	GIBRALTAR		HURN, UK	GROUND CREW ON FLIGHT	C	3.35	11.25	HAL DT 276
24.09.1943	BLIDA, ALGERIA		GIBRALTAR	GROUND CREW ON FLIGHT	C	15.30	18.30	HAL DT 276
01.10.1943	PROTVILLE, TUNISIA		BLIDA, ALGERIA	GROUND CREW ON FLIGHT	C	14.40	17.20	HAL DT 276
02.10.1943	YUGOSLAVIA		PROTVILLE, TUNISIA	GEISHA 1	NC	20.58	05.00	HAL DT 276
03.10.1943	YUGOSLAVIA		PROTVILLE, TUNISIA	GEISHA 2	C	21.55	07.40	HAL DT 276
09.10.1943	BLIDA, ALGERIA		PROTVILLE, TUNISIA	GROUND CREW + AIR COMMODORE H R VAUGH ON AIRCRAFT	C	14.50	17.35	HAL DT 276
11.10.1943	GIBRALTAR		BLIDA, ALGERIA	GROUNDCREW AND R CHURCHILL ON AIRCRAFT	C	13.25	16.30	HAL DT 276
12.10.1943	LYNEHAM, UK		GIBRALTAR	GROUNDCREW AND R CHURCHILL ON AIRCRAFT	C	00.15	08.15	HAL DT 276
13.10.1943	TEMPSFORD		LYNEHAM, UK		C	12.05	13.05	HAL DT 276
16.10.1943	FRANCE	F	TEMPSFORD	WHEELWRIGHT 32	NC	20.30	03.55	HAL M 161

BARTTER FLIGHTS AND OPERATIONS FROM 21 AUGUST-10 DECEMBER 1943								
18.10.1943	FRANCE	F/RF	TEMPSFORD	DICK 51/TINKER 3	NC	22.50	04.15	HAL T284
21.10.1943	FRANCE	F	TEMPSFORD	DIRECTOR 57	NC	21.15	02.33	HAL H
7.11.1943	FRANCE	F	TEMPSFORD	SPRUCE 17	NC	20.25	03.50	HAL L
09.11.1943	FRANCE	RF	TEMPSFORD	TRAINER 95	C	19.40	04.40	HAL D
10.11.1943	FRANCE	RF	TEMPSFORD	TRAINER 41	NC	19.40	02.15	HAL 'O' 275
12.11.1943	FRANCE	F	TEMPSFORD	WHEELWRIGHT 38	C	19.42	03.05	HAL T
25.11.1943	FRANCE	RF	TEMPSFORD	JOHN 36/GENARME	C	20.35	03.35	HAL 'O' 275
10.12.1943	DENMARK	SD	TEMPSFORD	TABLE JAM 18/ TABLE JAM 19	NC	NO TAKE OFF TIME LISTED	FLEW FOR 4.5 HRS BEFORE SHOT DOWN	HAL BB378

THIS LIST DOES NOT INCLUDE ALL TRAINING AND/OR BOMBING OPERATIONS

KEY

SEC – SECTION, F = F SECTION/SOE, RF = RF SECTION/BCRA

STATUS – C = OPERATION COMPLETED, NC = OPERATION NOT COMPLETED, PC = PART COMPLETED

Appendix II

Bombing raids

In the summer of 1943, the increasing might of the Luftwaffe meant that industrial targets related to aircraft production were highlighted as targets for Bomber Command. Air Chief Marshal Sir Arthur Harris, known as 'Bomber' Harris, concentrated efforts on large cities with industrial areas. Harris had the ear of Churchill and is said to have visited him almost weekly at Chequers to gain his support for these operations. Substantial bombing operations were undertaken, with each operation consisting of hundreds of aircraft and thousands of aircrew. Losses for the RAF were substantial, but those in charge believed these bombing raids to be vital. Hamburg would be the first city to be targeted.

Brian Atkins, in his IWM interview, confirms his crew participated in the Hamburg Firestorm raids which were concentrated over four nights, 25, 27, 29 July and 2 August 1943.[226] We believe they may have been part of number 3 Group under Air Vice Marshal Harrison based in Exning, Newmarket, Suffolk.

To give a general idea of the casualty rates for aircrew in the Second World War, from 125,000 airmen, 51 per cent were killed, 13 per cent were either captured or evaded, with 12 per cent killed in non-operational accidents. Only 24 per cent survived the war without incident.[227]

Harris at strategic command ordered a maximum strength of heavy bombers for a raid on Hamburg on 24 July 1943. This was the beginning of the Battle of Hamburg, or as it was known in Hamburg: *die Katastrophe*.

The Bartter crew, along with other inexperienced crews, found themselves on the Firestorm raids which Atkins described as 'frightening ... to see hundreds of other aircraft in the air at the same time and distressing to witness aircraft shot down in flames and crews bailing out'. These mainstream bombing raids are vividly described by Miles Tripp in his book *Eighth Passenger*, the eighth passenger being fear.[228] Tripp, like Atkins, was a bomb aimer.

Bomber Command had 871 operational bombers and 957 full crews, not on leave at 6pm on 24 July; 792 bombers with full crew took off for the main Hamburg raid on the night of 25 July. The various aircraft that set off that evening were crewed by a total 5,959 men. Officially called 'Operation Gomorrah', it would last eight days and seven nights and at the time would be the heaviest aerial bombardment in history. The conditions for a successful bombing raid were in place, excellent meteorological conditions, a warm summer night and the introduction of 'window'. Otherwise known as 'chaff', these metallised strips were thrown from the aircraft in order to confuse the German radar.

Bomber Command had sent out an order on 17 July to each bomber group, they were to prepare to receive deliveries of 'window' ready for use on the upcoming raids to Germany. By 20 July, under strict secrecy, every bomber airfield was storing stacks of brown paper parcels containing 'window'. Each parcel contained 2,200 strips of metallic material, which when dropped would cause enemy radar to become close to useless as false echoes would confuse the system.

The first use of 'window' to disrupt German radar had encouraged more than half the Wing Commanders to join the operation. The introduction of 'window' also had the effect of sending a maximum number of new pilots and crews on the raids. Bartter and his crew were one of seventy-six new crews who flew on that first night.

Of the industrial targets hit, which numbered almost 600, almost 300 were mentioned by name. The civilian cost was immense, with over 40,000 dead and 37,000 injured. The firestorm which erupted in the city incinerated more than eight square miles (twenty-one square kilometres) and forced a million people to flee the city. Those who remained took shelter where they could, often in the basements of burnt-out buildings, and also witnessed the clearing of the dead, who were buried in mass graves. Eighty-seven Allied aircraft were lost, including twenty-nine Halifax aircraft, with 552 Allied airmen killed. There followed several further raids on Hamburg after this initial bombardment. Atkins specifies that, having become used to operating on their own, 'suddenly finding yourself in a bomber stream with hundreds of bombers/aircraft which you could see at times was quite frightening'. Crews were very aware of the German defences and there were times when they had to take strong evasive action, which hints at the extreme circumstances. He said it was distressing to see other bombers going down in flames and to see the crews bailing out; it was possible for some of the crew to see parachutes opening. It would have been particularly disturbing for Atkins in his position within the aircraft.

Those raids left vivid memories for those who took part. Martin Middlebrook, in his authoritative book, *Battle of Hamburg*, interviewed crews in their later life with one bomb aimer recalling 'we had treated this window, all these bundles in the aircraft with some levity. But it was a magic effect. The German flak and searchlights were all over the place'.

It was decided not to attack Hamburg the following night due to the heavy smoke covering the city. The result of the night of bombing on 27 July with 2326 tonnes of bombs with 98 per cent of aircraft returning was viewed as another success. It was during this raid that the Firestorm occurred. The bombing lasted for less than an hour, with three factors indicated as the main factors which led to the Firestorm.

First, there was unusual concentration, marking and bombing by the RAF with cratered roads preventing firefighting. Second, there was an unusual concentration of very high temperatures, there was a heatwave, and low humidity. The third factor was that the German Civil Defence had ordered that fires which had been smouldering in the west of the city for several days should be dealt with and extinguished. The RAF, on this evening, concentrated on the east of the city. Firefighting appliances and personnel were on the wrong side of the city.

After an hour of the first bomb being dropped, hardly any of the resulting fires were being tackled and burned out of control.

In total 55,000 German civilians perished in the Battle of Hamburg.

Berlin was next on the list, with the press in Great Britain pushing for further bombing raids, following the perceived success at Hamburg. Records suggest that there was an attempt to impress the Russians. On 19 August, Churchill pressed for bombing on Berlin following Hamburg; he had also suggested bombing the administrative district with delayed-action bombs.

Berlin was home to a substantial number of industrial sites, which included three aircraft plants as well as the Siemens company, whose site was so large they had their own town, Siemensstadt. The raids on Berlin began on 23 August, with three raids until 4 September. Over 1,600 sorties were flown, and 125 aircraft lost. Another sortie on 31 August saw over 600 aircraft take part. The impact of the bombing resulted in approximately 150 deaths on the ground, with the Germans believing that there were only 150 aircraft as the damage sustained was not significant. Stirling aircraft were the most vulnerable as they could not fly above about 14,000ft

(4,267 metres), but the Halifax aircraft was only slightly less vulnerable. On the first night, 251 Halifax aircraft were involved with twenty-five lost.

Situated deep within Germany, Berlin had a geographic advantage and was well defended. There were substantial Allied losses, with many aircraft lost before they even reached their target. The damage to Berlin was not as significant as that to Hamburg. The effect of the bombing on morale, though, was substantial, with over a million people evacuated from the city and food supplies dwindling for those who remained. While the physical damage was less, the impact on morale was meaningful. Bomber Command left Berlin alone until November, when they launched another group of bombing raids, and Halifax aircraft took part in three of these; 234 Halifax aircraft took part in the Berlin raid on 22 November, and it is possible that the Bartter crew were involved. Twenty-six aircraft were lost on this night, including ten Halifax aircraft; the loss of personnel was 167, with another twenty-five captured.

In his interview, Atkins is clear that they targeted factories and railway communications. When asked during his Imperial War Museum interview about civilian casualties, he responds: 'At that stage of the war [*long pause*] I don't think it entered our minds to any great extent.' He remarks on their training, and that this was what they had signed up for, but his pauses suggest that training took over and that an appreciation of the reality of war perhaps hit afterwards. He also reminds the generations that followed that 'one has to remember that the bombing of Germany was the only effective way that the population of Great Britain could see positive action being taken against the enemy'. He acknowledges the success in North Africa, but that was a long way from home. He also stated that 'a lot of comments post-war have to take account of the atmosphere in 1943/44'. This is a vital comment, as judgements cannot be made by taking the knowledge and sensibilities of today and applying them to events in the past. Those within cities such as London and Coventry would have felt that there was justification for bombing German cities.

The young men, including the Bartter crew, had volunteered to join, but you could not volunteer to leave. While our crew did not know of anyone who refused to fly, there was the threat of being marked as LMF: 'lacking moral fibre'. By 1943 any crew on their second tour would not face this ignominy, but it remained a threat to those on their first tour. The term 'lacking moral fibre' was used only by the RAF. It was brought in during 1940, where a lack of aircrew combined with the threat of invasion meant that senior members of the service felt they had to impose stringent penalties on those who refused to fly.[229] The consequences of refusing to fly were severe; men would be removed to assessment centres and suffered loss of rank and privileges. There was no opportunity to redeem oneself and many were discharged from the service. While harsh, many within the service felt it was a necessary deterrent to ensure the service retained experienced crews on the front line.

Those in the services were at the mercy of both political and military leaders; they couldn't choose their operations. Orders were given and the crews had a duty which they were bound to carry out. There was a belief that, in carrying out these raids, they were not only dismantling the economy of Germany but were offering hope to those at home who had suffered through raids on their towns and cities. While the destruction of transport and industrial targets was of primary concern, these raids also aimed to lower the morale of the German people. The firestorms were controversial and tainted the memory of many brave men for decades.

Atkins said he was involved in these raids around the time of the firestorm in Hamburg, and it would seem that it was while he was completing his training at RAF Riccall, as bombing operations were undertaken from this location and those training at the HCU were utilised. Nick Anderson's log makes no reference to flights to Germany, which suggests these raids might have been before the crew had fully formed and were still in final training.

Appendix III

Denmark and the blanket of radar

While the German forces made use of radar in an attempt to fortify their Atlantic Wall, which ran in parts from Norway to Southern France, it was Denmark which was particularly well covered. Flying over Denmark became extraordinarily dangerous for Allied crews due to a sophisticated system of radar stations. From the early days of the occupation, Allied forces started to fly over Denmark. This prompted the Germans to build radar stations, especially along the coastline, with the result that, at the end of the war, twenty-two stations were operating in Denmark, with a range which covered the whole country. Their primary purpose was to detect and track Allied aircraft and to guide German night fighters until they were sufficiently near the Allied bombers to see them directly or to detect them with their on-board radar. Allied aircraft were often located as they were flying over the North Sea.

The Germans gave their radar stations the names of animals whose first letter was also the first letter of the place where the stations were located. And so *Seehund* ('seal') was the station located in Zealand, *Krokodil* ('crocodile') was the name of the Copenhagen station, and *Faultier* ('sloth') was the station located on the island of Falster. The *Seehund* station in Tybjerg stood high above the countryside between Ringsted and Næstved, about twelve miles (20 kilometres) in a direct line from the Table Jam 18 drop zone in Skjoldenæsholm Forest. The station was built on parts of the fields of Tybjerggård Farm, which had been requisitioned by the Germans in 1941. Construction started in 1942, and the station grew bigger over the years. Traffic on a nearby road, the Klintemarksvej, was overseen by a checkpoint, and you could pass through only if you had special authorisation. Tybjerg's inhabitants had to live with the radar station, and, according to local reports, the Germans managed to maintain a peaceful relationship with the locals; they would even buy their groceries from the local market. That being

222

said, none of the locals in and around Tybjerg knew what the actual use of the radar station was.

The Seehund station manager (*Kompaniefführer*) was a man named Ludmann, the fighter controller (*Jägerleitoffizier*) was called Protby, and the platoon commander (*Gerätezugführer*) was called Metzler. In addition, the station hosted 105 soldiers and 118 assistants of the Luftwaffe from two distinct military units for detection and control (first the 20th / FlugmeldeLeitKp IV / LnRgt 222, then the 30th / FlugmeldeLeitKp IV / LnRgt 222). The station consisted mainly of a set of wooden barracks converted into housing, and various military facilities. It was equipped with only small-calibre weapons, but the whole station was fenced with barbed wire. A *Jagdschloss* Ver 2, a Freya LZ, a Freya MOT, and two Würzburg-Riese GEMA (Wasserman M radar), as well as a set of Heinrich/Hans direction/range finders were among the radar systems used in Tybjerg. The radar equipment was positioned approximately 1,500ft (500 metres) apart. The Wassermann M radar was 150ft (50 metres) high and had high transmission power as well as a detection range of approximately 200 miles (300 kilometres).

The *Seehund* station received information from the *Krokodil* and *Faultier* stations, as well as the Fluko station in Copenhagen. It would then transfer all observations for general coordination to Gyges, the German

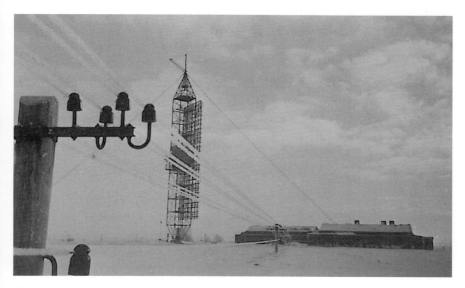

Figure 94. Wassermann M IV radar, 164 feet (50 metres) tall, at Seehund, Winter 1945/1946. (the Museum of Danish Resistance 1940–1945)

Figure 95. Seehund radar station, located in Tybjerg near Ringsted, 1945/1946. (The Museum of Danish Resistance 1940–1945)

bunker located in Gedhus near Karup. Because of its gigantic dimensions, the bunker was called Kammhuber's Opera, after the German army corps' General Josef Kammhuber. As soon as an aircraft from the Allied forces was located, the Germans could order a night fighter to be sent up, guided by radio from Gyges or by one of the radar stations such as *Seehund*. Once the night fighters were informed of an enemy aircraft being spotted, and of its course, they would try to get a visual on the plane. Most of the FuG 10 wireless equipment installed on the German aircraft was connected to an antenna fixed between the main fuselage and the tail, transmitting on mid-range (120–300 miles [200–500 kilometres]) to long-range (600–1,200 miles [1,000–2,000 kilometres]) frequencies. Once the pilot had established visual contact, he would, in general, aim for the tanks and the wings of the Allied aircraft. The night fighters were specially equipped to attack Allied aircraft from below, and from only 300–450ft (100–150 metres) away, where they could not be seen and hit.

Appendix IV

Responsibilities of PoW card

3

Remember that the person talking to you may be an enemy. The only man you can be sure is a friend is the man you knew before capture

3. By use of microphones, which must be expected may be in every room at every stage of your imprisonment.

Because you can't find the microphone don't think there isn't one. We know there is, and that the enemy will be listening. So, never talk shop

4. By suggesting that another officer or man has talked freely, giving the impression that silence is no longer of value.

5. By friendly reception and good treatment on capture, such as being offered drinks.

6. By renewed interrogation long after capture, not necessarily by direct inquiry but casual and seemingly friendly interest.

Say nothing and go on saying it

PART IV

DONT'S

1. **Don't** carry or allow anyone else to carry any papers, official or private, on a flight. An envelope may give away information. Everything gives something away, even an old tram ticket or a bill. Turn out your pockets as a matter of routine before going up even if you don't expect to go over the enemy lines.

2. **Don't** allow your kit to bear any tradesmen's tabs or labels of your school or station, or have any marks, other than official, on your identity disc.

Above and overleaf: Figure 96. The Responsibilities of PoW card which was given to all aircrew. Crews never took this on board an aircraft. (Tangmere Military Aviation Museum)

9. **Bogus Forms** may be produced in the hope that the prisoner will answer the questions which they ask. They may appear to be genuine Red Cross forms or official documents. Put your pen through every question except Name, Rank and Number—otherwise the Enemy may fill in the answers above your signature in order to bluff other prisoners. (*Note.*—Failure to fill in a Red Cross form does *not* delay notification to relatives, who are informed through official channels.)

10. **Propaganda.** From the moment a prisoner is captured he is subjected to enemy propaganda. He will continually be told lies about the war situation, and about his country and her Allies, in the hope that his resolution will weaken, and that his courage will fail.

These are only ten of the Enemy's tricks. Be on your guard. He has many others up his sleeve.

Do's and Dont's

1. **Do** give your Name, Rank and Number, *but nothing else.*
2. **Do** convince your interrogator from the very outset that you are the type who will never talk under any circumstances. Therein lies the whole secret of successfully withstanding interrogation.
3. **Do** behave with dignity and reserve under interrogation, so that you command the respect of your captors.
4. **Do** maintain your resolution and morale; and encourage your comrades to do the same.
5. **Do** empty your pockets before going on operations.
6. **Do** destroy your aircraft, maps and documents whenever possible. Remember that incriminating articles and papers can often be disposed of before the Enemy has a chance to search you.
7. **Do** keep your eyes and ears open after capture—you may learn much which may be of value both to your country and yourself if you succeed in escaping.

1. **Don't** be truculent or aggressive under interrogation. You may regret it.
2. **Don't** try to fool your interrogators. They will be experts at their job, and in any battle of wits you are bound to lose in the end. Once you begin to talk, they have got you where they want you. *Say nothing and go on saying it.*
3. **Don't** imagine that you can find every microphone. You can't.
4. **Don't** talk shop. A careless word may cost old comrades their lives. If you have plans to discuss, do it in the open air—but remember, even trees have ears!
5. **Don't** accept old prisoners on trust.
6. **Don't** believe enemy propaganda, and don't let your comrades do so either.
7. **Don't** broadcast, no matter what inducement is offered.
8. **Don't** fraternize. The Enemy is not in the habit of wasting his time, whisky and cigars on those who have nothing to give him in return.
9. **Don't** give your parole, except under special circumstances.
10. **Don't** betray those who help you to escape. A careless word after you have reached safety may cost them their lives.
11. **Don't** write direct to any Service address in the U.K., and don't reveal in your letter that the addressee is in any way connected with the Services. Remember that the German censor will closely examine all your correspondence, and will note what you write and to whom you write.
12. **Don't** carry these instructions on you or in your aircraft. They are to help you and not the Enemy. *Trust no one.*

A prisoner is always surrounded by his Enemies. Trust no one.

Rights of a prisoner

1. The rights of a prisoner of war are fully safeguarded by the Geneva Convention of 1929, and this should be displayed in every Camp. Insist on this being done.
2. There is a neutral Protecting Power to whom all serious complaints can be addressed through the Camp Commandant.
3. If you escape to a neutral country, claim your freedom and report to the nearest British representative.

(514) 33189 Wt. 30944/L1943 25M 9/44 W.P. Ltd. Gp. 454

Appendix V

The metal detection search for BB378, 72 years after the crash landing

In 2015, under the auspices of the Vestsjælland Museum Group, around thirty-five volunteers of all ages, including Jan Christensen, began searching a field in Bonderup.[230] In order to avoid disrupting the crops, searches were carried out on 12 February and 3 October. This was the location where the Bartter crew and the Halifax BB378 aircraft had made their crash landing. The museum had undertaken this task as they knew there was a great story to be told. The excavation was newsworthy, with the story appearing on Danish television mentioning that Muus had also been on board. The use of metal detectors would produce valuable information and artefacts which are now within a permanent exhibition at the Holbæk Museum.

Figure 97. Wreckage of BB378 after it crashed in 1943. (Holbæk Museum)

Figure 98. Volunteers at the excavation of the crash site. (Jan Christensen)

THE METAL DETECTION SEARCH FOR BB378

The researchers from the Vestsiælland Museum knew which field to direct their volunteers to, and after only thirty minutes the exact crash site was identified. Over the two days, more than 1,000 pieces of the aircraft were found. Most were near the surface with a few pieces up to 20 inches (50 cm) below the surface. While the metal detectors were necessary for the majority of finds, a few items were simply lying on the surface of the field. Although the Germans had cleared the site, it had been impossible for them to collect everything. Uffe Thulstrup, who was only 9 years old at the time of the excavation, was one of the enthusiastic and knowledgeable volunteers, and for him it was a real treasure hunt. His father, another volunteer, had told him the story of BB378. When the local TV station, TV2east, covered the story, Uffe was interviewed. He explained: 'The Germans took the aircraft as they wanted the aluminium, because to them, it was like gold.' The metal would be taken away to be melted down and was therefore valuable. The volunteers came from a large area, with some driving for several hours to reach the field. It was a rare opportunity to look for a Second World War aircraft and understandably drew considerable interest.

An unexploded hand grenade saw the authorities brought in to make it safe. The volunteers asked that it be detonated in such a way as to allow it to be displayed.

While the fire onboard no doubt destroyed a great many items, and the Germans took away what they could to melt down, the items located during just a couple of days of excavation provided a treasure trove. The number of artefacts recovered was substantial, with items such as pieces of melted aluminium weighing more than 11lb (5 kilos), demonstrating the intensity

Figure 99. Flags marking the locations of individual items. (Jan Christensen)

229

Figure 100. Grenade from BB378 on the left was made safe during the excavation. (Jan Christensen)

Figure 101. Bullets recovered from the site. (Jan Christensen)

of the fire on board the aircraft. It was noted earlier that the crash site was still smouldering more than twelve hours after the crash. The photos show just a few of the items unearthed during the excavation. It is not possible for the museum to display all the items, but many of the most interesting form part of the permanent exhibition.

Figure 102. Bullets which melted together with aluminium from the aircraft during the fire. (Jan Christensen)

Figure 103. Part of the fuel gauge. (Jan Christensen)

Figure 104. An aluminium plate with identifying numbers. (Jan Christensen)

Figure 105. The cockpit switch for the landing lights. (Jan Christensen)

This was a fantastic project which captured the imagination of young and old alike: the story of an RAF crew carrying an important figure of the Danish Resistance. The volunteers worked enthusiastically and diligently over just two days to locate so many interesting items. The opening of the exhibition in the Holbæk Museum was attended by many visitors, including Nigel Atkins. A second excavation took place in 2017 to ensure that everything possible could be recovered from the site.

Figure 106. Display of Brian Atkins's items, Holbæk Museum. The collection includes his medal miniatures. (Jan Christensen)

Appendix VI

Biographies

Author

Jan Christensen, born in 1967, is a Danish freelance writer, a researcher in both Denmark and the UK, and a public speaker. He specialises in the Special Operations Executive (SOE), the Danish Resistance, and the air-drops to them, as well as the air war over Denmark. He has regularly attended Tempsford for the annual remembrance service and has written for the Tempsford Veterans and Relatives Association (TVARA) newsletter. He undertook numerous visits to the National Archives at Kew to research the Bartter crew and their story. He lives in Næstved, Denmark.

Contributors

Maxine Harcourt-Kelly contributed to several chapters of the book. She returned to education as a mature student, gaining a first in BA (Hons) History, then completed an MA in Cultural History, both at the University of Chichester. Her interest in the Second World War was ignited by her father-in-law, who was in the Jedburgh section of the SOE. She was the volunteer archivist at Tangmere Military Aviation Museum for over three years. She is a freelance researcher and writer, is married with two adult children and lives in West Sussex, UK.

Abigail Exelby contributed to the chapter 'The War is over for you – Stalag IVB'. She obtained her BA (Hons) in History as a mature student in 2017, gaining a First. She continued to complete her MA in Cultural History, and is currently researching for her PhD. Areas of interest and research are Anglo/Jewish history from the 1930s onwards, Jewish gender history, and Holocaust studies. She is an independent researcher and writer from West Sussex, UK.

Editor

Adrian Stenton has been a freelance copy-editor for longer than he cares to remember.

Contributor and Foreword/Afterword

Nigel Atkins is the son of Brian Atkins. It was Nigel's interest in the crew that created this project. He has visited numerous areas of France, as well as Denmark, the former Yugoslavia, and the site of Stalag IV B, all of which has been vital research for the book. He has guided and contributed to the entire project. Nigel, a dual British-French national and Czech resident, is an advisor to several French municipalities in Strategic Planning and a past Associate Professor in Urban Planning at the Sorbonne University, Paris, where he lives with his family.

Appendix VII

Glossary

Abwehr German Military Intelligence

The Allies
The Allies consisted of the British Empire and Commonwealth, the Dominions of Australia, Canada, India, New Zealand and South Africa, plus the colonies in the Caribbean, Africa and Asia. The only member of the Commonwealth that was neutral was the Irish Free State. The Soviet Union was attacked by the Axis powers on 22 June 1941 and became an ally of Britain. Following the Empire of Japan's attack on the US base at Pearl Harbor in Hawaii on 7 December 1941, the United States joined the Allies.

The Axis powers
The Axis powers were created following the signing of the Tripartite Pact between Italy, Germany and Japan on 27 September 1940. Bulgaria, Croatia, Hungary and Slovakia subsequently joined. The French colonies of Algeria, Tunisia and Morocco in North Africa were loyal to the Vichy regime in occupied France but came under Free French control after the success of Operation Torch in November 1942.

Bureau Central de Renseignements et d'Action (BCRA) Free French Organisation under de Gaulle

Chetniks Serb guerrilla force

Clams Small limpet mines

Free French Forces Armed Resistance led by de Gaulle

Gammon Bombs Grenade

GLOSSARY

Gee
A radio navigation system which entered service with Bomber Command in 1942. Initially developed by Robert Dippy as a short-range blind-landing system, it was discovered to work well over longer distances. It worked by measuring the time delay between two radio signals and thereby produced a fix. Dippy began working on radar development in July 1936 at Bawdsey Manor in Suffolk. His proposals for a radio navigation system, Gee fix, were not initially taken up, but by 1942 they were being urgently developed. It was very successful as a general navigation system assisting bombers on their return flights, but was also very useful for Special Duties in assisting them in confirming drop zones. The system is credited with saving many lives and aircraft.

Gestapo Official secret police of Nazi Germany

Jedburgh
Three-man teams sent in behind enemy lines to harass the enemy. Part of F section, they were sent in wearing uniforms, so were particularly at risk of discovery.

Mills Bombs Hand grenades

Rebecca/Eureka System
This was a short-range radio navigation system which had only come into service during 1943 and which allowed a ground-based unit (Eureka) to communicate with an airborne device (Rebecca). Rebecca would calculate the range from the Eureka transponder, allowing pinpoint accuracy for crews dropping supplies.

S-phone
A radio system developed by SOE with Captain Bert Lane and Major Hobday of the Royal Signals. It allowed communication between the ground receiver and the aircraft. It was direction dependent and worked at heights below 10,000ft, so suited Special Duties flights. It allowed for fairly secure communication.

Special Duties Squadron
Those squadrons tasked with flying to occupied territories to deliver both supplies and agents into the field.

Sten guns
A simple and lightweight sub-machine gun which was cheap to produce. They were used particularly by those undertaking insurgency, because they could be easily hidden under clothing.

Ultra
The codename given as a fictional agent to hide the work done at Bletchley Park decoding messages sent via the Enigma machine.

Vichy
The initially unoccupied area of France under Marshal Philippe Pétain

Wehrmacht The German armed forces

Appendix VIII

Ranks in the Royal Air Force mentioned in the book

AVM	Air Vice Marshal
Gp Capt	Group Captain
W/Cdr	Wing Commander
S/Ldr	Squadron Leader
F/Lt	Flight Lieutenant
F/O	Flying Officer
P/O	Pilot Officer
W/O	Warrant Officer
F/Sgt	Flight Sergeant/Sergeant Pilot
Sgt	Sergeant
LAC	Leading Aircraftman
AC	Aircraftman
AC1	Aircraftman No 1 Class
AC2	Aircraftman No 2 Class

Other service ranks mentioned

Lt Col	Lieutenant Colonel
Lt	Lieutenant
Capt	Captain
Flt Off	Flight Officer
Acting Sgt	Acting Sergeant
Cpl	Corporal

Bibliography

Primary sources

House of Commons Hansard
Imperial War Museum, Oral History of Brian Atkins
<https://www.iwm.org.uk/collections/item/object/80012151> National Archives, Kew
National Archives, France
<https://www.archives-nationales.culture.gouv.fr>

Interviews

Anderson family
Brian Atkins, Imperial War Museum, Oral History
  <https://www.iwm.org.uk/collections/item/object/80012151> Nigel Atkins
Margaret Fradin Fry Family
Julia Castelli Gair
René Gimpel
Inge Sofie Ibsen
Krügermeier family
Marc Serritrice

Newspapers

Bedfordshire Times and Independent
Dansk Daad, Halifax BB378 Capture, January 1944
London Gazette
Ringsted-Haslev-Sorø newspapers

BIBLIOGRAPHY

Secondary Books

Anon, *After the Battle: Dulag Luft* (London: BOB International, No.106, 1999)

Ashdown, Paddy, *The Cruel Victory* (London: William Collins, 2015)

Bailey, Roderick, *Forgotten Voices of the Secret War* (London: Ebury Press, 2008)

Bennit, Poul, *Danish Police behind Barbed Wire* (Demark: Skandinavisk Bogforlag, 1945)

Biondich, Mark, *The Balkans: Revolution, War and Political Violence since 1878* (Oxford: Oxford University Press, 2011).

Bloch, Marc, *Strange Defeat* (New York: W.W. Norton, 1968) [reissued by Oxford University Press, 1999]

Body, Robert, *Runways to Freedom* (Lulu, 2016)

Bourne-Paterson, *Major Robert, SOE in France 1941–1943* (Barnsley: Frontline Books, 2016)

Bowman, Martin, *Voices in Flight: The Heavy Bomber Offensive of WWII* (Barnsley: Pen and Sword, 2015)

Buckmaster, Maurice, *They Fought Alone* (London: Biteback Publishing, 2014 edition)

Churchill, Winston, *The Second World War* (Boston: Houghton Mifflin, 1948– 1953)

Clark, Freddie, *Agents by Moonlight* (London: Tempus Books, 1999)

Collins Weitz, Margaret, *Sisters in the Resistance* (Chichester: John Wiley and Sons, 1995)

Dear, Ian, *Sabotage and Subversion: The SOE and OSS at War* (London: Cassell Military Paperbacks, 2002)

Dixon, Peter, *Setting the Med Ablaze: Churchill's Secret North African Base* (London: Cloudshill Press, 2020)

Elkin, Jennifer, *A Special Duty: A Crew's Secret War with 148 Squadron* (London: Mention the War, 2015)

Fogg, Shannon, L., *The Politics of Everyday Life in Vichy France* (New York: Cambridge University Press, 2009)

Foot, M.R.D., *SOE in France* (London: Her Majesty's Stationery Office, 1966)

Gammon, V.F., *Not All Glory! True Accounts of RAF Airmen Taken in Europe, 1939–1945* (London: Arms and Armour Press, 1996)

Goldsmith, John, Accidental Agent (London: Lee Cooper, 1971)

Grehan, John, *RAF and the SOE: Special Duty Operations in Europe during World War Two, an Official Account* (Barnsley: Frontline Books, 2016)

Guéhenno, Jean, translated by David Ball, *Diary of the Dark Years, 1940–1944* (Oxford: Oxford University Press, 2016)

Guiet, Jean Claude, *Dead on Time: The Memoir of an SOE and OSS Agent in Occupied France* (Stroud: The History Press, 2016)

Heslop, Richard, Xavier: *A British Agent with the French Resistance* (London: Biteback Publishing, 2014)

Jackson, Julian, France: *The Dark Years 1940–1944* (Oxford: Oxford University Press, 2001)

Jones, Benjamin F., *Eisenhower's Guerrillas: The Jedburgh, The maquis and the Liberation of France* (New York: Oxford University Press, 2016)

Kaiser, Charles, *Cost of Courage* (New York: Other Press, 2015) Kedward, H.R., In Search of the maquis (Oxford: Clarendon Press, 1994)

Kedward, H.R., *Occupied France: Collaboration and Resistance 1940–1944* (Oxford: Blackwell, 1985)

Kedward, H.R., *La Vie en Bleu: France and the French since 1900* (London: Allen Lane, 2005)

Krentz, H., *To Hell in a Halifax* (Meaford, Ontario: Kent Publishing, 2006)

Lett, Brian, *SOE's Mastermind: An Authorized Biography of Major General Sir Colin Gubbins* (Barnsley: Pen and Sword, 2016)

Levie, Howard S. (ed), International Law Studies—Volume 60, Documents on Prisoners of War < https : //digital-co mmons.us nwc.ed u/cgi / viewcontent. cgi?article=1923&context=ils>

Lloyd, Christopher, *Collaboration and Resistance in Occupied France* (Basingstoke: Palgrave Macmillan, 2003)

Lucas, Laddie (ed), *Wings of War* (London: Hutchinson, 1983)

Lytton, Neville, *Life in Occupied France* (London: Macmillan, 1942)

Maclean, Fitzroy, *Eastern Approaches* (London: Penguin, 2019)

Malraux, André, *Femmes Dans la Guerre* <www.books.google.co.uk>

Merrick, K.A., *Flights of the Forgotten* (London: Arms and Armour Press, 1989)

Michel, Henri, *The Shadow War: Resistance in Europe 1939–1945* (London: History Book Club, 1972)

Middlebrook, Martin, *The Battle of Hamburg: The Firestorm Raid* (London: Penguin, 1984)

Middlebrook, Martin, *The Berlin Raids: RAF Bomber Command Winter 1943–44* (London: Penguin, 1990)

Miller, Russell, *Behind the Lines* (London: Pimlico, 2003)

O'Connor, Bernard, *Blackmail Sabotage: Attacks on French Industries during World War Two* (Lulu.com, 2016)

BIBLIOGRAPHY

Ousby, Ian, *Occupation: The Ordeal of France, 1940–1944* (London: Pimlico, 1999)

Rayment, Sean, *Tales from the Special Forces Club* (London: Collins, 2013)

Ricks, Thomas E., *Churchill and Orwell: The Fight for Freedom* (London: Duckworth Overlook, 2017)

Roberts, Walter R., Tito, *Mihailović and the Allies, 1941–1945* (New Brunswick, NJ: Rutgers University Press)

Serratrice, Marc, *Avoir 20 ans au maquis du Vercors* (France: Editions Anovi, 2014)

Simon, Paul, translated by W.G. Corp, *One Enemy Only: The Invader* (London: Hodder and Stoughton, 1942)

Swallow, T. & Pill, A.H., *Flywheel* (Waltham Abbey: Fraser Stewart Books, 1987)

Taylor, G., *Piece of Cake* (London: Peter Davies, 1956)

Tripp, Miles, *The Eighth Passenger* (Ware: Wordsworth Military Library, 2002)

Vercoe, T., *Survival at Stalag IV B: Soldiers and Airmen Remember Germany's Largest PoW Camp of World War II* (Jefferson, NC & London: McFarland & Co, 2006)

Walters, Anne-Marie and Hewson, David, *Moondrop to Gascony* (London:Macmillan, 1946) [republished by Winsley, Moho, 2009, with a new introduction, postscript and notes by David Hewson]

Ward, Chris with Hodyra, Piotr, *138 Squadron: Volume 6, RAF Bomber Command Profiles* (Farsley: Mention the War, 2017)

Weitz, Margaret Collins, *Sisters in the Resistance* (Chichester: John Wiley and Sons, 1995)

Williams, Heather, *Parachutes, Patriots and Partisans: The Special Operations Executive and Yugoslavia, 1941–1945* (London: Hurst and Co, 2003)

Wylie, Neville, *The Politics and Strategy of Clandestine War* (London: Routledge, 2012)

Articles

Freeman, Paul J., The Cinderella Front: Allied Special Air Operations in Yugoslavia during World War II (War College Series, 2012)

Imperial War Museum, Air Ministry Instructions and Guide to all Officers and Airmen of the Royal Air Force Regarding Precautions to be Taken in the Event of Falling into the Hands of the Enemy, 1941, LBY K. 88 / 1110

Jones, Edgar. LMF: The Use of Psychiatric Stigma in the Royal Air Force during the Second World War. *Journal of Military History*, 70(2), 2006

Rasmussen, Nicholas, Blood, Meth and Tears: The Super Soldiers of World War II. Medical Science and the Military: The Allies' Use of Amphetamine during World War II, *Journal of Interdisciplinary History*, 42(2), 2011

Rollings, Charles, After the Battle, *Dulag Luft*, 106, 1999

Websites

<https://www.49squadron.co.uk>
<https://www.aircrashsites.co.uk>
Alliance Francaise <https://www.alliancefrancaise.london>
BBC Peoples War <https://www.bbc.co.uk/history/ww2peopleswar>
The Interrogators <www.merkki.com>
Musée de la résistance <www.museedelaresistanceenligne.org>
Tempsford Veterans and Relatives Assocation
<http://www.tempsford-squadrons.info/TVARA%20history.htm>
US Naval War College <www. usnwc.edu>

Photographs

Photographs from the following sources have been used with permission:
Amicale Action
Jean-Marc Atkins
Nigel Atkins
Kevin Britchfield
British Red Cross
BT Newspaper, Denmark
Bundesarchiv, German National Archive
Jan Christensen
Margaret Fraden
Fry Family
Peter Haining
Holbæk Museum
Hollingworth Family
Bishop Jovan of Ulpiana
Krügermeier Family

BIBLIOGRAPHY

Ali Lamport
Paul Mellen
Svend Aage Mortensen
Varinka W. Muus
Næstved Archives
l'Ordre de la Libération
Ringsted-Haslav-Sorø Newspapaers
Royal Air Forces Association
Marc Serratrice
Tangmere Military Aviation Museum
The Danish Museum of Resistance 1940–1945
The National Archives, Kew
The National Museum of Denmark WikiMedia Commons
Wikimedia / Lutz Bruno

Acknowledgements

Thanks go to the team who have worked and supported to assist in writing and producing this book, across three countries. Thanks as well to Heidi Sommerstedt-Rasmussen, Jan's wife, for her encouragement.

Special Thanks are extended to the following:

The Gerry Holdsworth Special Forces Charitable Trust, whose objective is to preserve and promote the heritage of the SOE and special forces. The Trust accorded generous financial support for the research and the preparation of the manuscript.

Mark Seaman MBE, a renowned historian with the Cabinet Office and an authority on the SOE and the French Resistance. Mark, from the beginning encouraged the writing of this book with an emphasis on the human angle of a Special Duties crew.

Dr Andrew Smith, Lecturer in Liberal Arts, Queen Mary University of London. Andrew has been the academic who has offered encouragement throughout the writing process and reviewed the research.

Karen Munk-Nielsen, the Curator of the Holbæk Museum Denmark. A room has been dedicated to the RAF and the crash of BB378. Karen devotes considerable time to educating local schoolchildren on aspects of the Danish Resistance. Once a year she takes a group of children in the middle of winter at midnight to the intended dropping zone of the BB378 at Bonderup to experience how the reception committee must have felt.

The Anderson family, for sharing their father's story and PoW letters which gave detailed insight into the life of a PoW in Germany.

Julia Castelli, Peter Bartter's adopted daughter, for corresponding, both by email and phone, from her ranch in Costa Rica! Thanks to Julia the

ACKNOWLEDGEMENTS

personality of this exceptional man was better understood. Thanks also to Margaret Fradin, Peter Bartter's niece, for sharing her material and photos of Peter. She played a major role in tracing Julia, which took several years.

Several members of Joe Fry's family have engaged during the writing of the book, providing valuable insights. Joe's family in Canada kindly donated Joe's leather bomber jacket to the Holbæk Museum.

Stan Smith's relative, Paul Mellen, for providing photographs and information.

Rene Gimpel has given detailed information on his father Charles [Ernest] Gimpel, the agent flown in on Operation John 36. Nigel Atkins has represented the Gimpel family at official ceremonies in Paris on several occasions.

Ralph Hollingworth's daughters aided further understanding of the work of SOE in Denmark from 1940–45.

Marc Serratrice, one of the few remaining maquis from the Vercors, who kindly provided a great amount of detail for the operation to the Vercors region.

Bernard Doerflinger, who provided invaluable research and assistance on the Vercors.

Elizabeth Buchan who, in 2015, published a novel on the Danish Resistance and the SOE: *I Can't Begin to Tell You*. Elizabeth kindly corresponded and gave her thoughts on the SOE in Denmark.

John and Duncan Evans of Books Express, Saffron Walden.

Author and researcher Paul McCue from the WW2 Secret Learning Network.

Denmark

Alsønderup-Tjæreby Archives
Historical resources on Occupation, Esbjerg
Holbæk Museum
Næstved Archives

Roskilde Archives
Stenlille Archives
The Danish National Archives
Tølløse Archives

UK

British Airways Speedbird Heritage Centre
National Archives, Kew, England
Royal Air Force Club, London
Shropshire Family History Society
Tangmere Military Aviation Museum
Tempsford Veterans and Relatives Association (TVARA)
The Gerry Holdsworth Special Forces Trust

Canada

Canadian Armed Forces, Directorate of History and Heritage

Thank you to the following for their support and assistance:
John Anderson
Jean-Marc Atkins
Ken Atkins
Nigel Atkins
David Barry
Mogens Bencard
Julian Beynon-Lewis
Bishop Jovan of Slavinia
Bob Body
Dines Bogø
Kevin Britchfield
Karyn Burnham
Julia Castelli Gair
Poul Christensen
Emily Clarke
Bernard Doerflinger
Rosemund Durrant

ACKNOWLEDGEMENTS

Duncan Evans
John Evans
Pauline Evans
Abi Exelby
Margaret Fradin
Jørgen Fredslund
Alison Fry
John Fry
René Gimpel
Maxine Harcourt-Kelly
Sofie Ibsen
Major Mathias Joost
Julie and Leo de Jourdan
Andrea King, Ardingly College
Kai Krügermeier
Lisa Krügermeier
Søren and Gudrun Lund
Henrik Lundbak
Ulla Lunn
Paul McCue
Paul Mellen
Karen Munk-Nielsen
Bent Nielsen (Niller)
Bent Nielsen (Vandløse)
Rita Nielsen
Lise Nørgaard
Martin Pavon
Maureen Pelletier
Mark Seaman
Marc Serritrice
Dr Andrew Smith
Heidi Sommerstedt-Rasmussen
Adrian Stenton
Libby West
Beverley Whittington

Endnotes

1. The Gerry Holdsworth Special Forces Trust is a charitable endeavour founded in 1989 to help preserve and promote the heritage of the wartime Special Operations Executive and related special forces.
2. The National Archives (TNA).
3. Thomas E. Ricks, *Churchill and Orwell: The Fight for Freedom* (pp. 132–133).
4. This position required an exam and was considered a responsible post.
5. *Dad's Army* was a BBC television comedy series broadcast between 1968 and 1977, recounting the days of the Home Guard in the Second World War.
6. Imperial War Museum (IWM), oral history, Brian Atkins, catalogue number 12419.
7. The Arnold Scheme ran from 1941 to 1943, training RAF pilots in the US, and was named after US General Henry H. Arnold of the USAAF.
8. M.R.D. Foot, *SOE in France* (p. 2, quoting recommendations on control of para-military activities, 5 June 1939).
9. Foot, *SOE in France* (p. 3).
10. Churchill had become Prime Minister on 10 May 1940.
11. Foot, *SOE in France* (p. 8).
12. Patriot Forces referred to those within the occupied territories who, in whatever form, were resisting the occupiers. Special Operations Directive for 1943. Chiefs of Staff memorandum 20 March 1943. OCS (43) 142(0), CAB 80/68.
13. KCMG: Knight Commander of St Michael and St George – awarded in 1946; DSO: Distinguished Service Order – awarded in 1940; MC: Military Cross – awarded in 1916.
14. Brian Lett, *SOE's Mastermind: An Authorized Biography of Major General Sir Colin Gubbins* (p. 133).
15. Lett, *SOE's Mastermind* (p. 48).

ENDNOTES

16. Maurice Buckmaster, *They Fought Alone* (p. 3).
17. Further details are given within the operations section of Chapter 3.
18. IWM.
19. Danmarkbesat.
20. Foot, *SOE in France* (p. 13).
21. John Grehan, *RAF and the SOE: Special Duty Operations in Europe during World War Two, an Official Account* (p. 5).
22. K.A. Merrick, *Flights of the Forgotten* (p. 56).
23. Grehan, *RAF and the SOE* (p. 209).
24. Professor M.R.D. Foot, quoted during a speech at the Royal Air Force Historical Society, February 1989.
25. Rubber shortages were due to the Japanese capture of major rubber-producing regions in the Far East.
26. Grehan, *RAF and the SOE* (pp. 120–125).
27. IWM, oral history, Brian Atkins.
28. Grehan, *RAF and the SOE* (pp. 108–114). SIS = Secret Intelligence Services.
29. Tangmere is no longer an RAF site but remains home to the Tangmere Military Aviation Museum.
30. A Squadron consists of a number of Flights; a Flight consists of a number of aircraft. For 138 Squadron, there were two Flights. Each Flight had approximately ten aircraft at its disposal at any one time.
31. Robert Body, *Runways to Freedom* (p. 97).
32. IWM.
33. Personal communication, Rosemund Straw, November 2019.
34. Sean Rayment, *Tales from the Special Forces Club* (p. 175).
35. Beef olives is a dish consisting of thin strips of beef wrapped around stuffing and braised in a gravy-like sauce. It contains no olives.
36. TNA.
37. Grehan, *RAF and the SOE* (p. 111).
38. Freddie Clark, *Agents by Moonlight* (p. 303–318).
39. Julian Jackson, *France: The Dark Years 1940–1944* (p. 385).
40. Paul Simon, *One Enemy Only: The Invader* (p. 69).
41. Simon, *One Enemy Only* (p. 27).
42. Christopher Lloyd, *Collaboration and Resistance in Occupied France* (p. 25).
43. Jackson, *France* (p. 386, quoting Frenay, *La nuit finira*, p. 16).
44. Jackson, *France* (pp. 402–405).
45. Jackson, *France* (p. 453).
46. Jean Guéhenno, *Diary of the Dark Years, 1940–1944* (p. 232).
47. Jackson, *France* (p. 476).

48. H.R. Kedward, *In Search of the Maquis* (p. 22).
49. Guéhenno, *Diary of the Dark Years, 1940–1944* (pp. 221–222).
50. Ian Ousby, *Occupation: The Ordeal of France, 1940–1944* (p. 211). Francois Mauriac was a famed French novelist who had been a member of the Resistance. He won the Nobel Prize in Literature in 1952 and was a member of the Académie Français, a council which deals with matters related to the French language.
51. Jackson, *France* (pp. 483–487). This was not an actual fortress, but a region where the Maquis could hide and train. Anyone approaching on the roads would be visible, and the Maquis could disappear into the areas around the plateau.
52. Guéhenno, *Diary of the Dark Years, 1940–1944* (p. 217).
53. IWM, oral history, Brian Atkins.
54. TNA.
55. TNA.
56. https://aircrashsites.co.uk
57. General Giraud worked secretly for the Allies under the Vichy regime. He was at one time a serious rival to de Gaulle but his influence waned before the end of the war. The Carte circuit was too big and insecure to continue. Donkeyman was the largest of the fragments when the circuit was broken up. Foot, *SOE in France* (pp. 250–251).
58. Foot, *SOE in France* (pp. 272–273).
59. Chris Ward with Piotr Hodyra, *138 Squadron: Volume 6, RAF Bomber Command Profiles* (pp. 180, 183).
60. TNA.
61. Nicholas Rasmussen, *Blood, Meth and Tears: The Super Soldiers of World War II* (pp. 205– 233).
62. TNA.
63. Ward with Hodyra, *138 Squadron* (p. 195), and TNA.
64. Foot, *SOE in France* (p. 121).
65. Ward with Hodyra, *138 Squadron* (p. 197).
66. Nicholas Anderson logbook and TNA.
67. Personal communication, Marc Serratrice, 27 August 2021, interview with Nigel Atkins in Grenoble.
68. Pilot report, TNA.
69. Operation John 35 was lost in the Vercors with all on board killed. All were buried in Autrans but due to conditions on the ground the bodies were not recovered until August 1944. Serratrice lamented this episode during Nigel Atkins's interview with him.

ENDNOTES

70. Marc Serratrice, *Avoir 20 ansau maquis du Vercors*.
71. Personal communication, Marc Serratrice, 27 August 2021, interview with Nigel Atkins in Grenoble.
72. Not to be confused with Dr Leon Martin, founder of the Franc Trieur and Vercors activist.
73. Paddy Ashdown, *The Cruel Victory* (pp. 71–74).
74. Personal communication, Marc Serratrice, 27 August 2021, interview with Nigel Atkins in Grenoble.
75. Personal communication, Marc Serratrice, 27 August 2021, interview with Nigel Atkins in Grenoble.
76. Personal communication, Marc Serratrice, 27 August 2021, interview with Nigel Atkins in Grenoble.
77. Ward with Hodyra, *138 Squadron* (p. 201).
78. TNA.
79. Foot, *SOE in France* (p. 42).
80. Paul McCue, notes on Sevenet, quoting official documents.
81. Foot, *SOE in France* (p. 284).
82. Kedward, *In Search of the Maquis* (p. 272).
83. Foot, *SOE in France* (p. 285).
84. Major Robert Bourne-Paterson, *SOE in France, 1941–1943* (p. 177).
85. Kedward, *In Search of the Maquis* (p. 272).
86. Foot, *SOE in France* (p. 311).
87. Bourne-Paterson, *SOE in France, 1941–1943* (p. 177).
88. TNA.
89. TNA.
90. TNA.
91. IWM, oral history.
92. Bernard O'Connor, *Blackmail Sabotage: Attacks on French Industries during World War Two*.
93. TNA.
94. Charles Kaiser, *Cost of Courage* (pp. 14–15).
95. Personal communication, Réne Gimpel.
96. Kaiser, *Cost of Courage* (p. 187).
97. Grehan, *RAF and the SOE* (p. 165).
98. Body, *Runways to Freedom* (p. 143, quoting TNA, March to October 1943).
99. This concept is not recorded in any speech by Churchill, but he is reported as having used the analogy when speaking with Stalin in Moscow in August 1942.
100. IWM, oral history, Brian Atkins.

101. Paul J. Freeman, *The Cinderella Front: Allied Special Air Operations in Yugoslavia During World War II*.
102. Heather Williams, *Parachutes, Patriots and Partisans: The Special Operations Executive and Yugoslavia, 1941–1945* (p. 206).
103. Walter R. Roberts, *Tito, Mihailović, and the Allies, 1941–1945*.
104. TNA.
105. TNA.
106. Freeman, *The Cinderella Front* (p. 23).
107. TNA.
108. Fitzroy Maclean, *Eastern Approaches* (p. 226).
109. Maclean, *Eastern Approaches* (p. 281).
110. Maclean, *Eastern Approaches* (pp. 294–298).
111. Maclean, *Eastern Approaches* (pp. 402–403).
112. TNA.
113. TNA.
114. TNA.
115. Winston Churchill, House of Commons, 22 February 1944, Hansard
116. TNA.
117. Tropicalizing an aircraft involved making adjustments to the mechanics of the aircraft to allow for operation in more extreme circumstances.
118. TNA.
119. TNA and Nick Anderson's logbook, by kind permission of his family.
120. TNA.
121. TNA file.
122. Williams, *Parachutes, Patriots and Partisans* (p. 182).
123. Maclean, *Eastern Approaches* (p. 385).
124. IWM oral history, Brian Atkins.
125. Personal communication.
126. The crisis of August 1943 / SOE Denmark 8, TNA.
127. TNA.
128. Joe Fry's personal journal.
129. Jan Christensen was able to contact Ibsen's widow, who shared her husband's very detailed memoirs and the following is gratefully drawn from them. Personal communication, Inge Sofie Ibsen, 2016. Personal memoirs of Holgar Henning Finn Ibsen.
130. Joe Fry, personal account.
131. Lise Nørgaard, interviewed by Jan Christensen, 8 July 2014.
132. Joe Fry's personal account, also letters to Atkins's family.
133. TNA.

ENDNOTES

134. TNA.
135. David Hewson, in Anne-Marie Walters, *Moondrop to Gascony*.
136. Confirmed by Major Mathias Joost, RCAF, personal communication, 29 May 2020.
137. Major Mathias Joost, RCAF, personal communication, 29 May 2020.
138. *London Gazette*.
139. IWM, oral history.
140. *Dansk Daad*, 'Halifax BB378 Capture', January 1944.
141. IWM, oral history.
142. IWM, oral history.
143. IWM, oral history.
144. IWM.
145. IWM.
146. TNA.
147. TNA.
148. IWM, oral history.
149. Anon, *After the Battle: Dulag Luft* (p. 6)
150. *After the Battle* (p. 18).
151. Howard S. Levie, *International Law Studies – Volume 60*.
152. IWM, *Air Ministry Instructions and Guide to all Officers and Airmen of the Royal Air Force Regarding Precautions to be Taken in the Event of Falling into the Hands of the Enemy, 1941*.
153. IWM, oral history.
154. H. Krentz, *To Hell in a Halifax* (p. 27).
155. Krentz, *To Hell in a Halifax* (p. 28).
156. V.F. Gammon, *Not All Glory! True Accounts of RAF Airmen Taken in Europe, 1939–1945* (p. 20).
157. Gammon, *Not All Glory!* (p. 20).
158. IWM, oral history.
159. TNA.
160. IWM, oral history.
161. TNA.
162. TNA.
163. *Air Ministry Instructions and Guide to all Officers and Airmen of the Royal Air Force Regarding Precautions to be Taken in the Event of Falling into the Hands of the Enemy, 1941*.
164. IWM, oral history.
165. IWM, oral history.
166. G. Taylor, *Piece of Cake* (p. 104).

167. T. Vercoe, *Survival at Stalag IV B: Soldiers and Airmen Remember Germany's Largest PoW Camp of World War II* (p. 10).
168. Taylor, *Piece of Cake* (pp. 100–111).
169. TNA.
170. TNA.
171. Vercoe, *Survival at Stalag IV B* (p. 32).
172. Vercoe, *Survival at Stalag IV B* (p. 32).
173. IWM, 12419, Reel 4.
174. Taylor, *Piece of Cake* (p. 121).
175. Vercoe, *Survival at Stalag IV B* (p. 36).
176. Personal communication, Ken Atkins, Cambridge, November 2019.
177. Taylor, *Piece of Cake* (p. 109).
178. TNA.
179. TNA.
180. Poul Bennit, *Danish Police behind Barbed Wire* (pp. 175–176).
181. Taylor, *Piece of Cake* (p. 114).
182. Taylor, *Piece of Cake* (p. 115).
183. Taylor, *Piece of Cake* (p. 115).
184. Taylor, *Piece of Cake* (p. 115).
185. Vercoe, *Survival at Stalag IV B* (p. 41).
186. Vercoe, *Survival at Stalag IV B* (p. 54).
187. T. Swallow and A.H. Pill, *Flywheel*.
188. Swallow and Pill, *Flywheel*.
189. Ernesto Howell, personal communication, correspondence from Ernesto Howell to Nicholas Anderson's family, 20 January 1944.
190. George Anderson, personal communication, letter from George Anderson to his parents, date unknown.
191. Wing Commander Richard Douglas Speare, personal communication, correspondence from RAF Tempsford, 11 December 1943.
192. George Anderson, personal communication, letter from George Anderson to his parents, date unknown.
193. Vercoe, *Survival at Stalag IV B* (p. 10).
194. Vercoe, *Survival at Stalag IV B* (p. 10).
195. An international charitable organisation offering healthcare, first aid, and support services.
196. Anderson family letters.
197. Anderson family letters.
198. Vercoe, *Survival at Stalag IV B* (p. 42).
199. Personal communication, Ken Atkins, Cambridge, 9 November 2019.

200. Vercoe, *Survival at Stalag IV B* (p. 100).
201. TNA.
202. TNA.
203. IWM, oral history.
204. IWM, oral history.
205. IWM, oral history.
206. TNA.
207. TNA.
208. IWM, oral history, Brian Atkins.
209. Taylor, *Piece of Cake* (p. 149).
210. IWM, oral history.
211. Vercoe, *Survival at Stalag IV B* (p. 177).
212. IWM, oral history, Brian Atkins.
213. IWM, oral history, Brian Atkins.
214. TNA.
215. TNA.
216. TNA.
217. Taylor, *Piece of Cake* (p. 253).
218. TNA.
219. IWM, oral history, Brian Atkins.
220. TNA, telegram from Lisbon 340 (Z/4416/4416/36), plus book and Carlos Guerreiros.
221. 5 May 1995, *Venstrebladet.*
222. 5 May 1995, *Berlingske Tidende*
223. Mark Biondich, *The Balkans: Revolution, War and Political Violence since 1878* (p. 181).
224. Ibid
225. TNA.
226. IWM.
227. Martin Middlebrook, The Battle of Hamburg: The Firestorm Raid (p. 110)
228. Miles Tripp, The Eighth Passenger
229. Edgar Jones, LMF: The Use of Psychiatric Stigma in the Royal Air Force during the Second World War (pp. 435–458).
230. The Vestsjælland Museum is an umbrella organisation incorporating eleven museums in West Zealand.

Index

INDEX

INDEX

INDEX

INDEX

INDEX